# Perspectives on Good Writing in Applied Linguistics and TESOL

# Perspectives on Good Writing in Applied Linguistics and TESOL

Edited by
Robert Kohls and Christine Pearson Casanave

University of Michigan Press
Ann Arbor

To my mother
—Robert

To my past and present doctoral students:
Keep writing after you get that PhD!
—Chris

# Acknowledgements

The idea for this edited book grew out of Robert's PhD dissertation on tutor and tutee beliefs about good writing and a writer's voice. A debt of gratitude goes to Alister Cumming, his supervisor, for his mentorship and encouragement. Thank you, Alister! We would like to acknowledge the guidance and support provided by Kelly Sippell on the early stages of this edited collection. Kelly was both knowledgeable of the fields of applied linguistics and TESOL and personally acquainted with many of the authors in this volume and their work. Without her, this collection would not have seen the light of day. We would also like to thank Katie LaPlant and the team at University of Michigan Press for their patience as we worked to prepare these chapters, our anonymous reviewers for the excitement they showed about the contributions of this book, and Rosa Manchón and Merrill Swain for their generous endorsements. Most of all, we would like to thank our authors for their superb contributions and for helping advance the conversation about good writing and good writers in the field of language education and beyond.

# Contents

# Part IV
## Readers, Reading, and Writing      255

# Preface

## Our Perspectives on the Need for This Book

*Robert Kohls and Christine Pearson Casanave*

Many educators would agree that scholars and writing teachers alike need to have a clear and explicit idea of what we mean by "good" and "not-so-good" writing in order to teach, evaluate, and research the activity of writing in multilingual academic contexts. In an audience comment at the American Association for Applied Linguistics (AAAL) conference in Toronto in 2015, Alan Hirvela noted that second language (L2) writing scholars have yet to conceptualize what "good" writing means for multilingual writers, teachers, and evaluators and made a spirited call for researchers to unpack this complex and contentious notion. We are still attempting to fulfill this challenge today, and this book takes a step in that direction.

One reason that it is difficult to conceptualize good writing is that "good" is a value judgment, so its definition will differ according to who holds this value. Therefore, defining "good academic writing" in English-dominant university contexts clearly and unambiguously turns out to be pretty much impossible. This is so even though Helen Sword (2009, 2012) has gotten us halfway there with her work on "stylish academic writing," as have several others (Becker, 1986; Billig, 2013; Huck, 2015; Mewburn, 2019; Pinker, 2014a, 2014b; Reichelt, 2003; Strunk & White, 2000; Williams & Bizup, 2015; Wong & Godfrey, 2022; Zinsser, 2006). But we can probably all agree that good writing makes us want to turn pages and keep reading.

Even though they don't discuss much about the importance of page-turning, the canonical writing style guides, some of which are listed above, have a great deal to say about good writing, mostly to first language (L1) writers of academic and literary English across the disciplines.

These guides urge authors to write prose that is clear, simple, and jargon-free to the extent possible. They want authors to understand the logic of how one sentence needs to follow from another in a way that helps readers comprehend without obstacles. They also want authors to avoid pretension and obfuscation rather than trying to impress readers with their erudition. Many guides also list common misspellings and misuses of words, phrases, and grammar that even first language users of English fall victim to and urge us to correct them. In short, they are full of good advice and examples.

But academic writers who follow all this advice still might not be very good writers. Even teachers and scholars of second language writing in fields like applied linguistics, fields that are fundamentally about language, might not have a concrete, explicit sense of what they mean by good writing, beyond writing that is mechanically and rhetorically "correct." As Ilona Leki (1995) said long ago, "I know it when I see it." But still, "bad" academic writing persists. Steven Pinker (2014b) does not mince words when he says that "the familiarity of bad academic writing raises a puzzle. Why should a profession that trades in words and dedicates itself to the transmission of knowledge so often turn out prose that is turgid, soggy, wooden, bloated, clumsy, obscure, unpleasant to read, and impossible to understand?" (p. 1).

If Pinker is correct, then teachers and scholars of L1 and L2 academic writing have some responsibility in improving matters, both through instruction and through modeling in their own writing. This means that teachers and scholars need to have an explicit idea of what we mean by both "good" and "not-so-good" writing in order to be able to teach, evaluate, and research our subject and, dare we say, to practice it ourselves in our own writing. We suspect that many native English-speaking teachers (NESTs) who are not trained as writing teachers use their native intuitions to teach, evaluate, and practice writing without being able to explain their intuitions. Good academic writing will thus be deemed native-like in the sense that nothing odd or jarring jumps out for L1 English readers. This is a regrettably narrow and problematic view of good writing.

We also suspect that many non-native English-speaking teachers of writing (NNESTs), and perhaps NESTs too, teach writing from a base in English grammar and conventional paragraph and essay organization in the way they themselves learned to write in English. "Good" academic writing for these teachers will be writing that is grammatically, lexically, and organizationally appropriate according to some standard, often found in textbooks or writing guides. It is likely that many teachers of L2 writing of all kinds will be more concerned with helping students learn how to put grammatically and lexically correct sentences together in a competent way (i.e., that will earn them a passing grade) than with helping them write in ways that go beyond the advice in a conventional guide to usage. The chapters in this book go beyond this conventional view of good writing. The contributors challenge our thinking about what counts as good writing, inviting us to investigate writing beyond our obsession with correct (standard, conventional) grammar and vocabulary to find other ways to characterize, teach, and practice good writing. The chapters will thus serve to enrich readers' understanding of attitudes, beliefs, and values about this underrepresented concept in L1 and in particular L2 writing scholarship.

Despite differences, everyone seems to agree that good writing is readable, engaging, and accessible, even if the language is complex and even if it deals with complex ideas, and that it is free of gratuitous jargon. We also believe, as we said above, that good writing in any field will inspire readers to keep turning pages (electronic or print), whether that writing is linguistically and rhetorically simple or complex and whether the topic written about is known and transparent or novel and dense.

In this book, therefore, we do not seek fixed ideas of what good writing might mean. Instead, we bring together many voices of those involved in the multilingual writing enterprise—educators, assessment experts, and students—who offer their insightful perspectives on the nature and practice of teaching and learning good writing in colleges and universities around the world. They provide conceptual ideas on the nature of writing and academic publishing and more practical ideas on how perspectives on good writing shape teacher feedback, assessment practices, and writing curricula. Importantly, the essays offer writing scholars and teacher-educators ideas for new areas of writing research beyond the well-traveled practice of written corrective feedback (WCF), a topic we do not cover in this collection. For all readers, the chapters in this book will help them explore their own beliefs, values, and assumptions about what good writing means to them.

In particular, the chapters in this book cover the following areas connected to writing practices with and by multilingual students and faculty: (1) teaching, learning, and assessing; (2) mentoring, supervising, and publishing; (3) personal perspectives; and (4) readers and reading.

# Part I: Teaching, Learning, and Assessing

Part I brings together chapters that complicate the very notion of good writing in theory and practice. The authors contest the idea of generating a universal definition of "good writing," instead finding good writing to be a fragile construct, one largely dependent upon and defined by genre, audience, and purpose rather than simply on grammatical accuracy. To this end, readers are encouraged to look beyond the limitations offered by written corrective feedback (WCF) as a way to good writing and more toward the promise of responding at the discourse level in which nurturing the intellectual, ideational, and rhetorical needs of novice writers is prioritized over correcting sentence-level errors. Part I concludes powerfully with insights from a longitudinal self-assessment project of undergraduate writing that rejects the very idea of good writing and instead replaces it with nurturing the characteristics of a good writer.

# Part II: Mentoring, Supervising, and Publishing

Developing an awareness of good writing involves examining the role that mentorship plays in becoming a good academic writer. Part II takes a broad look at the ways in which good writing is rooted in and nurtured by the various relationships we have with writing including how our parents, teachers, supervisors, and editors socialize us into becoming academic writers and into developing a powerful voice. Building on the characteristics of the good writer and the importance of feedback in nurturing writers discussed in Part I, the chapters in Part II explore both the emotional connections and practical considerations between experts and novices around the writing enterprise.

# Part III: Personal Perspectives

Part III takes a deep dive into the personal beliefs, values, and experiences of accomplished academic writers in the fields of Applied Linguistics and TESOL. Authors share their struggles, setbacks, and successes writing and publishing in their first or second language. Building on Parts I and II, Part III spotlights the emergent nature of good writing, in which dialogue, agency, and reflexivity become essential characteristics of the accomplished academic writer.

# Part IV: Readers, Reading, and Writing

All writing, including academic writing, is storytelling. In Part IV, the final two chapters in this collection characterize good writing as a byproduct of astute and well-read writers who know their audience and can deliver a message that informs, inspires, and identifies them as full members of the discourse community. The benefits of extensive reading across multiple genres equip writers with an arsenal of tools, strategies, and approaches to making writing meaningful to the readers they want to reach. The importance of writers both connecting with readings and knowing their own audiences becomes critical, especially for graduate students and junior scholars who must meet the expectations of supervisors, editors, and reviewers in order to get their work accepted.

## References

Becker, H. S. (1986). *Writing for social scientists: How to start and finish your thesis, book, or article*. University of Chicago Press.

Billig, M. (2013). *Learn to write badly: How to succeed in the social sciences*. Cambridge University Press.

Huck, G. (2015). *What is good writing?* Oxford.

Leki, I. (1995). Good writing: I know it when I see it. In D. Belcher & G. Braine (Eds.), *Academic writing in a second language* (pp. 23–46). Ablex.

Mewburn, I. (2019). *Becoming an academic: How to get through grad school and beyond*. Johns Hopkins University Press.

Pinker, S. (2014a, September 26). Why academics stink at writing. *The Chronicle of Higher Education*. http://chronicle.com/article/Why-Academics-Writing-Stinks/148989/

Pinker, S. (2014b). *The sense of style: The thinking person's guide to writing in the 21st century*. Viking.

Reichelt, M. (2003). Defining good writing: A cross-cultural perspective. *Composition Studies, 31*(1), 99–126.

Strunk, W., & White, E. B. (2000). *The elements of style, fiftieth anniversary edition*. Longman.

Sword, H. (2009). Writing higher education differently: A manifesto on style. *Studies in Higher Education, 34*(3), 319–336.

Sword, H. (2012). *Stylish academic writing*. Harvard University Press.

Williams, J. M., & Bizup, J. (2015). *Style: The basics of clarity and grace* (11th ed.). Pearson Education.

Wong, M., & Godfrey, J. (Eds.). (2022). *What is good academic writing? Insights into discipline-specific student writing*. Bloomsbury Academic.

Zinsser, W. (2006). *On writing well*. HarperCollins.

# Part I

# Teaching, Learning, and Assessing

Chapter 1

# In Search of "Good" Argumentative Writing: A Traveler's Tale

*Alan Hirvela*

## Introduction

The best way for me to start is by establishing a few parameters. On the one hand, I doubt that we can define, conclusively, good L2 writing in a generic sense. Writing itself is just too large in scale. There are so many specific kinds of writing, for one thing. And there are so many contexts in which writing occurs, as well as so many people teaching it across the globe. Given these circumstances, among others, generating a "one size fits all" notion of good writing seems like a futile quest. On the other hand, I would not want to see the quest abandoned, and I believe we can make progress by narrowing the quest to good writing as it applies to specific types of writing. In the course of doing so, we might uncover approaches to the good writing quest that can be generalized to the larger search for an understanding of good writing. Even if we can't, in the end, conclusively define good writing in a broader sense, there's no harm in trying.

My engagement with this topic begins with one of my favorite pieces of L2 writing scholarship: Ilona Leki's still relevant and important 1995 book chapter, "Good Writing: I Know It When I See It." Very early in that chapter, she makes the following comments:

> When we teach freshman writing courses, implicit in the enterprise is the notion that we know what good writing is and that we can teach it

to our students within the confines of a non-discipline-specific writing course. . . . Yet as writing instructors we also know that the concept of writing is context-bound, that what is good writing in one instance is not as successful for all circumstances, that different contexts impose different, even contradictory constraints on writers. (pp. 23–24)

Here I want to use the notion of "context" to refer to different types, or genres, of writing. This is because what constitutes good writing for, say, a narrative essay is not the same for a type such as a synthesis essay. Such core features of academic writing as a thesis statement, introduction, and conclusion, as well as notions of organization and development, carry different expectations for quality relative to the type of essay being written. From this perspective, it seems almost pointless to try to construct generic notions of "good" L2 academic writing. A better idea is, as mentioned earlier, to tailor definitions of good writing to specific essay types. In that spirit, I have selected perhaps the most complex and challenging essay context of all for my focus: the argumentative essay.

I've made this choice for a couple of reasons. One is the widespread use and importance of argumentative writing in academic settings, a point acknowledged by many scholars over the years (e.g., Wolfe, 2011). This point applies to school-based writing as well as the high-stakes assessment context. It is commonly understood that argumentative writing matters, and yet, as I have asserted elsewhere (Hirvela, 2017), in the L2 writing field we are still pretty much "missing the boat" with respect to argumentation. Although there is good work being done, it is scattered across the scholarly and pedagogical landscape, and there is no centralized understanding of what we're dealing with. This is in sharp contrast to what I have called the "argument industry" in the L1 context, where a vast body of literature exists, including numerous textbooks and teacher resource books devoted solely to argumentative writing (Hirvela, 2020). This very large corpus of L1 literature has helped form something of a common understanding concerning argumentative writing in school contexts. The net result is that we have a conundrum in the L2 field: We agree that argumentative writing is important but are struggling in attempts to capture it fully. That includes establishing a consensus as to what represents "good" argumentative writing. A discussion of it relative to the "good writing" debate is one way of grappling with this situation while also contributing to the broader "good writing" discussion.

The other reason is my own longtime and significant engagement with argumentative writing as both a writing teacher and a scholar.

Argumentative writing has been on my professional radar screen for nearly a half century, and I'm still wrestling with it. But within that ongoing struggle lies a tale that I believe is worth telling. Furthermore, I think that many of us in the L2 writing community have interesting and useful argumentative writing tales to tell, tales that directly or indirectly involve an understanding of good writing, and that belief leads to the core viewpoint I want to convey in this chapter: that we can gain a great deal by gathering and analyzing these tales.

In this chapter I approach the "good writing" task in two ways. The first is by introducing the notion of "travelers' tales" and telling something of my own tale as it applies to argumentative writing. The second is to discuss a few tools we might use to shed light on the effort to characterize "good" argumentative writing.

## Travelers' Tales

To be honest, I don't know when the term "travelers' tales" entered the scholarly literature. I became aware of it around a quarter century ago while reading an article entitled "Adventuring into Writing Assessment" by Richard Haswell and Susan Wyche-Smith (1994) and have been intrigued by it ever since. In this article they explain how the writing faculty at their university successfully overcame administrative efforts to institute a writing assessment program that they opposed. They felt that a narrative account of that experience would be especially useful to other writing faculty facing similar circumstances. They characterized their effort "as a traveler's account with some travelers' advice rather than as an itinerary" on how to solve the kind of problem they encountered (1994, p. 221). This distinction between advice and itinerary, as well as the underlying belief in the power of narrative, strikes me as a very useful one. An important backdrop here is that, at that point in time, portfolios were beginning to gain popularity as a device to be used by individual teachers as well as by writing programs, and a number of writing scholars had published narratives of their adoption of the portfolio approach. As the number of these travelers' tales increased, the portfolio movement gained momentum, with informative and compelling narratives playing an important role in that process. Essential in this journey was the emphasis on offering insights on how to implement portfolio approaches rather than providing templates or rigid structures to be followed.

In the writing assessment field, an equivalent to the travelers' tales approach has been the publication of various attempts to validate schemes for assessing student writing. These accounts don't operate as narratives per se, but they perform the same basic function. That is, an assessment story is told, one that reflects the construct of "good writing" developed by the author(s). A prominent example of this kind in the argumentative writing context is Stuart Yeh's (1998) elaborate description of two studies he conducted of the argumentative writing composed by middle school students. Using Toulmin's (1958/2003) model of argumentative writing that has dominated argumentative writing pedagogy for several decades, Yeh tested the validity of two assessment scales he created, one more analytic in nature and one more holistic, each focusing on different aspects of argumentative writing. Through his detailed portrait of these validation efforts, Yeh was able to draw meaningful attention to many of the complexities associated with argumentative writing, especially an understanding of quality in such writing.

## My Traveler's Tale

I started my career as a writing teacher at a community college in the mid-1970s, and one of the essay types I had to teach was the argumentative essay. This was back in the days when writing courses were built around a progression from one essay type to another, i.e., the "rhetorical modes" approach. While no essay type was easy for me to teach as a novice in the profession of writing instruction, the argumentative essay was by far the most challenging. Indeed, I dreaded the argumentative unit each time I approached it. Whether it was due to my incompetence or the challenge of the essay type itself or a combination of the two, I'm not sure. But the bottom line is that the argumentative essay never stopped being the most difficult one for me to teach and assess, and the toughest one for students to learn.

Meanwhile, as a researcher, around twelve years ago, I began working with a few colleagues on what emerged over time as a major research agenda involving argumentation. Moving from small-scale, unfunded exploratory research to a tiny institutional grant and then to two large U.S. government funded projects, our team explored, in the L1 context, the teaching and learning of argumentative writing in over sixty local high school English Language Arts classrooms. (For detailed accounts of our research, see Newell, Bloome, & Hirvela, 2015; Bloome, Newell, Hirvela, & Lin, 2020.)

From a "good writing" perspective, what emerged from this significant engagement with argumentative writing over a long period of time? One point, or one part of the traveler's tale, was that there was anything but a unified understanding among the teachers we worked with as to what represented good argumentative writing. Instead, it was highly situated. This was partly because they were teaching students at different grade levels and for different lengths of time, along with different settings (urban and suburban). They were also teaching argumentative writing for different purposes: some for literary analysis and some as an academic essay type. They were also using different models of argumentation or basically different interpretations and adaptations of the ubiquitous Toulmin model introduced in 1958. Then, too, given how many students have struggled with this form of writing, just as research has long shown, the teachers often had to adjust their expectations for such writing, so that it was something of a moving target. Seeing all of this variability was enlightening, to say the least, and it highlighted how complex, and unique, argumentation is compared to other forms of writing taught to pre-college students.

Our classroom-based research involved working within specific settings over an extended period of time (usually an entire school year in which a researcher worked with the same teacher) and included audio- and videotaping of class sessions, gathering students' writing and teachers' instructional materials, and interviewing students and teachers. We also administrated pre- and post-tests of students' argumentative writing. What we saw was astonishing in its variety and its quality, especially after conducting intensive pre-study summer workshops with our participating teachers. We, the research team, thought that a common framework for argumentation had been established through our workshops. However, once the teachers were back in their schools and confronting the day-to-day realities of teaching and learning, they made constant adjustments to account for local needs and circumstances.

Under these conditions, a notion of "good" argumentative writing that would be accurate and applicable across contexts was unattainable. It was easy to recognize good teaching, and we saw a lot of it, but "good" writing was another matter. This was an important takeaway from our research that dominated our writing about it. That is, we could identify good (and not-so-good) teaching and articulate, in detail, what we saw as important features of expertise in argumentative writing instruction. This was an exciting and meaningful part of our collective travelers' tale.

The previous paragraph leads to the second part of this traveler's tale, the part that concerns assessment of the student writing we collected and attempts to recognize "good" argumentative writing. This was an especially illuminating part of our overall tale, and it proved to be an extraordinarily complicated and frustrating, though educational, experience. We were presumably the "experts," and though we may have done well with respect to the data-gathering activities we engaged in, the quest to score the pre- and post-test writing we had collected was a long series of trial-and-error attempts that illustrate how challenging it is to define quality in argumentative writing.

The process started with establishing a core model of argumentation to work with, as our assessment tool had to have some foundation to build on, and here we went in the direction most people go, for better or worse: Toulmin. And understandably so. There are reasons why Toulmin's model dominates in argumentative pedagogy, beginning with its common characterization as a "practical" model of argumentation (Bracewell, 1998, 153). Kunnan (2010, p. 14) explained that the "Toulmin model of argument structure is a method of practical reasoning with a structured mascrostructure of arguments." Teachers and assessors like this clarity. Or, as Yeh (1998, p. 127) noted, "A major advantage of Toulmin's model, from a pedagogical perspective, is the simple procedural representation of the basic layout of arguments . . . the model suggests both goals and procedures for writing a simple argument, facilitating instruction of novices." Thus, it is an especially teacher-friendly model to use, so it was no surprise to us to see our participating teachers' awareness of it and preference for using it.

Also worth noting is that there are different versions of Toulmin's model that can assist pedagogy and that add to the model's appeal. In his initial model presented in 1958, Toulmin's primary focus was on three core elements: claim, grounds (evidence), and warrants connecting the evidence with the claim. He eventually moved to what is often referred to as a secondary dimension that includes three additional components: counterarguments, rebuttals, and backing. Thus, depending on their instructional circumstances, teachers can opt for what our research team called the "simple Toulmin" three-component model he originally proposed, or what we labeled the "complex Toulmin" version that comprises all of the six elements he wrote about later.

The existence of these two versions of the Toulmin model was important for us, because each version was in use over the course of our research. This meant that we had to create an assessment tool, a workable rubric that would map onto what we were observing in the classrooms. We found no existing rubric that fit our parameters sufficiently, and so we set out to create our own. That is an unpleasant tale in itself. Because the different parts of the argument are so important in the Toulmin model and because we were interested in students' handling of each of the parts, we spent a considerable amount of time constructing and testing different versions of an analytic rubric in which points were awarded separately for each of these core elements of the argumentative essay. We then practiced using different versions of this rubric on selected samples of the students' writing.

In the end, we reluctantly rejected the analytic approach. It appealed to us as researchers, but no matter which version we used, it didn't account fully for how this large body of teachers had taught these argumentative features in the different instructional contexts at hand. Such a situation highlights the challenges involved in identifying "good" argumentative writing. If your assessment tool doesn't work, then how do you know what's good?

A particular area of concern that vexed us was warranting, which many of our teachers professed to not fully understanding or to feeling insecure about teaching and yet is a core element of argumentation in the Toulmin model. Warrants are basically statements of the assumptions that connect claims and evidence so as to strengthen the argument being made. We found that some taught it and some didn't, and those that did barely taught it. And it was clear from our classroom observations that students tended to be lost during the warranting-oriented instruction units. As such, we couldn't assume that all of the essays being scored would include it. The same issue applied to counterarguments and rebuttals. There was so much variation among the essays in terms of what was and wasn't taught and included in the writing that the analytic approach simply didn't work. The scores we obtained were too erratic to be useful because the essays varied so widely in terms of what they had and didn't have and in what quantities.

We then moved on, reluctantly, to holistic scoring, and here the going was not any easier. We once again developed and tried a number of versions of a holistic rubric, but scoring among the team members was scattered, even after considerable attempts to calibrate ourselves as well as others we brought into the assessment process because of the large volume of essays to be scored. Achieving acceptable levels of inter-rater agreement, as with our use of analytic rubrics, was difficult and frustrating work, though it did allow us to gain general pictures of the writing produced and was an improvement over our analytic rubrics. However, we realized that the holistic scoring wasn't really telling us much that we wanted (indeed, needed) to know about students' command of the architecture of argumentation. The impressionistic scoring of essays as a whole simply could not capture what we wanted to learn about.

In the final analysis, we were caught in a dilemma we never did resolve satisfactorily, which is partly why our publications have focused on the teaching and not the writing, including not directly articulating what constitutes "good" argumentative writing. With argumentation taught to so many students in so many different educational settings or contexts, locking onto a "one-size-fits-all" construct of argumentative writing would not have worked. On the one hand, we were keenly interested in how students handled the different components of an argumentative essay. After all, argumentative writing is rooted in these components, as is the teaching of argumentation. But this means there is more to account for in trying to characterize "good" writing. This is where argumentation separates itself from the other kinds of writing that are commonly taught; the other types don't include such discrete, and complex, parts.

Our assessment tale illustrates a conflict that Edward White captured long ago in a famous essay called "Holisticism" (1984) that was published as the analytic-holistic scoring debate was generating considerable heat:

> To proceed holistically is to see things as units, as complete, as *wholes*, and to do so is to oppose the dominant tendency of our time, the analytic spirit, which breaks things down into constituent parts in order to see how they work. Analytic reductionism assumes that knowledge of the parts will lead to understanding of the whole. . . . Holisticism argues against reductionism and denies that the whole is only the sum of the parts. (p. 400)

Our travelers' tale brought us into the heart of the search for a clear, indisputable understanding of "good" argumentative writing and good writing in general. A point worth noting here is that, in addition to our unhappy adventures with analytic and then holistic rubrics, we also tried scoring some essays using both our analytic and holistic rubrics. Interestingly, the outcomes were somewhat different. What was "good" with one rubric wasn't necessarily "good," or "as good," with the other. Not that there were large gaps between the two assessments, but there was enough of a difference to muddy the "good writing" waters.

In the end, for the most part we could eventually agree about the really outstanding and really poor writing. But nearly all of what we saw fell in between those two poles on the assessment scale, and that is where our assessment tale is also useful. This is perhaps the dilemma that many writing teachers and specialists run into and that we are confronting in the "good writing" debate, whatever type of writing is involved: how to work with the large amount of writing that falls between the often more obvious top and the bottom? What are the finer distinctions to be made between different levels of quality? And how do we make them in acceptable ways? In my mind, these are the central questions concerning identification of good writing.

In the final analysis, my hope is that this traveler's tale as it applies to argumentative writing sheds some light on how complex such writing is and why we struggle to agree on what constitutes "good" argumentative writing. There are so many parts to account for and so many variables at hand.

## Options for Attempting to Define "Good" Argumentative Writing

Regarding the questions I just posed with respect to argumentative writing, I would need far more space to address them meaningfully than I have here. Instead, I want to briefly discuss two tools that I believe could prove to be useful in chipping away at the notion of "good" argumentative writing for both teachers and students. These can be applied across the grade level board, from pre-university contexts to undergraduate writing courses. Each of them operates from a developmental perspective. That is, each takes into account the complexity involved in learning how to compose arguments as well as the many contexts in which argumentative writing may be attempted. Because we are so often teaching novice L2 writers and argumentation is so challenging, this developmental view seems to me to be essential.

### Emergent Arguments

One of these tools I find intriguing is the notion of "emergent arguments" proposed by Pessoa, Mitchell, and Miller (2017). They note that "University students across disciplines are often expected to write argumentative texts. However, many students, particularly L2 writers, struggle writing arguments and teachers may not be prepared to scaffold argumentative writing" (p. 46). Under these circumstances, as they see it, students' argumentative essays can be viewed from an "emergent arguments" angle that calls for viewing these essays as "texts that meet some of the expectations for argumentative writing but not others" (p. 46) and working *with* such limitations where they appear. These are the texts that fall within the important gray area I noted earlier: that complicated and large space *between* poor and very good writing. This is where I feel our most important work can occur. Utilizing this emergent argument construct would allow teachers to differentiate between what works and what doesn't in an argumentative essay and thus better understand the different levels of quality between good and poor.

The Pessoa et al. approach, which is illustrated in their work through the lens of first-year university students writing arguments in a history class, draws on resources provided by Systemic Functional Linguistics (SFL) that can be applied to the exploration of specific genres of writing across different disciplines. Pessoa et al. developed what they called an SFL-based "toolkit" teachers can use as they respond to students' argumentative writing. This tool makes it possible to "highlight these texts' mixed effectiveness in meeting genre expectations" (p. 46). In their view, "under this conceptualization of writing, instructors can isolate particular resources to help students meet genre expectations more effectively" (p. 54).

This approach operates like an analytic rubric, but as applied to instruction rather than assessment. By focusing on specific elements typically included in an argumentative essay from an "emergent arguments" framework, teachers can not only tease out what works and what doesn't work but also develop a more finely grained understanding of what "good" writing is for novice writers grappling with the many nuances of argumentative writing. Such an approach may make it easier to distinguish between, say, an adequate or fairly good essay and a good one and help address our issues concerning the understanding of good writing.

## "Good-Enough" Writing

Another tool I want to discuss, and one that is part of my own traveler's tale, is the notion of "good-enough" writing. I have been fascinated by this idea for many years after reading, in 1997, an article by Margaret Mackey called "Good-Enough Reading: Momentum and Accuracy in the Reading of Complex Fiction." As the article's title suggests, it has no connection to writing. However, I've long felt that there is value in applying the "good-enough" idea to writing and have made various attempts to do so in my own teaching.

Mackey states that her article "illustrates how readers of complex fiction engage in a good-enough reading in which they strike a balance between the need for momentum and the need for accountability to the text" (p. 428). The article discusses what she found when she had a wide range of readers—eighth and eleventh grade students, undergraduates, and a doctoral student—read the same young adult novel. At the core of her observations was what amounted to compromises some of the readers made as they engaged with the reading task. In their case, it was the need to keep moving through the text—instead of stalling—while also trying to decode the author's intentions. While doing so, many of them found it difficult to fully complete both acts and so they cut corners where they could and, perhaps more importantly, could live with the compromises they made. In short, they lowered their expectations and were comfortable with "good-enough" readings of the text. From an assessment perspective, the "good-enough" category made it possible to arrive at more meaningful evaluations of their reading.

As a writing teacher, I have envisioned similar elements in writing. That is, writers need to complete the writing task and try to meet the expectations associated with the task. However, many writers will be unable to do so when the writing task is a challenging one. In the case of argumentative writing, this could mean constructing a workable claim or thesis but adopting (and accepting) shortcuts in supporting the claim with suitable evidence or failing to present warrants linking the evidence persuasively to the claim. What comes out of this still looks superficially like an argumentative essay, albeit an incomplete one. It is "good-enough" at that point in time and for the struggling writer.

This, in fact, is what we often saw, or suspected, in the writing we analyzed in the argumentative writing research I described earlier. For instance, we saw many instances in which students, knowing they were expected to engage in warranting, made half-hearted attempts to do so. It appeared that, in their eyes, this was good enough. Even if what they did was incomplete, there were traces of attempts made, and they were presumably comfortable with these compromises between task expectation and task execution.

As a traveler in the world of argumentative writing, I have, over the years, come to see how a notion of "good-enough" argumentative writing would help in making the distinction I noted earlier: between writing that is adequate and writing that is fairly or reasonably good—that exasperating gray area in argumentative writing that both analytic and holistic rubrics seem unable to account for meaningfully.

Mackey explains that "scholars, teachers, and readers need to develop a vocabulary that will permit an acknowledgement of the tentative and the unfinished in readers' approaches to complex text" (p. 428), and I would argue that we have the same need in trying to define "good" argumentative writing. Given how challenging such writing is for many students, knowing how to account for the "tentative" and the "unfinished" in their argumentative essays might help us in our engagement with defining good writing. As I said earlier, we are often on reasonably safe ground when it comes to knowing what is really good or what is poor. It is all that space in between that I think we're really wrestling with in the good writing quest. Not that we have fixed ideas of good or poor. But, as Leki observed, we somehow know the good writing when we see it, even if we can't explain why it's good. The same is probably true with the poorer writing. What is harder to explain is the sort of good and the nearly good, i.e., the good-enough, and what separates them from the really good, especially in a demanding form of writing like the argumentative essay.

Here it might be said that "good-enough" argumentative writing is similar to the "emergent arguments" idea, and that is probably the case. Each, as noted earlier, takes a developmental view toward argumentative writing and students' journey toward good writing. At a broader level, the terms may overlap. However, there may also be circumstances in which one of the terms is more suitable than the other. Whatever the case may be, I see these two notions as potentially useful contributions to our efforts to define "good" argumentative writing and other kinds of writing as well. I believe each, in its own way, can help explain the important and vexing space between the poor and the good, and the more we know about that space between, the better we understand each end of the continuum: the poor and especially the good.

## Conclusion

When Liz Hamp-Lyons became editor of the journal *Assessing Writing*, she wrote in her introductory article (2002) the following observations that still resonate strongly as we address the search for an understanding of "good writing" that motivated the formation of this edited collection on good writing:

> When writing is assessed, that which is assessed is less well-understood than many other constructs. The questions: What is good writing? How do we know? According to whom? and similar ones, remain intriguing because they remain unresolved. (pp. 5–6)

I think these questions may always be unresolved, especially if we focus too heavily on the definitions themselves and not the means by which we attempt to answer them. This is where I feel that travelers' tales can play a helpful role, as they did when portfolios entered the writing field. Much was learned, and gained, as we heard different tales of attempts to adopt effective portfolio schemes. The same is true for me in my own tale of making sense of argumentative writing over a long period of time. Gathering and then analyzing travelers' tales of efforts to define or categorize good writing, especially within a framework in which we focus on specific types of writing instead of one generic brand, may help us construct a way forward that would make the good writing quest more manageable and effective.

In my case, looking back over my own traveler's tale with respect to argumentative writing, I can pinpoint lessons learned and insights gained. Constructing such a tale involves identifying and sorting out important information and key moments that contribute to the evolving narrative, and this is where learning occurs.

Where we can make progress in this quest to come to terms with good writing, in my view, is by taking a closer look at *how* we go about this quest instead of focusing so much on the end product of a definition of good writing. I think that creating, collecting, and comparing more travelers' tales would be a useful step in that process.

## References

Bloome, D., Newell, G., Hirvela, A., & Lin, T-J. (2020). *Dialogic literary argumentation in high school language arts classrooms: A social perspective for teaching, learning, and reading literature.* Routledge.

Bracewell, R. J. (1998). Commentary on "Validation of a scheme for assessing argumentative writing of middle school students." *Assessing Writing, 5,* 151–157.

Hamp-Lyons, L. (2002). The scope of writing assessment. *Assessing Writing, 8,* 5–16.

Haswell, R., & Wyche-Smith, S. (1994). Adventuring into writing assessment. *College Composition and Communication, 45,* 220–236.

Hirvela, A. (2017). Argumentation and second language writing: Are we missing the boat? *Journal of Second Language Writing, 36*, 69–74.

Hirvela, A. (2020). Argumentative writing and textbooks: Implications for teaching, learning, and development. In L. Grujicic-Alatriste & C. Crosby Grundleger (Eds.), *Second language writing in transitional spaces: Teaching and learning across educational contexts* (pp. 237–262). University of Michigan Press.

Kunnan, A. J. (2010). Test fairness and Toulmin's argument structure. *Language Testing, 27*, 183–189.

Leki, I. (1995). Good writing: I know it when I see it. In D. Belcher & G. Braine (Eds.), *Academic writing in a second language: Essays on research and pedagogy* (pp. 23–46). Ablex Publishing Company.

Mackey, M. (1997). Good-enough reading: Momentum and accuracy in the reading of complex fiction. *Research in the Teaching of English, 31*, 428–458.

Newell, G., Bloome, D., & Hirvela, A. (2015). *Teaching and learning argumentative writing in high school English language arts classrooms*. Routledge.

Pessoa, S., Mitchell, T. D., & Miller, R. T. (2017). Emergent arguments: A functional approach to analyzing student challenges with the argument genre. *Journal of Second Language Writing, 38*, 42–55.

Toulmin, S. (1958/2003). *The uses of argument*. Cambridge University Press.

White, E. M. (1984). Holisticism. *College Composition and Communication, 35*, 400–409.

Wolfe, C. R. (2011). Argumentation across the curriculum. *Written Communication, 28(2)*, 193–219.

Yeh, S. S. (1998). Validation of a scheme for assessing argumentative writing of middle school students. *Assessing Writing, 5*, 123–150.

# Chapter 2

# "It Depends. . . ."

*Penny Kinnear*

Language and writing teachers need to have conversations. We need to delve into the terms we use on a regular basis but that we assume everyone understands. A discussion of "good" as applied to writing seems like a good place to start. Currently, I work within the context of a specific set of genres, "engineering communication," at a university where the majority of engineering students arrive with complex linguistic profiles and proficiencies but must learn to speak, read, and write in "English engineering." My students have equally complex and diverse experiences with writing and writing instruction. On the occasions I have had the opportunity to raise the question of "good" writing with colleagues, the conversations have been limited to lexicogrammatical mechanics, coherence and cohesion, and argument structure and clarity in engineering writing. The meanings of the terms used in the conversations were tacit. We assumed that everyone shared an understanding of exactly what each of those terms meant and the mechanics of achieving them. When multilingual student writing was understood to be the object of my inquiry, the criteria veered almost completely to lexicogrammatical accuracy, vocabulary, and citation practices. Pushing a little further into, "Well, how can we teach students how to better meet the criteria you mention?" the response would usually focus on improving the use of proofreading and editing practices (learning to use spell-check), adhering to citation norms, identifying topic sentences, using shorter paragraphs, using more active verbs, and meeting the requirements of the assignment. Suggestions like these all have merit but provide only a partial answer to a perplexing question.

**17**

Although I agree with the premise of engaging in (and even stirring up) these conversations about "good writing," I also think we need to include our students as we build an understanding of not just what good writing means but also how we as teachers and students can teach and learn to recognize and produce "good writing." I have played with this idea for several years, prompted first by an experience in a course I taught in a professional writing program. I asked my class in one of our first meetings to provide criteria we could use to judge "good writing." Out of the class of seventy-five, a few students volunteered "no grammar mistakes," "no spelling or punctuation mistakes," "good language," and "has a hook." And then the class fell silent. When I asked for details, the students met me with averted looks and more silence.

I dropped the topic until the next class. I began that class by playing three music selections—a classic jazz vocal by Billie Holiday, a hip-hop piece by Meshell Ndegeocello, and a bubblegum pop piece. I asked the students to listen, and I watched them respond. Next, I asked them to decide which was "good" music. They had been divided into small groups of four or five students, and the ensuing conversations were lively! I gave them about ten minutes and then asked for a report. The students talked about styles, beats, melody, harmony, lyrics, images in the lyrics, political references, unexpected turns in rhythm, and on and on. The students actively listened to one another and competed to have their ideas heard. I waited a bit longer and then interrupted and asked, "Why can't you talk about writing with such detail and nuance?" It temporarily stopped the discussions, but it also started students thinking about writing both inside and outside the classroom.

I explicitly state at the beginning of a course that I will have met my teaching goals if I have made the need for me to assess their writing obsolete by the end of the course. I put that into practice in one course by requiring that students submit their final written assignment during the scheduled final exam time. After the students took their places in the exam room, I distributed the marking rubric we had used all term and instructed them to mark their papers, including in-line comments and feedback. They also had to assign a mark to the paper and justify it with reference to the rubric and their feedback. Most of the students, once they got over the shock of the "exam," provided detailed critiques and marks that matched or were within a half-letter of the mark I had assigned. I was most interested in reading their critiques, as they often clarified how the students had been able to "step back" and read their work from a reader's perspective. However, on deliberation, I also realized that we had only come to an agreement about what counted as "good writing" for that specific class in that specific time and place. Would that really serve them in a different class or in a context outside of a university classroom?

Since then I have also played with the idea of collaboratively building rubrics by analyzing writing assignments through the lenses of Halliday's concepts of field, tenor, and mode (Halliday, 2002). This approach recognizes that part of the criteria does indeed acknowledge institutional expectations, but it only tickled the edges beyond the specific assignment within a classroom. The students used the rubrics to guide their writing and then the evaluation and feedback of peers' writing and eventually their own. The conversations during the analysis activity engaged the students and challenged them to clarify, prioritize, take positions, and commit to a definition of "good" in that context, at least. But even though the development of criteria in the class served to define "good writing" in that particular context, it did not provide a broader conceptualization of good writing. Serendipitously, I received the invitation to consider the question "What makes good writing?" at the same time I introduced a more systematic approach to developing students' ability to judge their own writing. This happened in a small class I teach that focuses on three questions: "What is language, what is meaning, and what are the relationships between them?" I asked the students if they would be interested in helping me to answer that question, and they responded enthusiastically, usually within minutes of the invitation going out. However, our endeavours were disrupted by the global COVID-19 pandemic that disrupted everyone's lives as well as our class. A year later I reached out again to set up online discussions. I learned that the question remained important to them, not just in terms of their marks but in terms of their professions, their own writing, and their own reading. They were all engineering students from different engineering disciplines and ranged from recent entrants to the program starting their second year of studies to the newly graduated preparing to begin their work careers. They were also a diverse group with interesting linguistic histories. Although none of them were monolingual English speakers, they all had most of their formal education in English medium institutions while maintaining various home languages and in many cases receiving varying degrees of literacy instruction in their other languages, which include Arabic, Mandarin, Hindi, French, Afrikaans, and Yoruba. . . . I found all the students thoughtful, willing to contest and explore ideas; they were all practitioners of writing and avid readers. They were interested in trying to understand this thing called "writing" and its qualities.

I was rewarded with six positive and enthusiastic responses when I reached out to my former students. Kerryn, who told me after the course that she had NEVER worked so hard in a course or enjoyed it so much, had been a second-year engineering science student when she took the course. She had been raised and educated in South Africa and was bilingual in Afrikaans and English. Nili had been a first-year student from India who had completed her mandatory calculus course the previous summer so had an opening in her schedule. She was multilingual and multiliterate in Hindi, English, and Urdu. Sahar was in the final semester of her electrical and computer engineering degree. She was multilingual in English, Arabic, and French, and a huge fan of K-pop so had begun learning Korean as well. Leo was in the last term of his engineering degree. He had been born in Canada but had been raised with both English and Mandarin and, of course, mandatory French at school. Victoria was a second-year student when she took the course. She had been raised in her parents' home languages and had been educated in English in Botswana. Michael was a first-year engineering student raised in China with Mandarin as his primary language. The students were scattered, so we arranged two separate meetings on Zoom to accommodate their availability and that didn't require anyone to meet online in the middle of the night or before dawn. I sent the students the following list of questions to think about:

- What is "good" writing?
- How do you know writing is "good"?
- What do you look for in good writing?
- Where have you encountered good writing? What did you respond to in that writing?
- How do you judge your own writing as "good" (or "good enough")?
- What disqualifies writing (yours or someone else's) from the "good" category?
- Who showed you good writing? How did they do that?
- What is the role of your other language(s) in defining/ confusing/clarifying your ideas and practices of making your writing good?
- How do you learn to be a good writer?

Once we got caught up on each other's recent accomplishments and whereabouts, we plunged into the conversation. As I had expected, they all had thought and prepared, and they all had much to say. We followed the conversation rather than letting the questions guide us. We looped between "prepared" thoughts and ideas that emerged from the conversations. There were thoughtful pauses, lulls, and animated overlaps (as much as Zoom made possible). Both conversations extended more than an hour over the planned time. With the students' permission, I have imposed some structure on the reproduction of our conversations as we all attempted to define "good writing."

As my students stated, the marks they receive are their first indication of the quality of the "goodness" of their work. If they get a high mark, then the writing must be good. Digging into this initial measure of quality, the students clarified that they understood "good" as a measure of how closely the writing met the requirements, the expectations of that professor, that course, or that TA but conceded that it really did not mean that it was "good." From here they suggested that because different kinds of writing serve different purposes and different readers, one measure of good writing would have to take into consideration how well the writing serves the purpose and meets the needs of the readers. "Good" is determined by who reads the writing for what purpose. A business major will judge the writing differently than a psychology major, who will judge it differently than a literature major and so on. "It depends" guided the deliberations of "good writing" and how to achieve it. As Kerryn put it, " 'Good' can and *should* have many meanings." "Good" is sensitive to time, to experience, to periods of life, to circumstances, and to contexts. Importantly, as we discussed the criteria for good writing, we continued to deliberate the ways the students learned to judge and produce good writing and the roles that their other languages and cultures played in the process.

All of these students confirmed that their criteria for good writing began with their school experiences. As Sahar summarized it, "In elementary and middle school, we are pushed to be expressive, to tell stories, be descriptive, be emotional but then when we go to high school it becomes all about making arguments and being logical, until we have to write our university essays and all of a sudden, we have to show emotions again. We get really mixed messages!"

Their early judgments of good writing focused on correct spelling, good grammar, a clear temporal order, and, (they ventured) long and complex sentences that would make a writer sound sophisticated. They paired this with striving to meet the teacher's expectations, or at least the expectations they perceived the teacher as having, usually expressed through rubrics, the rules paired with a certain genre, and the examples that were sometimes provided. The rules were easy to follow and usually, if followed carefully, garnered positive results. Nili recounted how her English teachers provided specific rules for writing a persuasive essay or presenting an argument that made it "easy" to produce a "good" piece of writing. But, as we all dug a little more into our experiences with "rules," they concluded that just following the rules will lead to rigidity in one's writing. Following a set of rules limits a writer. No one saw that as a sufficient way to determine if writing was "good"—perhaps necessary but certainly not sufficient.

But it is not just the words that a writer chooses to use or the sentences that a writer crafts but also the intentions behind those words—a balance between achieving clarity and ensuring that information, position, ideas, or images are clearly understood while simultaneously respecting a reader's knowledge and understanding of the subject and the context. It's not just about judging or "knowing your audience" but more of a balancing of two positions—the reader and the writer and how they see and respond to one another. The students explored their understanding of this reader-writer relationship throughout the conversation. Understanding and respecting that relationship stood out as a hallmark of good writing.

Acknowledging readers, the students agreed that a writer needed to communicate their intentions in some way. Perception of intent, with the understanding that a reader can never completely know what the writer's intentions were, was seen as necessary. However, how that might be accomplished becomes one of the writer's challenges. Kerryn added, "As a writer, and what I appreciate in a piece of good writing, is where I can feel the writer guiding me to understand their intentions." Intentions will come through in layers (as meaning is also layered). Part of that may be accomplished in how the writing is structured. Sometimes this is explicitly accomplished, one layer at least, in an introduction. But good writing guides a reader throughout a text. The writer doesn't just assume a reader will draw the same meanings from the writing. Writers may develop a signature way of doing this through their organization at both the paragraph and whole text level, their use of repetition, or their ability to circle back to main points or ideas. I interpreted this as a kind of "checking in with their reader to make sure everyone was still on the same page."

"Good writing" depends on who is reading the writing and for what purpose. The students brought up their own experiences to consider how a business executive, an English teacher, or a lawyer is not likely to draw the same judgments about what each consider good writing to be—or at least not in all genres, which took the students to a consideration of murder mysteries.

The business executive and the lawyer may well judge a murder mystery as good writing—but when judging that murder mystery, they employ a set of criteria specific to their expectations around being entertained, mystified, or challenged to "solve" the mystery before the answer is revealed. However, that same lawyer and business executive will both employ a different set of criteria when reading a brief or a contract—even the same brief or contract. Again, the students were cognizant of and concerned with the reader-writer relationship. Leo referred to his experience (and received several sympathetic nods of understanding) in preparing written documents for his co-workers shortly after he started a year-long internship. He had just started and was unsure of just how formally he should write, with what degree of technicality, how much background knowledge his readers (new work colleagues) would have. He was keenly aware that making the wrong choices in any of these categories could result in a judgment of his competence, his professionalism, his assumptions about his co-workers. He talked about feeling nearly paralyzed in those first weeks. This prompted the question of just how a writer makes those kinds of decisions.

The ability to make those decisions must come first from an awareness that a genre has multiple expressions that are often dependent on the context. The writer then has a responsibility to get to know that context and their potential readers. For Leo, that meant listening carefully to the ways his colleagues, his supervisors, and his managers spoke with him and with each other. It also included carefully reading and analyzing the written communication that he received, looking for the patterns, for the jargon, for the tone, even for the organization and formatting. As successful students, all of them had relied on doing this in different contexts, at first unconsciously and eventually consciously. Sahar, an avid writer of fan fiction, described her own learning by both reading what others posted and the comments they received as well as posting her own efforts and getting comments on her attempts. Although much can be learned from reading and observing, it is also necessary to be able to interrogate what is being observed and assumed. Depending on the context, a writer will ask a teacher, another student, a mentor, someone whose writing they admire in their attempt to gather the information that they can use to make decisions that will suit their readers and their needs and criteria for not just acceptable but actually good writing.

Another perspective of this reader-writer relationship was expressed as "Good writing *engages* a reader." Just what readers are engaged with also depends. It may depend on the topic, although the topic alone is usually not enough to maintain the engagement of every reader. Engagement may depend on the topic or the experiences shared in the writing because they resonate with a reader. Sometimes, the craftsmanship itself creates pleasure and appreciation of just how the writer has sculpted a sentence, a paragraph, or an entire piece, leading to the frank admiration of reading something and then responding with "Damn, that's good." Engagement can also flow from a sense of connection with the writer rather than the craftsmanship of the writing alone. The students acknowledged that depending on their feeling of connection with the writer, they might judge something differently. Which took us back to "It depends."

Turning back to the writing itself, the students listed the following qualities: flow, rhythm, meaning. Interestingly, in work-related writing, in personal writing, and in writing they read, meaning emerged as the primary criterion. As readers, they looked for meaning first because if they could find meaning, that indicated that they could begin a dialogue. As writers, they also prioritized meaning, although they also admitted that that had not always been the case. As Victoria and Michael had described, when they first began writing in English, it was about following the rules, checking the required boxes, and meeting the expectations of an assessor. However, as they began to master the mechanics, meaning-making began to take priority. They noted a tension between the writer's meaning and the reader's meaning and the role of conventions and expectations. Is writing still good if a writer violates some of the genre conventions in order to preserve or express the writer's meaning? There is a creative tension here, also an expressive tension even in their professional or student writing. How far can they push against the boundaries to express meaning, including expressions of their own personalities, without compromising the judgment of their readers? The answer came back to "It depends," but it depended on meaning not being obscured for a reader because the writer had bent the conventions. It also depended on the writer's meaning not being compromised because the writer had strictly adhered to the conventions. Sahar admitted to pushing the boundaries here, often placing something to please or entertain even in the professional documents that she had produced during her sixteen-month internship with a large software company the previous year. This balancing act requires a keen awareness of reader expectations, contextual expectations, and the writer's own intended meaning. It is not a foolproof process.

But how does a writer learn all of this? How does a writer learn to judge good writing, to produce good writing? Hands down, everyone agreed that you learn to write by engaging in the activity of writing, doing the writing. Even though that may be necessary, they also agreed that it is not sufficient. Experiencing good writing through reading; gaining sufficient competence with the mechanics of written language; engaging in a variety of critique and revision dialogues are equally necessary activities. They were unwilling to separate definitions and descriptions of good writing from the activity of writing in much the same way that they embraced the need to acknowledge and understand the nature of the relationship between reader and writer. It became necessary to explore just how someone learns to write in order to produce "good" writing.

Understanding good writing comes from the experience of good writing that comes from reading widely, both all the required school reading and exploring their own interests outside of the classroom. It is important to read with purpose and to read outside of your own "comfort zone." In our class I had required them to read selections from Bakhtin's essay, "Discourse in the Novel" from *The Dialogic Imagination* (Bakhtin, 1981), Vygotsky's *Thought and Language* (Vygotsky, 1986), and several research articles from the field of applied linguistics. All of these were far from the academic and technical text reading they were familiar with as engineering students. The readings were far outside the students' "comfort zone," but they accepted the challenge and engaged with the texts and learned from them. They learned the concepts, but they also learned more about writing. We even compared excerpts from two translations of Vygotsky's work that prompted a lively discussion of the differences in vocabulary choice, style, and organization. This exercise, along with discussions of their responses to their own explorations of different genres, helped the students articulate their criteria for good writing (from a reader's perspective) and the reasons for their preferences of one approach over another.

In classroom settings from elementary school to university, the students' instructors paid attention to the writing craft through analysis of an author's style, sentence structure, use of language, and literary techniques such as metaphor, simile, and alliteration. Looking at and using examples of good writing produces a tension. Examples, like rules, have value but also limitations. The students made a point of differentiating between blind and rigid imitation of examples (trying to write like Hemingway or Shakespeare or IBM's annual shareholder's report, because they had all tried at least one of these) and knowing what to pick out from the example that gives the example its genre or style character in order to make use of those structures, vocabulary choices, and organizational principles to gain acceptance and comprehension from their readers.

A tension often exists between instructors and students around the provision of "examples." Instructors often resist providing examples as they, accurately or not, assume students will unquestioningly imitate them. Students ask for examples to help them make the leap from decontextualized and abstract rubric descriptions to their own sentences and paragraphs. Examples have limits. Examples prove useful only if they are analyzed and discussed with a focus on decisions an author made and the impact of those decisions on meaning. Although it is impossible to know a writer's motivation for writing decisions, it is possible to analyze the impact of those decisions. In doing this, the students saw utility as they could make more intentional decisions with their own writing. They also noted that those kinds of discussions rarely occur in classes or in the feedback they receive.

Providing a little more nuance, especially around using literary examples from any culture or language's canon, the students argued that the examples were not so much a way to teach writing as samples of written art, time capsules that captured a society's use of language and values. Having exposure to such pieces provided an understanding of cultural and linguistic references and history, which then gave the students multiple ways of interpreting what they read. As this part of the discussion took shape, the students relied more on their multilingual experiences. Depending on the subject they were writing about and genre they were writing in, the students might call on their other languages (including their knowledge of the culture, historic as well as current), language practices, and historical and cultural references. The students understood that their other languages could help them by making them explain, search for, and try different expressions of an idea until they could find the word or expression that pleases the reader and captures the intended meaning. They also had found the limits to these explorations. Sometimes this exploration would take them to something they could only approximate in English, forcing them to acknowledge the limitations of any single named language.

Analysis and discussion serve only one function of examples. Examples can also be used as models for imitation, usually at the sentence level. Perhaps because we had spent time during the class differentiating between mimicry and imitation from a Vygotskian perspective, the students focused on learning from their imitations. Each had imitated different writers at different points in their writing lives. They imitated to learn. Sometimes it was to try out a technique such as Hemingway's short, direct sentences and then decide not to use it. Sometimes it was about incorporating expressions or even vocabulary words into their writing until they could appropriate them (in a Bakhtinian sense) as their own—or not. The examples were not simply to be mimicked; the students were adamant that unthinking mimicry limited, rather than strengthened, their ability to produce good writing.

Looking beyond the sentence to paragraphs and documents took us to genre conventions. These conventions that have been agreed upon can be useful when writers attempt to fulfill certain purposes. Learning the rules of the genres is easy; understanding why those conventions, those rules, those techniques work and create certain effects is more challenging. But without the discussions and the exploration to understand the genre conventions, a writer lacks the knowledge of how to apply them, how to use them to serve the making of meaning in written form. Victoria made the point that simply following rules creates rigidity and constraints for writers, not freedom. It helped her in the beginning but then became frustrating and confining. But understanding those rules, being able to see how they guide certain decisions can turn the rules into guidelines and techniques to be used as applicable depending on a writer's intentions, purposes, assumed readers, and writing context.

Reading and analyzing examples and learning and using genre conventions are necessary, but again, as the students said, not sufficient. Critique and the dialogue that accompanies the critique are equally necessary. Different readers bring different perspectives and strengths to the dialogue. A teacher, an editor, a peer all bring different levels of experience, of "connoisseurship," to the critique. Someone who has read many, many different pieces of writing over a long period of time for the purpose of understanding the craft will have a different repertoire of critique to draw on. And each of these responses has value. My students realized this. Getting a peer to critique something is useful but probably not sufficient, as your peer will not have the experience of reading good and bad, effective and ineffective writing, whereas a teacher or an editor will. But the peer will often be able to tell you when something doesn't make sense or when too much has been left unwritten. A teacher and an editor often read with the purpose of understanding why a piece of writing works or does not work in order to provide direction to improve. The students identified these dialogues as a critical step in learning how to produce good writing. Understanding why that beautifully crafted sentence fails to produce the intended meaning gives a student writer an opportunity to stand back and consider what decisions were made to create that sentence (paragraph, series of paragraphs), what assumptions were being made, and then to interrogate them. If you can begin to understand why something does not produce the intended meaning and response you anticipated, you can begin to understand how to make it work. Equally important were the opportunities to critique someone else's writing. Sahar talked about how she often acted as an "editor" for her classmates and how that sharpened her own ability to step back from her own writing. She also noted that she learned how others might achieve the same purpose, adding to her repertoire of potential techniques. Being someone else's editor allowed students to step back from the writing more easily than when they tried to edit their own work. It also allowed them to practice being the reader and being aware of how they responded to different vocabulary choices, sentence patterns, and paragraph and document structures from the reader's perspective. Feedback, critique, and responses to their writing emerged throughout the discussions to have equal importance, with practicing writing on a regular basis and reading, as critical components of learning to be a good writer.

As our conversations worked toward a conclusion, the students returned again and again to "Good writing depends." Through this discussion they had affirmed that it depends on the topic, the genre, the relationship between the reader and the writer. It also depends on the writer's own development. Early in their writing development, students often related good writing to matters of correctness of spelling, syntax, punctuation, and word choice. Gaining a degree of control over these mechanics afforded the students the freedom to play with expressive writing, storytelling filled with action, and descriptive writing. Elementary school experiences privileged more expressive writing, but middle school and especially high school thrust students into a different set of genres that required understanding and using rational, logical organization backed by evidence to argue a position or thesis or to persuade a reader. The intentionality required for these logically structured purposes clashed with the more free-form, expressive writing that had been rewarded earlier in their writing experience. Whereas the "good" judgment of their own writing was still awarded by an outside authority, the students' own criteria for "good" were expanded to include the criteria for a persuasive essay with an argument to defend a claim or to present a position. Both applying to university and then coming to university added further layers of complexity to the criteria. An application would be more likely to ask for a personal statement where the student was expected to express their own voice along with demonstrating their control of language and genre. Many of the students found that this confused rather than clarified their ideas around "good" writing at the time. As Sahar had stated, "We got really mixed messages!"

All the students agreed that good writing requires time, effort, and practice; it doesn't just happen, nor are only some people naturally good at it. It takes time to read and analyze why something sparks a response in you as a reader. It takes time to learn to use a variety of techniques, approaches, strategies, grammatical structures, and lexical choices to create meaning that a writer and a reader can share. It takes responses to the writing, written and oral, to help a writer find out what has worked, what comes close to working, and what didn't work. These students regularly reviewed current writing and feedback but would also return to their past work, analyze it for the patterns that seemed to be successful regardless of genre and those that were genre-specific and learn to recognize and use those patterns. When it comes to writing, "good" has many meanings. It also has multiple expressions, but good writing is intentional, thoughtful, and engages in a dialogue to make meaning with readers.

## References

Bakhtin, M. M. (1981). *The dialogic imagination: Four essays*. University of Texas.

Halliday, M. A. K. (2002). *On grammar* (J. Webster, Ed., Vol. 1). Continuum.

Vygotsky, L. (1986). *Thought and language* (A. Kozulin, Trans.). The MIT Press.

**Chapter 3**

# Developing "Good Writing" through Emerging Academic Genres: Considerations for Graduate Education

*Christine M. Tardy*

"... Scholarly work that makes us want to turn pages *is* important."
(Casanave, 2010, p. 12)

Our notions of good writing are often tightly wrapped in genre. If asked what "good writing" in their field is, for example, many academics may first think of writing that occurs in print-based research genres, such as scholarly articles or monographs. These are, after all, the most prestigious genres and the ones that academics tend to spend the most time on. Yet today's academics also communicate in a range of emerging multimodal genres, such as graphical or video abstracts (Hendges & Florek, 2019), videos and podcasts (Rowley-Jolivet & Carter-Thomas, 2019), and academic blogs written for public audiences (Luzón & Pérez-Llantada, 2019). These less formal genres do not hold the same importance as peer-reviewed research articles for hiring, promotion, or tenure, but they do facilitate academic networking and allow scholars to speak to wider audiences or to the same audiences in different ways. In these more public-oriented genres, academics repackage research to "discuss and share scholarly work, both with peers and the interested public, engage citizens in the research process, and increase the visibility and reliability of their research" (Luzón & Pérez-Llantada, 2019, p. 2). In attempting to reach less specialized readers (or viewers or listeners), scholars must consider how to engage them—how to make them "want to turn pages," in Casanave's (2010) words. As we consider what good academic writing is in our disciplines, we would do well to not ignore these emerging genres.

As the chapters in this book illustrate, definitions of good writing vary. Though many perceptions of what counts as good writing are grounded in vague terms like "clarity" or "organization," I have found more useful Sword's (2012, 2017) insights regarding what she says "stylish" academic writers do to engage and inform readers. For example, she highlights the importance of audience, noting that "attention to audience is a hidden but essential ingredient of all stylish academic writing" (2012, p. 44). Other techniques of stylish academic writing include the use of storytelling or a narrative arc to engage readers; "the ability to express complex ideas clearly" (Sword, 2012, p. 157) by helping readers see the bigger picture; attention to expression of their own identity (Sword, 2017); and a willingness to "stretch and break disciplinary molds" (Sword, 2012, p. vii) in creative and compelling ways.

Building on these insights, I believe there are several ways in which emerging digital genres can inform academics' understanding of good academic writing and, crucially, may also help scholars develop important tools that contribute to good—or stylish—writing. First, engaging in newer digital genres can allow academic writers to develop their rhetorical flexibility, as they learn to communicate effectively across audiences, media, and modalities. Flexible writers are able to draw on their repertoire of writing strategies and resources and then adapt those to new audiences and contexts, contributing to more effective writing. Writing in more publicly oriented genres can also help authors become more attuned to audience, engagement, and accessibility. Sword (2017) describes activities like blogging and community engagement as "muscle-building tonics," noting that "[t]he more you cross-train by writing across genres as part of your everyday academic work, the better prepared you will be to adapt to new audiences when you write for publication" (p. 121).

Emerging academic genres also often allow writers to bring additional identities and values into their writing. For example, in tweets or blogs, academics can use humor and personalized viewpoints to discuss research, and they can highlight aspects of their identities (as, for example, an advocate or as a minority scholar) that are often less visible or even invisible in traditional genres. Given the alienating experience that many scholars, especially novices, have with academic writing, opportunities to personalize their scholarship and make it more accessible to a wider range of readers can be motivating and engaging, potentially contributing to the passion that characterizes good writing. When asked about her most effective writing, sociologist Michèle Lamont described it by saying "There's a little bit of twinkle in the eye" (Sword, 2017, p. 109). Public genres may help scholars develop that "twinkle in the eye" because they tend to allow for more options to do so.

Finally, emerging, public genres also give writers a chance to break away from some of the more rigid conventions of many academic genres and to consider how to communicate their work in alternative ways. For instance, an introduction to a research article commonly grounds the research in previous scholarly work, while an introduction to a science blog might ground the research primarily in a single paper or even a personal anecdote (Luzón, 2013). Much academic research writing also tends to use densely packed noun phrases and jargon and less personal language, while public-facing academic genres may use more features of conversational discourse, include humor or emotional reactions, and avoid or at least explain jargon (Hyland, 2010; Luzón, 2013). These alternative conventions are not always appropriate in formal academic genres, but they give writers a chance to express meaning in audience-sensitive ways. In addition, emerging academic genres are often heavily multimodal, so writers can draw on many semiotic resources to communicate scholarship. As Belcher (2017) notes, "The huge semiotic toolkit that multimodal design makes available can empower students with an appealing array of learner-centric, autonomy-motivating, voice-enhancing, audience-engaging options" (p. 84). Through multimodal practices, academic writers can expand their writing repertoires and their "toolkit" for writing persuasively and relevantly to different audiences. Many of these same tools can also support scholars as they write in more traditional academic genres.

Decades ago, Limerick (1993) wrote that many professors see it as a duty to "enforce a standard of dull writing" (p. 74) with graduate students because they think this is what is necessary for publication. I disagree with Limerick's claim that "[p]rofessors are often shy, timid and fearful people" who use dull prose as "a kind of protective camouflage" (p. 54), though I agree with her that faculty have a responsibility to support graduate student scholars in developing their academic writing. In recent years, I have started to see a place for emerging genres in this developmental process. In an attempt to help newer scholars (as well as myself!) build their academic genre repertoires and to develop expansive views of "good academic writing," I now ask graduate students in my courses to create texts that allow them to consolidate and disseminate knowledge in *multiple* ways—including traditional academic papers but also emerging, lower-stakes, often digital genres. In this chapter, I describe three examples of course assignments that engage graduate students with subject-matter content through writing beyond traditional academic genres. The goal of having students write in these "less academic" genres is to give them an opportunity to focus on clear and engaging communication with attention to audience and the use of linguistic and other semiotic resources that may aid in such communication.

## Three Examples

The three assignments I share here—a video abstract, a listicle, and a podcast—are quite distinct but share several important features. First, these assignments all rely fairly heavily on multimodality to create and express meaning. In these genres, writers gain practice in communicating information through a range of semiotic resources and often through narratives about their work. In addition, each of these assignments engages students in authentic genres that communicate academic scholarship to less specialized audiences. These assignments also ask student writers to carefully consider audience as they identify intended readers, listeners, or viewers (including, possibly, class members) and compose a text that is meaningful and appropriate for them. Finally, and perhaps most importantly, these less formal genres oblige students to communicate complex ideas in accessible—and hopefully engaging—ways. Given these features, I believe that giving graduate students the opportunities to write in these ways can help draw their attention to elements like audience, identity, creativity, storytelling, and the bigger picture of their work—elements that good academic writers also attend to.

## Video Abstract

Traditionally, academic abstracts have been used to provide a short overview of a longer text, such as a proposal, research article, or thesis. Abstracts can help readers determine whether the research is relevant for them and also serve a persuasive function of attracting readers to the research (Hyland, 2004). Abstracts also allow (or require!) writers to step back and share the bigger picture of their work in limited space (Sword,

2012). In the digital age, new versions of the abstract have emerged, including the graphical abstract (a visual that represents a concept or process from the research) and the video abstract (a three- to five-minute video that shares a project overview). These multimodal abstracts are not necessarily substitutes for a traditional abstract, which provides more detail than a visual alone and can be read in far less than three to five minutes. Instead, they offer an alternative or supplemental text for describing a research project. They share some similarities with the three-minute thesis (3MT®), in which graduate students give an extremely short TED-style overview of a doctoral thesis, using language accessible to nonspecialists. The texts often blend movie-like features (pictures, video, voices, music) with more traditional abstract conventions (use of specialized terminology, obligatory rhetorical moves, figures or graphs, acknowledgment of funding sponsors). Given this hybridity, video abstracts can be found not only in academic journals but also on the websites of scholars and their research teams. In other words, they can take on an additional public relations function. The high-impact medical journal *The BMJ* describes video abstracts in this way:

> The tone of your video should be relaxed and friendly. If you're writing something you're going to read out, write it as you would say it and not as it would be written in an article. It might be difficult to put scientific terms into conversational language, but imagine you are telling the story to a lay person. Video abstracts are aimed at the scientific public but are open to anybody and will reach a wider audience, including journalists, if they are more accessible. (BMJ, n.d.)

The editorial page of *Theory, Culture, & Society* guides authors to "direct your [video abstract] remarks to a non-expert and whenever possible unpack elaborate theoretical and technical terminiology" (*Theory, Culture, & Society*, n.d.).

I first began incorporating video abstracts into my graduate courses in 2014, when the genre was still quite new. As the final assignment for a seminar on genre theory and pedagogy, class members created a video abstract of their major projects in lieu of a more traditional class presentation. Working up to this assignment, we collected examples of video abstracts and discussed common conventions, successful and unsuccessful features (ranging from audio and background to content), and some of the goals the genre was used to carry out. We also discussed our own local use of the genre, including what we would like it to accomplish in our setting. From there, the students were encouraged to consider how they could use or exploit the video abstract for our purposes, creating a video of three to five minutes (I have since limited them to three minutes, with the knowledge that many will still exceed that timeframe by a bit). The activity resulted in some of the most engaging "presentations" of research that I have ever seen.

In sharing their work in this medium, writers must consider how to communicate scholarly information visually and orally, with both modes encouraging less formal and often more accessible text. I stress to my students that they can keep their videos technologically simple (e.g., just recording themselves on a smartphone) or they can make more sophisticated use of the technology if they'd like to spend more time. Through this process, they attend to audience, identity, narratives, and telling the bigger picture—and the results are often stunning as they share accessible, engaging, and informative representations of scholarly work. Students have also taken liberties in this assignment to represent a different aspect of their identity than they can in a traditional presentation. For example, one student's video playfully began like the start of a *Star Wars* movie with text moving outward to the galaxy. Another video presented the project in ways that resembled a movie trailer. Still others have used animations to tell a story about their research, or they have featured themselves describing the research as though they were sharing information with colleagues in a relaxed setting. Some have used voiceover audio and others have relied on written words and images—there are so many options available to them for self-representation. In other words, there is a tremendous variety in how students approach the assignment and how they try to achieve the goal of sharing their project with the classroom community.

The video abstract also gives students valuable practice in communicating their research with a wider audience. Some have made their video abstracts publicly available on YouTube, and one revealed to me that this was the only project from graduate school that she shared with her family. Because the video assignment is typically due at least one week prior to the submission of the final written paper, students also often note that having to tell a story about their project in video form helps them to find the story they want to tell in their written text as well. Finally, I must note that our showcase of the video abstracts on the last day of class is a real course highlight. One student found that it built confidence in her work in a way that, for her, presentations did not. She reflected to me on "the delight of sharing a video abstract and observing classmates' rapt attention or laughter in response, which is very different from the traditional peer review experience."

## Listicle

The listicle is another relatively young genre, with the label (a blend of *list* and *article*) highlighting its hybridity. Although such lists have long been featured in popular magazines, internet culture and the rise of blogs and social media have made listicles more visible. In the United States, the popular website *Buzzfeed* is closely associated with the listicle. A quick search for "lists" in *Buzzfeed* yields hundreds of examples, with titles such as "16 Things You'll Understand Only If You Love Dogs" or "17 Reasons Why the Australian MacDonald's Is Better Than the American Version." While some lists are limited to numbered items, many include paragraphs of explanation under each item heading.

Despite the lighthearted and even trivial content of many listicles, I think they are a valuable genre that is well suited to popular dissemination of academic scholarship. Listicles synthesize information, they are quick to read (facilitated by the use of headings and an elimination of transitions), they often use visuals to convey meaning and engage readers, and they highlight main points (as numbered items) often supported by a short prose paragraph. As such, they also encourage authors to attend to many aspects of good writing, such as attention to audience, storytelling, and the bigger picture. Recognizing the potential value of listicles, I started incorporating them into my graduate courses as short in-class activities a few years ago. I initially found them to be a useful aid for students in consolidating material from a unit or even the entire course but have since been intrigued by how they might support development of good writing. A recent advice article by Rachel Toor in *The Chronicle of Higher Education* (Toor, 2019) similarly argues that listicles have several benefits for academic writers: They can help writers to make bolder claims ("This is good practice for academics who tend to pad, wander, and get lost in our own thickets of prose"), to produce arguments that are attuned to readers and that hold their engagement, to support arguments with explanations and examples, and to make arguments more immediately visible.

I have recently begun introducing a listicle as a culminating out-of-class assignment in my graduate course on Global Englishes. The assignment prompt guides students through several steps to complete the project, including (1) reviewing the listicle genre (explanations and samples are provided); (2) finding a focus and curating sources (suggestions of course assignments and readings to review are shared); (3) creating their list and adding details; and (4) designing the listicle to make it reader-friendly and to resemble a published listicle, possibly incorporating visuals. Students are also encouraged to think of their list as a kind of story, carefully considering what it is they want their readers to know about their topic and how they can share that information in a compelling way.

Class members have created a range of informed, audience-sensitive, and engaging texts in response to this assignment. Titles have included, for example, "6 Things I Wish I Had Known about Global Englishes Before Joining the Peace Corps" and "12 Principles for Teaching about World Englishes in Writing Classes." One pair worked together to create an entire website that included three separate listicles, all related to Global Englishes and language teaching. Sarah, a high school Spanish teacher who completed the course, wrote a listicle titled "Nine Things Every K-12 School Administrator in the US Should Know About Language Variety," from which her first list item is quoted:

1.Language changes.

> You probably already know that all spoken languages change and
> have variation, including English or other languages that may
> be spoken or taught as a second language at your school, such
> as Spanish. The question is, how does this relate to your school
> environment? That question will be answered throughout the rest of
> this list, so keep reading! In the meantime, take a look at this quote
> regarding language change and teaching: "One direct outcome of this
> perpetual shift has been the increasing number of recommendations
> that the teaching of English be made to reflect local identities
> and incorporate local as well as worldwide norms."[2] How do the
> English or other languages your students speak reflect your students'
> identities? How can the teaching of these languages at your school
> reflect local and global norms?

Sarah's listicle demonstrates an awareness not only of what topics would be relevant to her audience but also of using writing features that engage directly with readers (such as the use of questions and the second person) and a less formal style.

# Podcast

Podcasts have been available in MP3 (audio file) format since 2000, but the roots of the genre go back further to radio talk shows and news broadcasts, especially the narrative radio features of the 1920s and 1930s (McHugh, 2016). Podcasts often include dialogue between two or more hosts (or a host and guests) and are available in single episodes that make up a series. They typically emphasize storytelling and are often described as "audio narratives" (McHugh, 2016).

Academic podcasts are now growing in popularity, addressing topics from science to psychology to language to history. Journals and professional organizations have also begun to produce podcasts, often interviewing academics about a publication or an area of research. Podcasts are one of several genres that Rowley-Jolivet and Carter-Thomas (2019) categorize as "scholarly soundbites"—brief oral recordings in which scholars discuss their current or recent research. Because podcasts often take the form of a dialogue, they are generally conversational. Through a podcast, an academic has the opportunity to share their work in an accessible, relatable, and even entertaining manner, reaching a wider audience than they would in a typical scholarly publication, and attending to many features of good writing. Podcasts also allow for more personalization of the research, including the expressing of emotion that is often omitted in scholarly publications (Rowley-Jolivet & Carter-Thomas, 2019) but that may allow researchers to highlight their passion for their work, another hallmark of good academic writing (Sword, 2012).

I had avoided implementing podcasts in my classes until very recently, because I questioned the time it would take for students to produce such a text. But in my ongoing quest to expand novice professionals' academic genre repertoires, I recently assigned podcasts in my graduate course on second language writing. My goal was for students to gain practice in sharing course content with an audience of their choice: peers in their graduate program, colleagues in their teaching contexts, a wider audience of teachers beyond their local context . . . whoever they thought might be interested! To ensure that the project would not require them to spend unnecessary hours on production and editing, I first produced my own short podcast. As a brand-new podcaster, I spent a total of three hours (from conception to final product) creating a simple ten-minute podcast.

To introduce the project to students, I shared my own podcast on the first day of class; this example included an interview with Paul Kei

Matsuda, the author of one of our readings in that class session. I then provided relevant links and guidelines for creating a simple podcast and asked students to create a one-minute podcast for the next class, responding to one of our readings. All of the students were able to complete the assignment without trouble, with most even incorporating music at the start and end of their recording. Next, students were paired up and assigned a topic aligned with a set of weekly readings in the course. Their job was to read ahead and create a podcast that provided a new perspective on the topic, extending the readings for the week in some way. With eight pairs in the class, we listened to a student-produced podcast roughly every other week of the semester, supplementing our readings. Students listened to their peers' podcasts at home (along with the assigned readings), and a discussion forum was set up in our course management system where they could discuss the podcast with each other and the authors.

Students have approached the podcast in a variety of ways. Some have discussed questions from fictitious listeners, and some have adopted the frame of a game show, discussing course content through a fun competition. One pair, Anuj and Violet, explored the sociopolitical dimensions of teacher feedback through a dialogue in which they each shared how they might respond to the same examples of student writing. They began their podcast by explicitly describing themselves as non-experts, adopting the identity of engaged and informed learners themselves:

> **Anuj:** Welcome to *Burnt Out*, the podcast for burnt out teachers of writing, who do not always have the time or energy to read through cutting-edge research work on pedagogy, which is why we—that is me, Anuj—
>
> **Violet:** —and me, Violet, bring to you each week a quick summary and discussion of best ideas in pedagogy that you ought to know about.
>
> **Anuj:** Hi Violet!
>
> **Violet:** Hi Anuj!
>
> **Anuj:** So, what do we have in store for our burnt-out teachers today?
>
> **Violet:** A podcast on sociopolitical and contextual dimensions of response.
>
> **Anuj:** Whoah! That's quite a mouthful. What does that really mean though?
>
> **Violet:** Good question, Anuj. So, before I get to that, a couple of disclaimers. First, we are only grad students and are still learning

> about these theories. So, in case we are not 100% correct about what we say, and some of our listeners are experts in the field, please be kind. Second, while today's podcast will be used to address readings that will be of direct use to ESL and composition teachers, it could potentially have something to offer, I think, to teachers of all disciplines, since feedback is something that happens in almost all disciplines.

This novice identity is often discouraged in academic writing, but by adopting it here, Anuj and Violet were able to share with their audience a valuable learner perspective on the issue. Their podcast was relatable, insightful, and accessible while also telling a more personal story about teachers' experiences with feedback. In other words, their podcast displayed many features of good academic writing though through a less traditional academic genre.

## Final Thoughts

It is probably worth emphasizing that I am not advocating for the assignments described here to replace writing in print-based genres like research articles or proposals. Those are challenging genres that require a great deal of practice and support, and graduate courses and faculty can play an important role in providing that in their courses. But I believe there are many reasons to *also* give graduate students an opportunity to engage in "smaller" genres that academics increasingly use to communicate with wider audiences. As a teacher, one of the benefits that I have seen is that these more public-oriented genres give students practice in communicating disciplinary content in ways that are engaging, relevant, and meaningful. Through such practice, writers build the skills of storytelling and focusing on the bigger picture and become alerted to audience sensitivity. At the same time, they have the opportunity to foreground their various identities and perhaps to acknowledge how their own values impact their scholarly work. Providing students with opportunities to practice writing in these ways—making prose accessible and engaging, sharing scholarship through narratives, and perhaps bringing some of themselves into their texts—may also help to build writing muscles that can strengthen students' more traditional academic writing. Assessment criteria for such assignments can also draw on such features, highlighting their value to students. Additionally, to help writers see the connections between these assignments and their traditional scholarly writing, classroom discussions or reflections may consider how they might adapt these tools across genres.

I would finally note that seasoned scholars may be the greatest impediment to expanding our views and practices of good writing in the ways I have described here. I suspect many academics will find podcasts or listicles to be too light or trivial to be worthy of serious scholarly work, let alone to give them time and space in graduate education. Some may even see emerging digital genres as detrimental to literacy more generally. Yet it is unlikely that society will close the door on public writing in the digital space anytime soon. And given the increasing importance of communicating scholarly ideas in persuasive, accessible ways to the public, we would all do well to expand our academic genre repertoires and to develop new tools for sharing our work. We might even improve our traditional academic writing in the process.

## References


Belcher, D. D. (2017). On becoming facilitators of multimodal composing and digital design. *Journal of Second Language Writing, 38,* 80–85.

BMJ. (n.d.). Video abstracts: Top tips for a good video abstract. *BMJ Journals.* https://authors.bmj.com/writing-and-formatting/video-abstracts/top-tips/

Casanave, C. P. (2010). Taking risks? A case study of three doctoral students writing qualitative dissertations at an American university in Japan. *Journal of Second Language Writing, 19,* 1–16.

Hendges, G. R., and C. S. Florek (2019). The graphical abstract as a new genre in the promotion of science. In M.-J. Luzón and C. Pérez-Llantada (Eds.), *Science communication on the internet: Old genres meet new genres* (pp. 66–86). John Benjamins.

Hyland, K. (2004). *Disciplinary discourses: Social interactions in academic writing.* University of Michigan Press.

Hyland, K. (2010). Constructing proximity: Relating to readers in popular and professional science. *Journal of English for Academic Purposes, 9,* 116–127.

Limerick, P. N. (1993, October 31). Dancing with professors: The trouble with academic prose. *New York Times Book Review,* 54, 74, 75.

Luzón, M.-J. (2013). Public communication in science blogs: Recontextualizing scientific discourse for a diversified audience. *Written Communication, 30,* 428–457.

Luzón, M.-J., & Pérez-Llantada, C. (2019). Connecting traditional and new genres: Trends and emerging themes. In M.-J. Luzón & C. Pérez-Llantada (Eds.), *Science communication on the internet: Old genres meet new genres* (pp. 1–18). John Benjamins.

McHugh, S. (2016). How podcasting is changing the audio storytelling genre. *The Radio Journal—International Studies in Broadcast and Audio Media, 14*(1), 65–82.

Rowley-Jolivet, E., & S. Carter-Thomas (2019). Scholarly soundbites: Audiovisual innovations in digital science and their implications for genre evolution. In M.-J. Luzón & C. Pérez-Llantada (Eds.), *Science communication on the internet: Old genres meet new genres* (pp. 88–113). John Benjamins.

Sword, H. (2012). *Stylish academic writing*. Harvard University Press.

Sword, H. (2017). *Air & light & time & space: How successful academics write*. Harvard University Press.

*Theory, Culture, & Society*. (n.d.). Video-abstract guidelines. https://www.theoryculturesociety.org/video-abstract-guidelines

Toor, R. (2019, June 11). 7 ways that list-making helps you produce scholarly work. *The Chronicle of Higher Education*. https://www.chronicle.com/article/7-ways-that-list-making-helps-you-produce-scholarly-work/

## Acknowledgments

My sincere thanks to all my graduate students for helping me develop my own understanding of "good writing," and especially to Sarah Albrecht, Violet Chabko, and Anuj Gupta for allowing me to share their work in this chapter.

**Chapter 4**

# "Good Writing" and "Good Feedback": A Look at the Genre of Teacher Written Feedback at the Discourse Level

*Lynn Goldstein*

When exploring what makes "good writing," teachers of multilingual writers need to examine the pedagogies that help multilingual writers produce "good writing." Teacher written feedback at the discourse level is one such pedagogy. Discourse-level feedback focuses on genre, rhetorical moves, organization, development, use of sources, content, audience and purpose, and language choices (both lexical and grammatical) for specific genres and specific content as well as language choices tied to different Englishes. Like many others, I have used teacher written feedback at the discourse level (subsequently referred to as discourse-level feedback) to help the multilingual writers I work with to produce more effective texts and become stronger writers. In addition, beginning in 1977 when I first started teaching multilingual writers, I have worked toward understanding what makes for effective discourse-level feedback.

As part of developing these understandings, my experiences teaching and researching multilingual writers have led me to conclude both that discourse-level feedback is a "pedagogical genre" (Rodway, 2018) and that effective instantiations of this genre possess certain core characteristics. My intent in this chapter is therefore to call on my experiences as a teacher of multilingual writers, a multilingual writing feedback researcher, and a teacher educator of multilingual writing teachers in order to describe the discourse-level feedback genre and enumerate what makes instances of such feedback "good," i.e., what characteristics of this genre help multilingual writers become more effective writers. In short, if we want to help multilingual writers move toward producing "good writing," we need to consider what characteristics of discourse-level feedback will help students to do so no matter how "good writing" is defined for particular discourse communities, who the authors and audiences are in these communities, and what the contents and genres are within these communities.

Let me begin by saying what this chapter is not. First, it isn't about written corrective feedback (WCF). The second language writing literature is replete with research, papers, and books addressing WCF (see, for example, Bitchener, 2021; Bitchener & Ferris, 2011; Ferris & Kurzer, 2019; Manchón & Polio, 2021). In fact, in our empirical look at publications and presentations over the past twenty years, Robert Kohls and I found that published work and conference presentations overwhelmingly focus on WCF, with substantially less work examining discourse-level feedback (Goldstein & Kohls, 2019), thus creating an imbalance that can lead researchers, teacher educators, in- and pre-service multilingual writing teachers, and multilingual writers to believe that good writing is by definition sentence-level correctness. Given this imbalance and given that good writing involves more than sentence-level correctness, I've chosen to focus this chapter on discourse-level feedback. That said, it is important to note that discourse-level feedback does not ignore language, but its focus is not on sentence-level correctness. Instead, its focus is on helping students appropriately and correctly incorporate language needed for particular genres and content (Worden, 2019). Discourse-level feedback also does not ignore language problems in instances where the writer's meaning is obscured, given that it isn't possible to give discourse-level feedback if a teacher cannot understand what the writer has written.

This chapter is also not a research-based review of what we know about discourse-level feedback and its role in helping multilingual writers produce "good writing." Although examining this is a valuable endeavor, and one that I have participated in (Goldstein, 2016), I want to consider instead my accumulated learning from having engaged in discourse-level feedback since 1977 in a variety of settings (intensive English language programs, community college programs, undergraduate programs, content-based reading-writing courses for pre-matriculated graduate students, adjunct writing courses for graduate students, content courses for graduate students) for a variety of multilingual writers, including matriculated and non-matriculated students, generation 1.5, international, and immigrant students. Through these experiences, I have consistently and concertedly engaged in reflection in and on action regarding my feedback practices (see, for example, Goldstein, 2010), and these reflections along with my experiences inform my discussions below.

As I began to reflect on my past experiences, I concluded that discourse-level feedback is a genre, a text type, rather than, as it is often portrayed, a set of comments. These reflections helped me realize the importance of both describing the discourse-level feedback genre and setting out what makes for effective instantiations of this genre. Before I do so, let's first look at the basic characteristics of genres where writers are writing to and for specific audiences. In each rhetorical situation, there is an author and an audience (either real or imagined) and a discourse community within which the author communicates to the audience through the author's text. Authors have intentions (i.e., purposes) for how they want their texts to be read, what they want to communicate, what they want their text to do, and what they want their audiences to think, feel, know, and do. In turn, audiences interact with the author's text discerning what is meant and what the author's purposes might be and also making decisions about their own purposes for how they will make sense of and make use of the text. Thus, the creation of a text and the use of a text is an interactive process. In addition, there are various possible relationships that may hold for specific genres between the author and the audience for a text, from highly conventionalized ones (such as a textbook passage intended to teach, with the author as teacher and the audience as learner) to more loosely defined ones (for example emails, given that the authors of and audiences for an email can have a range of relationships and purposes). There are also degrees of conventionalized structure, content, and language for some very loosely defined genres, as in the case of a personal diary, while others are highly conventionalized, such as an abstract for a professional conference. As well, genres can create, reify, or change relationships between the author and audience, relationships such as expert and novice, and can also create, reify, or change relationships of solidarity, power, distance, and trust between the writer and the reader within the community where the genre is being produced and shared. In addition, these processes of relationship creation, reification, and change can be one of the fundamental purposes of a genre. More generally, as Tardy (2019) points out, "Genres are used by social groups or discourse communities to carry out repeated activities. . . . It's also useful to emphasize that genres do things, typically responding to common situations (also referred to as rhetorical situations)" (p. 13).

The discourse-level feedback genre meets the hallmarks of a genre delineated above given that

1.  it is a repeated activity;

2.  it responds to a rhetorical situation that includes the teacher (author) and the teacher's purpose(s) for the feedback; the student (audience) and the student's purposes for making use of the teacher's feedback and how the student makes use of it; the context within which the feedback takes place, i.e., the student's immediate text, the student's previous text(s), and the teacher's feedback on the student's previous texts; instructional content in the writing course and the feedback topic, namely, what the feedback addresses;

3.  it takes place within particular social communities (e.g., an undergraduate multilingual writing course), and in so doing its author (a teacher) has particular purposes, some of which may be conventionalized such as being "instructive," and some that may be more individual (providing a listening ear or learning about content or disciplinary genres from the writer, for example);

4.  its author (a teacher) has particular purposes, some of which may be conventionalized, such as being "instructive," and some which may be more individual (providing a listening ear or learning about content or disciplinary genres from the writer, for example);

5.  the audience (students) also has specific purposes for reading/ using the discourse-level feedback text such as using the feedback to strengthen their texts and move developmentally toward good writing and toward becoming a more independent writer; getting a sense of an audience reading and engaging with their texts; receiving validation for their ideas and/or their emotions; getting good grades and/or meeting course requirements. Likewise, the audience may also choose not to make use of the teacher's discourse-level feedback text;

6.  just as for some other genres, the author's (teacher's) purposes may be prescribed and even proscribed within particular discourse communities by those who hold the power to do so, such as program administrators requiring program exit exams that focus on specific discourse features and thus encourage teachers to respond to specific aspects of their students' texts;

7.  feedback texts display a range of possible linguistic and structural patterns, such as the use of certain syntactic forms (e.g., questions or imperatives), certain pragmatic intents (e.g., requests for action), feedback placement (e.g., within the students' texts, at the beginning, at the end, or some combination), and the use of stance markers such as hedging or modals or praise;

8.  there are also possibilities for different written modes such as handwritten feedback or written electronic feedback;

9.  there is a range of possible foci for discourse-level feedback, i.e., what gets commented on: the writer's content, the writer's emotions, the use of sources, genre needs, the use of elemental and complex genres, coherence, cohesion, organization, development, support, and/or language needed for particular contents and language needed for particular genres;

10. the teacher's purposes for and the content, structure, and the mode of discourse-level feedback as well as the student's purposes in using and not using discourse-level feedback take place within and both influence and are influenced by social relationships. These may include the traditional teacher as instructor and writer as learner but other relationships can also be in play, as when, for example, the multilingual writing student becomes the teacher regarding the students' content or discourse community (see, for example, Merkel, 2018). As well, purposes for giving discourse-level feedback and for how students use or even do not use discourse-level feedback influence and are influenced by relationships of equal power, unequal power, distance, closeness, trust, and so forth (Goldstein, 2006; Lee & Schallert, 2008; Tardy, 2019).

Just as we do with other genres, it's important to consider what makes any instance of the feedback genre a sound one, in other words what characteristics make instantiations of the discourse-level feedback genre "good" such that it fulfills a number of author and audience purposes within any particular rhetorical situation while scaffolding each writer within that writer's zone of proximal development (Vygotsky, 1986) in a collaborative process (Grabe & Kaplan, 1996; Murphy, 2000; Rodway, 2018). The characteristics I have arrived at include discourse-level feedback that

1. is **comprehensible**
2. is **selective**
3. is **usable and developmentally appropriate**
4. includes **intertextuality**
5. incorporates **multimodality** to provide **affordances**
6. **individualizes**
7. creates, sustains, and/or changes **relationships**
8. is **dialogic**.

**Comprehensibility** comes first, given that none of the other characteristics of good feedback matter if a writer cannot make sense of the discourse-level feedback. I'm using the term *comprehensibility* with three meanings: first, that the recipient can understand the sentence-level meaning; second, that the recipient can understand the pragmatic intent (Conrad & Goldstein, 1999); and third, that the comment exhibits text specificity (Goldstein, 2005). To illustrate the distinction between meaning and intent, consider the following feedback on a student's text: "I'm wondering why you don't believe in that idea." If the student does not understand the meaning of "wondering why," they will not understand the sentence-level meaning of this sentence. It goes without saying that teachers need to consider a student's language proficiency when they consider what lexical items, idioms, and syntactic patterns to employ in wording a comment so that its sentence-level meaning is comprehensible. Related to this is the use of technical terms so that if a teacher uses terms such as *coherence* or *organization* or *development* or *explanation,* students know what these terms mean. Thus, the lexical and conceptual aspects of comprehensible feedback also need to be tied to classroom instruction, where students, with their teachers' guidance, examine texts that illustrate what these writing-specific terms mean and also examine texts to see examples of how these aspects of good writing work in specific genres.

For students who do understand the sentence-level meaning, they still need to decide *why* the teacher is making this comment, in other words to determine its illocutionary force. Does the teacher's comment mean only that the teacher is simply wondering about why the writer doesn't believe in that idea? Or does the comment mean that the teacher wants the student to do something other than register the comment, for example to revise to explain why the writer doesn't believe in the idea in question? Teachers cannot assume that the pragmatic intent of their discourse-level feedback is readily understood, and here, too, classroom instruction is fundamental to teaching students how to make sense of a teacher's pragmatic intent (Goldstein, 2005). Thus, comprehensibility is neither static nor situated solely in the comments themselves. It is dynamic, dependent on each writer's language proficiency, each writer's deciphering of the commentary's pragmatic intent, and each writer's knowledge about what makes "good writing" for the genre and content of each student's text.

Last, comprehensibility is also related to text specificity. Compare the following discourse-level feedback to a claim in a student's paper that individuals are not doing enough to solve climate change:

A.  "Why do you believe this?" written at the top of the paragraph where this claim is embedded;

B.  "Why do you believe this?" where the claim is underlined and the comment is written next to the claim;

C.  "Why do you believe we are not doing enough to solve climate change?" written next to the claim or at the beginning of the paragraph.

A lacks text specificity—it is not clear what "this" refers/points to and is the type of generic comment that could be written on any text. Although B's wording is identical to A, B is text-specific because the placement and underlining provide the referent for "this." C is also text-specific, as instead of using "this," the comment references the writer's words.

**Selectivity** refers to the need to be selective about what we give discourse-level feedback on and to also make sure that students can make use of this feedback. In most cases, providing line-by-line feedback on a student's text can be counterproductive, risking overwhelming the student, risking providing feedback that the student may not be ready to enact, and risking that the student will not take away specific lessons that can guide their future composing. When I work with graduate students on the teaching of second language writing, we practice providing discourse-level feedback on samples of multilingual writers' texts (Goldstein, 2005). For each student essay that we practice with, I also include a synopsis about each author (such as their language background and their rhetorical and sentence-level proficiency), the text (details about the writing assignment as well as the author's audience and purpose), a previous text or draft, and the writing course (what has been addressed in classroom instruction). My students' first impulse is to begin reading the students' texts with pen/pencil in hand and to write comments as they read. Having done so, they end up commenting on everything without a plan that considers the writer's readiness to attend to and act on certain feedback, the patterns of rhetorical problems within the text, or the genre and the content. Often, they are also reading as teachers without being readers. So next I ask them to put their pens/pencils down and just read the student's text, no commenting, just read as they would read any text. After they read with pencils down, I ask them to read again, consider what they know about the student, the rhetorical situation, and the classroom instruction, and note whether or not they feel the writer has fulfilled their purposes and met their audience's needs and what patterns of rhetorical difficulty they observe. Only after that process do we strategize about what to give feedback on and what to wait on for future work. It is only after that process that we begin commenting, focusing first on places that revision will help the writers better meet their purposes and their audience's needs as well as addressing patterns of rhetorical difficulty. Informing this process of choosing what to provide discourse-level feedback on are the text's rhetorical situation, course content and foci, and student readiness to enact particular types of revisions.

**Usability,** a concept related to selectivity, refers to multilingual writers knowing how to revise in response to particular comments, an ability that is tied to developmental readiness and to classroom instruction. We need to consider usability because multilingual writers can understand the content and the pragmatic intent of a comment and still not be able to carry out an effective revision in response. My "aha" moment about usability came after Susan Conrad and I discovered in our case study of three of my undergraduate multilingual writing students that they struggled to successfully revise in response to discourse-level feedback focused on development and explanation (Conrad & Goldstein, 1999). From that point on, I've found it important to consider each student's developmental readiness to carry out particular revisions (see also Treglia, 2008). This consideration is multifaceted. For example, consider my student Phuoc, who, in response to an assignment asking students to write about a life lesson arrived at through particular experiences in order to sway others to either avoid or embrace this experience, narrated the experience but did not address the life lesson or argue for embracing or avoiding the experience. To determine how to give Phuoc feedback, I needed to ask whether I had examined with the students in our course the use of narration for particular purposes such as argumentation, whether Phuoc had had the same difficulty in previous texts, and whether I had given her this feedback on a previous paper or draft. In Phuoc's case, this was her first draft, but we had addressed the use of narrative to support an argument in class, and she had used argumentation successfully in previous papers. Given this, I gave Phuoc feedback indicating that although she had told her story, I didn't know what she wanted me to learn from it and that she needed, as we had discussed in class, to use her story as support for the argument she wanted to make. This was usable discourse-level feedback for her, and she successfully revised. But what if we had not had class discussions about narrative as support for argumentation? If that had been the case, I would have supplied Phuoc with "instructive" discourse-level feedback, giving her a mini-lesson about how to revise to do so. And what if I had given Phuoc instructive feedback on previous drafts and yet she had still struggled to use this feedback and revise successfully? As I'll discuss a bit later, instead of only giving her discourse-level feedback, I would have taken advantage of affordances provided by multimodality possibilities, in this case meeting with Phuoc face to face to address the difficulties she was having.

**Intertextuality** refers to the notion that a student's text that a teacher is currently reading and responding to does not stand alone but rather is a part of a set of interrelated texts that include previous papers that the student has written, previous drafts if this is not the first draft, as well as all previous discourse-level feedback the student has received and the revisions the student has made in response to that feedback. Given this, we need to provide "feedback," "feed up," and "feed forward" (Hattie & Timperley, 2007), i.e., to provide feedback on how effectively the student has made use of the feedback from the prior draft or from prior papers in writing the current text and to provide feedback that pushes the student and the student's learning forward toward the next draft and furthers their overall learning. Reading retrospectively and prospectively this way allows teachers to identify both successes and difficulties in the student's self-motivated revisions and the student's successes and difficulties using discourse-level feedback on previous drafts and previous papers and to identify patterns of composing success and difficulty over time. In essence, retrospective reading allows us to fine-tune discourse-level feedback to a student's zone of proximal development (ZPD) (Vygotsky, 1986), by determining (1) what the writer is successfully able to both compose and revise independently; (2) what the writer is having ongoing difficulty with and thus either is not developmentally ready to address or needs more incremental instruction on; or (3) where the writer has made progress over time and now needs discourse-level feedback that scaffolds the revision and moves the writer into the next stage of learning. Intertextuality highlights the idea that becoming more effective writers at the discourse level is a process that takes place over time, with discourse-level feedback both playing an ongoing role in that process and being sensitive to that process. One example that comes to mind is an adjunct reading/writing course for pre-matriculated international graduate students where several students had ongoing difficulties using sources appropriately for the source-based writing they were undertaking. It was only through retrospective reading that I was able to see the incremental progress they were making, able to uncover what they could do on their own, and able to see what they still needed to have scaffolded. It was this process that allowed me to provide ongoing discourse-level feedback fine-tuned to each student's ZPD to make my feedback contingent and graduated (Aljaafreh & Lantolf, 1994).

**Multimodality** and **Affordances** refers to providing affordances, or possibilities for action (van Lier, 2000), by making use of other feedback genres along with discourse-level feedback, where warranted. These genres include face-to-face conferencing, video feedback, directing students to reference books, feedback from real audiences, or interviews of others in their real audiences, and so forth. A student who immediately springs to mind regarding the need to augment discourse-level feedback with other genres is Jin, an ethnically Japanese student born and raised in Korea. He had written an essay about discrimination focused on what he saw as discriminatory graffiti in public restrooms at his university (Goldstein, 2005). I had great difficulty following his essay, as it was replete with writer-based prose (Flower, 1979), so much so that I felt it would be counterproductive for me to give him written discourse-level feedback. Instead, I asked him to come talk with me. Through our discussion, I learned about his experiences of discrimination and came to understand that his draft, through his word choices, phrasing, and content, reflected a deliberate distancing from discrimination. This conversation gave us the opportunity to talk about what his purpose was and who his intended audience was and, if he chose to do so, how he could keep his emotional distance while revising to make his text reader-based. Our meeting enabled him to make his second draft significantly more reader-based and effective, something that I believe would not have happened if I had provided only written feedback.

As can be seen in the above discussions, in essence comprehensibility, selectivity, usability, intertextuality and multimodality all focus on **individualization** in terms of (1) what to comment on and what not to comment on by taking into account a student's developmental stage and readiness for specific feedback foci and readiness to enact a particular type of revision; (2) how comments are worded (i.e., syntactic structure, pragmatic intent, $+/-$ the use of modals, $+/-$ the use of praise, $+/-$ hedges, and so forth); (3) whether written discourse-level feedback is accompanied by other feedback modalities; and (4) whether to include instructional feedback. In addition, other aspects of students' texts where feedback individualization is important include:

- students' language backgrounds and the choices they make to deploy varieties other than or in addition to "standard English";

- students' background knowledge regarding the content they are writing about and the genres of their texts;

- students' attitudes toward the content of their text, toward the course, toward previous feedback, toward the teacher, toward written feedback mode (handwritten, typed, or electronic using the comment function in Microsoft Word);

- the specific needs of the genre students are writing in and the content they are writing about; and

- students' expressed agendas/requests for discourse-level feedback foci or instruction for how to enact a revision.

My student Bingo immediately leaps to mind, as he opened my eyes to the power of individualizing feedback in response to a student's own agenda and requests (Goldstein, 2005). Unprompted, Bingo annotated his first draft of an essay, telling me who his audience was and what his purposes were and asking me a series of questions about whether or not he had achieved his purposes for his audience. In addition, he included a list of possible revisions and their motivations and asked for my advice about them. His request resulted in a direct change in my responding practices: Bingo taught me that I could best provide discourse-level feedback if I better understood each student's audience(s) and purpose(s), each student's needs, and each student's thought processes about their drafts and revisions. Thinking about individualization also reminds me of a multilingual writing class I taught early in my career. One of my students was from Nigeria and another from India, and I realized when reading their essays that both at the sentence level and at the rhetorical level they were making use of different Englishes, varieties up until then I had not been familiar with. After reading about Nigerian Englishes and Indian Englishes, I made the decision to work with them as my informants about their language and rhetorical choices and to find ways that would work to effectively do so. This required discourse-level feedback that was consultative, rather than discourse-level feedback that told them that their rhetorical and language choices were wrong.

Individualization also addresses **relationships** and **attitudes**. The wording and foci of discourse-level feedback can signal to students how teachers see their **relationship** to each student and their **attitudes** toward each student. Likewise, how a student engages with a teacher's feedback can send messages about how the student sees the teacher-student relationship as well as the student's attitudes toward the teacher. Years ago, as a writing program administrator supervising multilingual writing teachers, I would ask the teachers to share with me the feedback they provided to their students as one aspect of classroom/instructional observations to inform my in-service education with these teachers. One of the teachers I was working with had written the following on a student's paper: "Andrei, Andrei, Andrei, how many times do I have to tell you. . ." (Goldstein, 2005). The teacher's wording clearly signaled the teacher's frustration with the student's ongoing difficulties without considering why the student was having these difficulties. It also signaled an antagonistic relationship.

In addition to its wording, the foci of a teacher's discourse-level feedback can also send messages. Through examining the feedback of another multilingual writing teacher, I learned that in her content-based writing course for matriculated multilingual policy students she had provided a significant amount of WCF to one of the students while in many instances not providing the needed discourse-level feedback. In our discussions, the teacher shared that she did so assuming that sentence-level issues indicated a lack of ability to work with discourse-level issues. In turn, the teacher's overwhelming focus on WCF signaled to the student that the teacher saw the student as less than competent to deal with discourse-level issues and that the teacher saw her relationship to this student as an arbiter of sentence-level correctness. I contrast this with one of my graduate student's practice responses to Dang. Dang had numerous sentence-level errors but what was interfering with his ability to fulfill his purposes was rhetorical, especially his need to provide more sufficient and appropriate support for claims he was making. My student concluded that one aspect of her relationship to Dang should be her role as a reader, so her discourse-level feedback focused on what she needed to know as a reader to best understand what he wanted to convey.

How a student engages with teacher feedback sends messages about the student's attitude toward and perceived relationship with the teacher (see Lee & Schallert, 2008, for example). Consider a situation where the student in a multilingual content-based writing course did not trust the teacher's knowledge of the content the student was writing about. However, as she informed me, she did not communicate this to the teacher because she saw her relationship with the teacher as one of unequal power, with the teacher holding the power. Given this, the student revised in response to and consistent with all of the teacher's feedback in her revisions even where the student felt the feedback was not correct. In contrast, my student Tranh saw himself as having a negotiated relationship with me. This influenced how he engaged with my discourse-level feedback, including instances where he told me that my discourse-level feedback about his arguments was wrong. Tranh did not always use my feedback, explaining that to do so would contradict what he felt was correct (Conrad & Goldstein, 1999). I share these examples to raise awareness that relationships and attitudes can play critical roles in the ways in which and on what teachers give discourse-level feedback and how and if students engage with this feedback. Given this reality, teachers need to consider both the wording and foci of their discourse-level feedback and the underlying messages their feedback conveys about how they perceive their relationships to each student and their attitudes toward each student. As well, teachers need to give careful consideration to how students' engagement with their discourse-level feedback can be affected by their perceptions of their teachers' attitudes toward them, their own attitudes toward the teacher, and their own understanding of their relationship to the teacher (Goldstein, 2006).

I've left **dialogism** (Bakhtin, 1986; Merkel, 2018) for last, as dialogism is key for all of the above characteristics of "good feedback."

Dialogism acknowledges the fundamental notion that the meaning of all texts—the student's texts both current and past, the teacher's discourse-level feedback both current and past, the student's revisions in response to discourse-level feedback as well as revisions independently motivated both current and past—is negotiated between the reader and writer and does not reside solely within any one text. Thus, dialogism allows us to move away from seeing discourse-level feedback and student composing and revision using discourse-level feedback as a decontextualized, asocial, linear process to a highly contextualized complex social process and recognizes that this process relies on mechanisms for ongoing communication between teachers and students.

How do we foster dialogism? From the students' perspective, we can look for ways in which they can communicate with us about their needs, their successes, their difficulties, their questions, and their preferences (Goldstein, 2005). We can begin with questionnaires or individual meetings at the start of a course and then periodically query students about their feedback experiences, preferences, and concerns. In addition, students can attach cover notes to their first drafts informing their teachers about their audience(s) and purpose(s), what they see as their strengths and their difficulties, and asking for specific feedback. Students can also attach cover notes to their subsequent drafts or revise and resubmit letters or annotate their texts, as Bingo did, not only to address strengths and difficulties but also to address how they used their teacher's feedback, what feedback they chose not to use and why, and what feedback they did not understand or did not know how to enact. Teachers can provide opportunities for dialogism through conferencing, either face to face or through electronic means, through providing feedback to students on their revisions, through explaining their feedback practices and how to interpret their feedback, through tying feedback to classroom instruction, and through making careful use of their students' cover notes, annotations, and any other methods of communication to best understand each student and each student's needs and to best provide feedback within the student's stated rhetorical situation.

In sum, dialogism as a concept fundamental to good feedback is essential, as it:

- allows students and teachers to communicate with each other, helping teachers avoid second-guessing students and students second-guessing teachers;

- helps teachers individualize their feedback in terms of comprehensibility, selectivity, usability, multimodality and affordances, intertextuality, and structure, foci, and content;

- enables teachers to engage students through available means for dialogism so that students can take agency over their own texts. Such dialogism helps teachers provide appropriate discourse-level feedback, including not only feedback that scaffolds students' learning but also feedback that acknowledges when the student brings content expertise and/ or disciplinary rhetorical expertise that the teacher may lack;

- fosters students taking ownership of their writing and their revisions by communicating how they have used their teacher's discourse-level feedback, what discourse-level feedback they have not used and why, and what discourse-level feedback they are either having difficulty understanding or do not know how to enact;

- allows teachers to understand how each student sees themselves in relation to the teacher and the respective roles they see themselves and the teacher playing in discourse-level feedback and student revision and in so doing foster productive, supportive, and trusting relationships;

- helps uncover student attitudes that affect how/if students make use of discourse-level feedback and that allow teachers to work to ameliorate negative attitudes and to also recognize if they have played any role in these attitudes;

- allows relationships to evolve and change as needed, allowing, for example, a shift from teacher to learner for the teacher and learner to teacher for the student (see Merkel, 2018).

In concluding, I want to acknowledge that although providing "good feedback" is a central aspect of second language writing pedagogy that can assist students in working toward producing "good writing," doing so is not an easy task but rather one that takes thought and time and practice. It is my sincere hope that an understanding that feedback is a text/genre and not a set of separate comments and that the characteristics of "good feedback" I have described above and mechanisms and rationales for dialogism I have concluded with can provide multilingual writing teachers with guidance and in so doing make the process of giving feedback less daunting, more systematic, and more approachable for the teacher and helpful and productive for the student.

## References

Aljaafreh, A., & Lantolf, J. P. (1994). Negative feedback as regulation and second language learning in the zone of proximal development. *Modern Language Journal, 78*(4), 465–483. DOI: 10.1111/j.1540–4781.1994.tb02064.x.

Bakhtin, M. M. (1986). *Speech genres and other late essays*. University of Texas Press.

Bitchener, J. (2021). Written corrective feedback. In H. Nassaji & E. Kartchavka (Eds.), *The Cambridge handbook of corrective feedback in second language learning and teaching* (pp. 207–225). Cambridge University Press.

Bitchener, J., & Ferris, D. (2011). *Written corrective feedback in second language acquisition and writing*. Routledge.

Conrad, S., & Goldstein, L. (1999). ESL Student revision after teacher-written comments: Texts, contexts, and individuals. *Journal of Second Language Writing, 8*, 147–181. https://doi.org/10.1016/S1060-3743(99)80126-X

Ferris, D., & Kurzer, K. (2019). Does error feedback help L2 writers? Latest evidence on the efficacy of written corrective feedback. In K. Hyland & F. Hyland (Eds.), *Feedback in second language writing: Contexts and issues* (pp. 106–124). Cambridge University Press.

Flower, L. (1979). Writer-based prose: A cognitive basis for problems in writing. *College English, 41*, 19–37. https://doi.org/10.2307/376357

Goldstein, L. M. (2005). *Teacher written commentary in second language writing classrooms*. University of Michigan Press.

Goldstein, L. (2006). In search of the individual: Feedback and revision in second language writing. In K. Hyland & F. Hyland (Eds.), *Feedback in second language writing: Contexts and issues* (pp. 185–205). Cambridge University Press.

Goldstein, L. (2010). Finding "theory" in the particular: An "autobiography" of what I learned and how about teacher feedback. In P. Matsuda & T. Silva (Eds.), *Practicing theory in second language writing* (pp. 72–90). Parlor Press.

Goldstein, L. (2016). Making use of teacher written feedback: A critical analysis of 30 years of research. In P. Matsuda & R. Manchón (Eds.), *Handbook of second and foreign language writing* (pp. 407–430). deGruyter Mouton.

Goldstein, L., & Kohls, R. (2019, November 13–16). *More than treating errors: Teacher written feedback and neglect of discourse level writing.* Paper presentation at the 2019 Symposium on Second Language Writing, Tempe, AZ.

Grabe, W., & Kaplan, R. B. (1996). *Theory and practice of writing.* Longman.

Hattie, J., & Timperley, H. (2007). The power of feedback. *Review of Educational Research, 77,* 81–112. DOI: 10.3102/003465430298487

Lee, G., & Schallert, D. L. (2008). Meeting in the margins: Effects of the teacher–student relationship on revision processes of EFL college students taking a composition course. *Journal of Second Language Writing, 17,* 165–182. https://doi.org/10.1016/j.jslw.2007.11.002

Manchón, R., & Polio, C. (2021) (Eds.). *The Routledge handbook of second language acquisition and writing.* Routledge.

Merkel, W. (2018). Role reversals: A case study of dialogic interactions and feedback on L2 writing. *Journal of Second Language Writing, 39,* 16–28. DOI: 10.1016/j.jslw.2017.11.007

Murphy, S. (2000). A sociocultural perspective on teacher response: Is there a student in the room? *Assessing Writing, 7,* 79–90. DOI: 10.1016/S1075-2935(00)00019-2

Rodway, C. (2018). *Reconceptualizing feedback as interactional contingent scaffolding: Improving argumentation in second language undergraduate writing: A praxeology* [Doctoral dissertation, Griffith University, Brisbane-Queensland, Australia]. https://research-repository.griffith.edu.au/rest/bitstreams/747d7dd9-21f3-51a0-a988-055a255b94fa/retrieve

Tardy, C. (2019). *Genre-based writing: What every ESL teacher needs to know.* University of Michigan Press.

Treglia, M. O. (2008). Feedback on feedback: Exploring student responses to teachers' written commentary. *Journal of Basic Writing, 27*(1), 105–137. DOI: 10.37514/JBW-J.2008.27.1.06

Worden, D. (2019). Developing L2 writing teachers' pedagogical content knowledge of genre through the unfamiliar genre project. *Journal of Second Language Writing, 46,* 1–12. DOI: 10.1016/j.jslw.2019.100667

van Lier, L. (2000). From input to affordance: Social-interactive learning from an ecological perspective. In J. P. Lantolf (Ed.), *Sociocultural theory and second language learning* (pp. 245–260). Oxford University Press.

Vygotsky, L. S. (1986). *Thought and language.* MIT Press.

# Chapter 5

# Shaping Teachers' Writing Assessment Practices: The Effect of Teacher Beliefs about Good Writing

*Deborah Crusan*

Let me tell you a story about how my assessment practices were shaped—how my *beliefs* in particular affected my practice. A long time ago, in a classroom of a small community college in western Pennsylvania, my writing assessment practices and my beliefs about writing and writing assessment (which to be honest were at that time largely unformed, uninformed, and unexamined) were laid bare. I was a fledgling teacher, having just earned a bachelor's degree in Education/Secondary English, and had been fortunate to land an adjunct position teaching developmental English to community college students.

I was excited to be in the classroom, and I couldn't wait to assign the first writing task. Revealing all my inexperience, I asked my students to write a paragraph and submit it for the next class. I can't emphasize it enough: *That. Is. All. I. Asked.* I gave no criteria, no topic, no direction, no requirements for form or function, nothing. I asked them to simply write a paragraph, which showed an utter lack of critical examination of my practice and the dearth of an assessment philosophy.

During the next class, the students submitted their paragraphs. Feeling emboldened by their mere submission of an assignment, I was eager to go home and read what they had written. When I began to read and assess, I realized, "Just because I know how to write doesn't mean I know how to teach (and thereby assess) writing" (M. B. Sjostrom, personal communication, February 25, 2020). I learned immediately that my beliefs about the teaching of writing lacked a theoretical basis. I understood that because I had asked my students to write a paragraph (and nothing further), I could not in good conscience hold them accountable for anything else—they had fulfilled the criteria I had provided. What a learning experience that was, and although I was a bit oblivious at the time, it was one that began the reshaping of my beliefs about teaching, writing, and writing assessment (Crusan, 2010).

Karaca and Uysal (2021) claim that the impetus for teacher decisions and pedagogical practices is teachers' inveterate beliefs. When teachers realize the importance and impact of their beliefs, they can be "better equipped with the required knowledge and skills in the process of teaching and learning" (p. 15). Obviously, I had a lot of unraveling to do. I had a vague recognition that my beliefs shape my perceptions and perspectives, which ultimately shape my reality, but what I first needed to untangle was exactly what a belief is. Merriam-Webster (2021) defines a belief as a "conviction of the truth of some statement or the reality of some being or phenomenon especially when based on examination of evidence," such as a belief in the validity of scientific statements.

As it became more obvious to me that my assessment beliefs and training were limited and lacked real-life application, I gradually realized that my teacher training program had not afforded me a path through which I could undergird my naive, raw beliefs with theoretical and practical knowledge concerning assessment so as to inform the development of my assessment philosophy. My assessment philosophy would then shape my pedagogy and emerge in every action in my classroom; in other words, I would clearly demonstrate my assessment beliefs/philosophies by what I made happen in my classroom (Crusan & Ruecker, 2022). At that point in my career, however, I had no assessment philosophy. Struggling as a writing teacher and trying to establish what I believed, I began asking myself questions (albeit not so clearly expressed at the time) such as:

- *Am I able to articulate what was wrong with my first assignment?*

- *What is it that I believe about the teaching of writing and writing assessment?*

- *What is it that I should provide for my students to help them understand what is expected of them? That is, what do students need to know to be held accountable?*

- *How can I be a more equitable assessor of my students' work?*

- *How do (my) teacher beliefs about good academic writing affect my writing assessment practices?*

- *How can I help my students understand what I believe about good writing and writing assessment?*

- *What do I believe constitutes good writing?*

- *Why do we write?*

- *Am I a good writer?*

Clearly, I had a long road facing me with the list above, but I understood intuitively that answering these questions would essentially reshape and hone my beliefs about good writing. And I think I was right. I soon realized that probably the most important question on my list was *What do I believe constitutes good writing?* Writing teachers and those who are learning to write for academic purposes in both first and additional languages often ask that complex and complicated question. Interestingly, some scholars believe there is no such thing as writing in general; writing, according to Wardle (2017), is always "in particular" (p. 30). In other words, good writing is highly contextualized. Attempting to formulate *my* definition of good writing, I asked my own students—all prospective teachers of English learners—to articulate their definitions of good writing. Here is some of what they said.

Good writing

- fits the writer's purpose
- can be understood by those for whom the writing is intended
- demonstrates clear and efficient articulation of ideas
- meets criteria
- demonstrates voice and style
- engages the reader
- thoroughly examines the topic without deviating from it
- follows a clear, organized, and coherent structure
- is well-argued, explained, exemplified, smooth, and expressive
- contains diverse sentence style/structure, vocabulary usage meeting or exceeding language/educational levels of the student, and appropriate use of language conventions.

Baertschi, L., Booth, H., Crisler, B., Idrees, A., Pitzer, T., Price, M., Tyler, S., Yu, F., & Zhang, Y. (personal communication, 2021).

Tillema's (1994) congruence hypothesis asserts that "the effectiveness of training is dependent upon the correspondence between trainee's pre-existing cognitions (especially beliefs) and the knowledge that training is intended to convey" (p. 601). Plainly, my students had articulated their beliefs clearly, and these beliefs about good writing showed their progress toward developing their own assessment philosophies. I would argue that many of these beliefs had been informed, shaped, and reshaped by their training as students and as teachers. However, in the discussion that followed in that class, my students confessed to some frustration when these beliefs collided with the bureaucracies in which they were teaching. They became discouraged by institutional mandates that "influence notions such as the definition of good writing, student expectations of classroom activities, and teacher training" (Crusan, Plakans, & Gebril, 2016, p. 45). The students perceived that institutional mandates were forcing them to change their pedagogies in ways that defied their personal teaching philosophies.

The list my students produced also made clear the myriad definitions of good writing. In linguistics, there is something called an *idiolect*. An idiolect is a person's specific way of speaking; every person has their very own idiolect that differs from the way other people talk (Dawson & Phelan, 2016). To stretch an analogy, might this be the case for a person's beliefs about what good writing is? Fernando (2018) found that students move closer to their definition of good writing when they understand their highly individual writing processes and are provided formative feedback on both process and product. It is therefore likely that their definitions of good writing might also be highly individualized.

In their call for chapters for the manuscript for this book, Kohls and Casanave pose important questions: What is good writing? How do we know? Frankly, I admire this call to define good writing; however, I believe we face a monumental task, for as we are consistently reminded, beauty is in the eye of the beholder. Is it a matter of taste, though? Certainly, definitions of good writing exist. But can we really agree on a single definition of good writing? To begin to define the construct of good writing, I must ask myself for what purposes am I writing, so the question(s) for me then become *What does good writing look like*

- in an academic article?

- in a short story?

- in an assignment in a composition class?

- in an email to my professor?

- in a recommendation letter for a colleague or a student?

- in a cover letter for employment?

- in an opinion piece to a newspaper editor?

If I can establish why I write, I can then go about listing what good writing looks like for that reason. Given that there are countless reasons to write—many more than I have listed above—it's easy to see that our many and varied purposes for writing are complex and contextualized. This is not to lessen the importance of Kohls and Casanave's questions but, as all good academics do, to complicate them. Supporting the notion of the varied definitions of good writing, the burgeoning research into assessment literacy finds that the highly contextualized nature of writing and writing assessment and the presence of multiple stakeholders call for somewhat more individualized definitions of good writing based on context (Inbar-Lourie, 2017).

This brings up other important questions. Can teachers write? Are they good writers? Can they articulate what good writing is to them? If they cannot write well, and there is evidence that supports the lack of that skill, then we have an even bigger issue at play. Despite the importance of writing instruction and assessment in primary, secondary, and postsecondary education, very few teacher preparation programs include adequate instruction about writing instruction and assessment (Dockrell, Marshall, & Wyse, 2016; Martin & Dismuke, 2018) and fewer still provide any writing instruction beyond the required composition classes at the beginning of many bachelor's degree programs. In fact, in a survey of pre-service teachers, Gallavan, Bowles, and Young (2012) discovered teacher candidates' disinclination to write; they also found that teachers in their study were unacquainted with the benefits of writing and reflection. Further, teachers held the belief that they were poor writers and felt uncertain about teaching writing and integrating writing into their lessons.

As I have done in the past (Crusan, 2010, 2015), I want to argue that the definition of good writing is tied to the <u>assessment</u> of writing. As a writing assessment scholar, I have tried for nearly two decades to answer the questions *What is good writing?* and *How do we know?* through the lens of writing assessment, for it is through writing assessment that I am obliged to define and refine my criteria. That is, it is in the assessment of writing that I wrestle with and finally crystalize what I want my students to do in certain kinds of writing. I must then communicate those criteria to students clearly and concisely. For example, I need to define good writing for my students through criteria and scoring guides that inform them as they attempt to produce good writing. It cannot be simply "Good writing, I know it when I see it" (Leki, 1995). If I am unable to define good writing (and again, it should be good writing *for a given purpose*), my students are out of luck. In other words, I must be assessment-literate; I need a deep understanding of the principles of sound assessment. To assess my students' writing ability fairly, I need to be able to design unbiased assessments and develop scoring rubrics and assessment criteria.

My point is that the definition of good writing and the assessment of writing really go hand in hand. Once again, these two things are inextricably entwined. In fact, Todd Ruecker and I call it a marriage and claim that every assignment a teacher makes is an assessment (Crusan & Ruecker, 2022). One of the questions I asked earlier was *What is it that I should provide for my students to help them understand what is expected of them?* That is, *What do students need to know to be held accountable?* This is where creating assignment criteria and accompanying rubrics come into play. It is also where teacher-educators can press their prospective teachers in the formation of their beliefs and philosophy. And it is clearly "practice what you preach." In other words, if I expect my students to do something in their classrooms, I model it for them in my classroom.

Let's look at the skill of summarizing, often taught in beginning college composition classes for English learners. When I teach summary in L2 Composition, I use samples to demonstrate what a good summary includes. My students and I read summaries and identify the necessary parts. I then use what we have discussed as necessary parts of a summary to generate the assignment criteria and the scoring guide or rubric. We discuss the weight of each item, arguing for a lighter or heavier weight depending on the item. I create these materials with my students, for they are now very astute about summary parts. This co-creation of materials empowers students, engages them with the assignment, and encourages buy-in to the assignment. In fact, Alter and Haydon (2017) suggest that students who are involved in these processes show a greater understanding of and respect for assignments and assessment. When they feel heard, students see the classroom as a fair environment. Such involvement in the creation of assignment/assessment materials seems to enhance student ability to present their opinions and respect the opinions of others. Once the materials are created, I provide them to my students at the beginning of all assignments; consequently, students rarely have questions about what is required and how it will be graded.

I do the same for the prospective teachers I work with. I show them through my assignments to them and tell them through their assignment/assessment activity creation in class that each assignment needs a specifically created set of criteria and a rubric created from those criteria. When we create writing assignments together, we decide what good writing is for a certain assignment. We ask, "What is it that I want my student to be able to do?" I then create the assignment, the criteria, and the rubric with my students, so that I can expect them to do the same for their students. In this way, I get my students to realize the contextualized meaning of good writing and good assessment and that it is important to be assessment-literate. As teachers, we need to teach our students what good writing is and how to be good writers. Good pedagogy is giving students the keys to the castle in the form of rubrics and samples of good writing in whatever genre upon which we are currently focusing.

It seems that there are several different problems to solve. We are struggling to effectively define good writing. We have also discovered that some teachers' writing skills might be inadequate. Additionally, teachers also often struggle with the assessment of writing. The issue of teachers' writing skills is a tough one, for there are many pieces to this puzzle: teachers' education programs, the lack of practice of the skill of writing, the myriad conflicting ideas that still exist about the best ways to teach writing. The best we can do is to call for more professional development for writing teachers and maybe to increase the criteria necessary for becoming a writing teacher in the first place. As teacher-educators, we should clarify what we do in our classrooms to make sure that our prospective teachers understand how to teach writing and are also ethical assessors who recognize the importance of assessment, how to do it, why to do it, and how to make assessment practices transparent.

Unfortunately, teachers are often afraid of assessment. Some confess that they secretly hate grading papers and report that they have concerns about what to weigh, if they are equitable and fair, and how their evaluations compare to those of other teachers. If teachers were instructed in a clear process by which they could create assignments and rubrics, they might feel better about the issues of judgment, equity, and comparability. And they are right to worry; Fernando (2018) notes that students perennially struggle with understanding the requirements of writing assessment because many requirements are not clearly written. These students complain that "they weren't told *what* counts. If you [teachers] want to count something when assessing a writing assignment, then you need to tell your students what counts" (Crusan, 2010, p. 59), especially when students are unfamiliar with the codes or rules for participating in power. That is, there may be a culture of power in the classroom, which some students may have little idea about negotiating (Delpit, 1988).

## Rubrics

As teachers, we make many decisions when it comes to how we might assess our students' writing. We need to be clear about the weight of each item. My perspective on rubrics is couched in my struggle to provide fair and equitable assessment to my students; I am constantly reminded of that disastrous first assignment where I failed to inform students of assignment criteria, how they would be graded, what I would use to grade their work, what counted, what didn't. If rubrics are not used to assess writing, assignment criteria must be made available; an explanation of criteria that allows students to know what will be assessed and how it will be assessed is necessary. Without that, what is the alternative? I am not alone in positioning myself in this way. Dempsey et al. (2009) remind us that without criteria and feedback, it is difficult to convey to students what is expected of them. In the absence of these, students will view writing assignments as subjective and capricious. Once again, teacher beliefs affect teacher practices.

As is probably clear by now, my personal beliefs about good writing hinge on teacher beliefs and on the context in which that writing is done. In reality, a teacher's definitions of good writing are only as strong as their ability to write, their beliefs about what good writing is, and their ability to convey those definitions to their students. I also have always believed in the power of a rubric to help me convey that information. However, painting a rosy picture of the use of rubrics is not entirely fair; rubrics are not without their problems. While they generally agree that rubrics offer value to teachers and students alike, Li and Lindsey (2015) specify differences in teachers' and students' interpretation of rubric language; therefore, the language of the rubric must be discussed in class by teachers and students to clarify any misunderstandings. Further, if a rubric is not systematically created in conjunction with a specific assignment, the use of that rubric might lead teachers to standardize their assessments.

It is probably not surprising to note that there are some who do not look favorably on the rubric. Wilson (2006) believes that rubrics are problematic as they tend to standardize student writing. In her experience, rubrics do not help teachers assess and respond to writing in productive ways. She believes that rubrics produce uniformity in instruction, in student writing, and in teacher reading of the product, shutting down teachers' responses to the writing. Rubrics—which Wilson defines as templates placed over a piece of student writing—cause teachers to see writing in the same way and give rise to the loss of texture that makes the teaching of writing interesting. Wilson further believes that an interesting piece of writing often throws a rubric into chaos. A rubric, she contends, is based on a formula that falsely predicts good writing; she claims that good writing is much more complex because a multitude of factors react in unpredictable ways.

Kohn (2006) also sees rubrics as problematic. He opines, "Just as it's possible to raise standardized test scores as long as you're willing to gut the curriculum and turn the school into a test-preparation factory, so it's possible to get a bunch of people to agree on what rating to give an assignment as long as they're willing to accept and apply someone else's narrow criteria for what merits that rating" (p. 13). Of course, Kohn is referring to more standardized assessments and overlooks the classroom teacher who independently designs assignments, criteria, and rubrics for each individual assignment based on what they believe students need to be able to do with certain genres of writing. That teacher then guarantees that students understand the assignment, are totally aware of ways that their work will be assessed, and recognize that their work will be assessed according to a set of criteria that they have agreed upon rather than having their work compared to that of their classmates.

Others (Crusan, 2010; Crusan & Matsuda, 2018; Jonsson & Svingby, 2007; Lee, 2017; Saenkhum, 2020; Weigle, 2007) credit effective and ethical rubrics with doing some of the job of communicating assignment criteria and our definition(s) of good writing to our students; rubrics help teachers specify exactly what is expected in an assignment. Further, a good rubric can "provide feedback to teachers regarding instructional effectiveness and supply benchmarks upon which to measure and document progress" (Crusan, 2021, p. 432). Jonsson and Svingby (2007) claim that ". . . rubrics seem to have the potential of promoting learning and/or improve instruction. The main reason for this potential lies in the fact that rubrics make expectations and criteria explicit, which also facilitates feedback and self-assessment" (p. 130). Without a doubt, teachers can use assignment rubrics to tentatively score drafts of student papers, which will provide feedback to students about their writing. Using rubrics in this way allows teachers to "establish accountability to and credibility with their students by providing them with clear, accessible, and understandable assessment materials, which also provide necessary transparency. This kind of rapport . . . between student and teacher cannot be overestimated" (Crusan, 2021, p. 432). In other words, a rubric does a lot to help us tell our students what counts as good writing and does even more to build trust.

Because samples of good assignments, good rubrics, and good writing are important, let's look at a summary assignment including the assignment, the criteria, and the accompanying rubric. As we know, a summary encapsulates a writer's intentions in fewer words than the original. It is a brief expression with no elaboration, explanation, or opinion, presenting the author's main points while reducing length. Teachers should rehearse with students, collaboratively read a text, and then practice writing a summary together. Students need to know that a summary states the main concept of the text, includes important facts and details excluding the student's opinions, is in the student's own words, sparingly uses direct quotes from the text (these selections should have quotation marks). The summary should reflect underlying meaning and only the most important details in logical order. Students should also be made aware of formatting and other requirements such as length. Some teachers require the first sentence of the summary to include the text's title, author, and main point of the text. Students are often informed of the importance of using source material from the text to demonstrate their ability to defend claims with source material since they will be using this skill often in their writing courses. This information helps raise awareness of the importance of citation.

The first step that a teacher can take is to explain what a good summary writer does: The summary writer identifies the most important points in the text to be summarized and restates the text in the summary writer's own words. Identifying key points and restating them are two skills crucial for students. They should also be aware of the definition of a thesis statement. A thesis statement is a concise statement of the main point a writer wishes to make, and it sums up the text in a single statement. This definition can guide them in their recognition of thesis statements when summarizing a text and can help them when they need to write a thesis statement.

Next, the teacher should list and explain the steps in creating a summary. The Robert Gillespie Academic Skills Centre (Sjostrom, 2020) suggests six steps are involved in writing a summary: Identify the sections of the text, distinguish between major and minor details, remove minor details and examples, pay attention to transition words, reorder the ideas as needed, and reserve your opinions. Additionally, the Centre includes a checklist: Write in full sentences; shorten the original text; use your own words and sentence structure; and maintain the author's intent. All these steps and checklist items can be considered criteria and can easily be turned into a rubric.

The assignment might look something like this:

**Summary Assignment** due _________________(date)

You will write a summary of one of three short texts that we have read in class. Remember that your summary should be in the form of a paragraph. It should begin with an introductory sentence that states the text's title, author, and main point of the text as you see it. You should paraphrase ideas from the text (express the meaning of the writer using different words, especially to achieve greater clarity) and use quotes sparingly. Use source material to defend your claims. Write a last sentence that concludes your summary, which is often a simple rephrasing of the main point.

We have worked together to create the following rubric, so I will use it to assess your summary. We will re-review all rubric points in class to assure your understanding before you begin this assignment.

Summary Rubric:

| | 0<br>Missing | 1<br>Novice | 2<br>Apprentice | 3<br>Proficient | 4<br>Distinguished |
|---|---|---|---|---|---|
| The summary: | | | | | |
| includes a sentence stating title, author, and main point | | | | | |
| is written in student's own words | | | | | |
| includes main points of text | | | | | |

|  | 0 Missing | 1 Novice | 2 Apprentice | 3 Proficient | 4 Distinguished |
|---|---|---|---|---|---|
| does not include student's opinions |  |  |  |  |  |
| includes some source material to defend claims |  |  |  |  |  |
| presents points in logical order |  |  |  |  |  |
| includes paraphrasing of ideas from text |  |  |  |  |  |
| includes a concluding sentence that wraps up the summary |  |  |  |  |  |
| uses appropriate transitions |  |  |  |  |  |
| is approximately 1/3 length of original text |  |  |  |  |  |
| is grammatically and mechanically correct |  |  |  |  |  |

KEY:

0 Missing: information is missing from the text

1 Novice: skills are becoming apparent

2 Apprentice: skills are growing and becoming more advanced

3 Proficient: skills show greater level of competency

4 Distinguished: skills are accurate, efficient, and effective

When I was a graduate student, I would occasionally ask my advisor pedagogical questions about teaching writing. Once, several other members of my cohort and I asked her if we should teach grammar in our L2 writing classes. Instead of answering us, she asked *us* a question. She asked why we would teach grammar in our writing classes and asked us for our pedagogical purpose. That is, she asked us to come up with a rationale for teaching grammar, so we did. We realized that we had valid reasons for sometimes including mini-lessons on select grammar issues that we saw in our students' writing. She then told us that the answer to many questions is, "It depends," (Johnson, 1999) and that through working out our reasons, we would see why we would or would not do something (e.g., teach grammar, give a test) in our classrooms.

Because the definitions of good writing are so highly contextualized, when we ask what good writing is, we can answer that, in fact, it depends. Among many things, it depends on what we are writing and for whom; that is, it depends on the purpose for writing and the audience. But one thing is very clear—as teachers we need to make transparent to our students what we believe good writing to be, and that will be done by our use of ethical, efficient, comprehensive writing assignments and assessments. Our students deserve nothing less.

## References


Alter, P., & Haydon, T. (2017). Characteristics of effective classroom rules: A review of the literature. *Teacher Education and Special Education, 40*(2), 114–127. https://doi.org/10.1177/0888406417700962

Crusan, D. (2010). *Assessment in the second language writing classroom.* University of Michigan Press.

Crusan, D. (2015). Dance, ten; looks, three: Why rubrics matter. *Assessing Writing, 26,* 1–4. http://dx.doi.org/10.1016/j.asw.2015.08.002

Crusan, D. (2021). Writing assessment literacy. In H. Mohebbi & C. Coombe (Eds.), *Research questions in language education and applied linguistics: A reference guide* (pp. 431–438). Springer. https://link.springer.com/book/10.1007/978-3-030-79143-8

Crusan, D., & Matsuda, P. K. (2018). Classroom writing assessment. In J. I. Liontas (Editor-in-Chief), *The TESOL encyclopedia of English language teaching* (pp. 1–7). Wiley-Blackwell.

Crusan, D., Plakans, L., & Gebril, A. (2016). Writing assessment literacy: Surveying second language teachers' knowledge, beliefs, and practices. *Assessing Writing, 28,* 43–56. https://doi.org/10.1016/j.asw.2016.03.001

Crusan, D., & Ruecker, T. (2022). *Linking assignments to assessments: A guide for teachers.* University of Michigan Press.

Dawson, H. C., & Phelan, M. (Eds.). (2016). *Language files: Materials for an introduction to language and linguistics, 12th ed.* Ohio State University Press.

Delpit, L. (1988). The silenced dialogue: Power and pedagogy in educating other people's children. *Harvard Educational Review, 58*(3), 280–299. https://doi-org.ezproxy.libraries.wright.edu/10.17763/haer.58.3.c43481778r528qw4

Dempsey, M. S., Pytlik Zillig, L. M., & Bruning, R. H. (2009). Helping preservice teachers learn to assess writing: Practice and feedback in a Web-based environment. *Assessing Writing, 14*, 38–61. https://doi.org/10.1016/j.asw.2008.12.003

Dockrell, J., Marshall, C., & Wyse, D. (2016). Teachers' reported practices for teaching writing in England. *Reading and Writing: An Interdisciplinary Journal, 29*, 409–434. https://doi.org/10.1007/s11145-015-9605-9

Fernando, W. (2018). Show me your true colours: Scaffolding formative academic literacy assessment through an online learning platform. *Assessing Writing, 36*, 63–76. https://doi.org/10.1016/j.asw.2018.03.005

Gallavan, N. P., Bowles, F. A., & Young, C. T. (2012). Learning to write and writing to learn: Insights from teacher candidates. *Action in Teacher Education, 29*(2), 61–69. https://doi.org/10.1080/01626620.2007.10463449

Inbar-Lourie, O. (2017). Language assessment literacy. In E. Shohamy, I. Or, & S. May (Eds.), *Language testing and assessment* (3rd ed.), (pp. 257-270). *Encyclopedia of language and education.* Springer.

Johnson, K. E. (1999). *Understanding language teaching: Reasoning in action.* Heinle & Heinle.

Jonsson, A., & Svingby, G. (2007). The use of scoring rubrics: Reliability, validity, and educational consequences. *Educational Research Review, 2*, 130–144.

Karaca, M., & Uysal, H. H. (2021). The development and validation of an inventory on English writing teacher beliefs. *Assessing Writing, 47*, 1–19. https://doi.org/10.1016/j.asw.2020.100507

Kohn, A. (2006). Speaking my mind: The trouble with rubrics. *The English Journal, 95*(4), 12–15. https://doi.org/10.2307/30047080

Lee, I. (2017). *Classroom writing assessment and feedback in L2 school contexts.* Springer.

Leki, I. (1995). Good writing: I know it when I see it. In D. Belcher & G. Braine (Eds.), *Academic writing in a second language* (pp. 23–46). Ablex.

Li, J., & Lindsey, P. (2015). Understanding variations between student and teacher application of rubrics. *Assessing Writing, 26*, 67–79.

Martin, S. D., & Dismuke, S. (2018). Investigating differences in teacher practices through a complexity theory lens: The influence of teacher education. *Journal of Teacher Education, 69*(1), 22–39. https://doi.org/10.1177/0022487117702573

Merriam-Webster Dictionary (2021). Belief. https://www.merriam-webster.com/dictionary/belief

Saenkhum, T. (2020). Preparing writing teachers to use assessment rubrics. *NYS TESOL Journal, 7*(2), 7–25. http://journal.nystesol.org/july2020/02_FA2.pdf

Sjostrom, M. B. (2020, February 25). Personal communication. The Robert Gillespie Academic Skills Centre. (n.d.). Six effective tips to write a summary. University of Toronto. https://www.utm.utoronto.ca/asc/sites/files/asc/public/shared/pdf/tip_sheets_writing/Summary_6Tips_alt_v1.pdf

Tillema, H. H. (1994). Training and professional expertise: Bridging the gap between new information and pre-existing beliefs of teachers. *Teaching and Teacher Education 10*(6), 601–615. https://doi.org/10.1016/0742-051X(94)90029-9

Wardle, E. (2017). You can learn to write in general. In C. E. Ball & D. M. Loewe (Eds.), *Bad ideas about writing* (pp. 30–34). West Virginia University Libraries Digital Publishing Institute.

Weigle, S. C. (2007). Teaching writing teachers about assessment. *Journal of Second Language Writing, 16*, 194–209. https://doi.org/10.1016/j.jslw.2007.07.004

Wilson, M. (2006). *Rethinking rubrics in writing assessment.* Heinemann.

**Chapter 6**

# Charting a New Course: Organic Writing Program Assessment in Action

*Priyavanda Abeywickrama, Esther Chan, John Holland, Jennifer Trainor, and Todd Walker*

As a new college student, I was very anxious about what my professors were to expect from me. I was truly afraid that I was not going to meet their expectations or that my writing would not be at the level it is supposed to be. I realize now that before taking this class, I focused all of my energy [on making] my writing appealing to my teacher. All the pressures of meeting standards and expectations made writing harder than it needed to be. This class helped me find my own method to write papers that I actually feel confident with. (Maya, student reflection)

I still haven't entirely found my writing style, but I have been experimenting with and developing myself through what I learned in this course. I am also still figuring out who I am, and this course has pushed me to think deeply about who I am and who I want to be. I was able to plan and zoom out to see my life in perspective. . . . I learned that I am the only one that could control my future. (Nathan, student reflection)

This semester we created pieces of writing that connected with one another. I have not taken a class like this before. Usually, in an

> English class, there would be a sense of structure with how your essay
> should be portrayed; however, this semester English class was a way
> to express my writing where I included identity development and
> looking at my lifelong goal. (Aliza, student reflection)

Students often arrive in first-year composition courses with a well-practiced routine of writing at the last minute, writing to pass the test, and, like Maya, writing to please the teacher. They see "good writing" as conforming to teacher-determined standards and expectations. Nevertheless, writing is messy, and, as these students have discovered, it entails much more than the words on the page. Maya has learned to engage with writing in ways she could not imagine before, discarding the rules and expectations of what good writing looks like to find her way. Nathan and Aliza have taken steps toward adopting a writer's and college students' identity. All have begun to understand the power of agency, taking control of their writing and writing processes. As Linda Adler-Kassner put it in her 2017 Conference on College Composition and Communication (CCCC) Chair's Address, "writing is never just writing." Adler-Kassner's point helps explain why we have struggled with the question *What is good writing?* at the heart of this volume. Asking it raises the specter of those reductive standards, expectations, and judgments that students like Maya, Nathan, and Aliza have begun to complicate.

In what follows, we describe our efforts to reimagine—some of us might say revolt against—such judgments. We focus on an institutionally mandated program assessment where our values about writing—that writing is messy; that it is related to identity, culture, and power; that it is developmental and contextual—and reductive definitions of "good writing" came into sharp relief. We navigated the ensuing complexities by rejecting the "industrial" approach to assessment that our university requested. Instead, we took on the challenge of creating an organic approach (Broad et al., 2009) involving lecturer-faculty collaboration and aligning assessment with our values as a program. We eschewed external rubrics that attempt to encode standards of "good writing" that, as others have written, are based on tautologies that uphold gatekeeping and linguistic racism (Gallagher, 2016; Inoue, 2015; Matsuda, 2006). We attempted to shift the emphasis from definitions of "good writing" toward an understanding of "good writers"—their practices, knowledge, development, struggles, and self-understanding. The insights we gained shifted teachers' identities in our program, as together we discovered new ways to answer the question of what we mean by "good writing."

# Pushing Back Against Industrial Assessment: Origins

We teach at a large, public, urban university located in the western United States serving diverse students, many of whom are multilingual or international or have been determined to need extra literacy support by our state university system. As Bruce Horner (2015) writes, deficit-oriented discourses about literacy circulate on campuses like ours. These discourses can create a lingering sense of failure among students and teachers, who feel pressure to ensure students' "mastery" of linguistic and academic standards. This pressure is even more pronounced for L2 learners, as Matsuda (2012) has argued. However, these discourses do not serve students' needs, address their lived experiences, or speak to their literate identities. Indeed, judgments about "good writing" are fraught with complexities of genre and context, identity and culture, power and privilege. Such judgments can unintentionally support linguistic ideologies and gatekeeping practices that stand in tension with our efforts to achieve educational equity. Moreover, these judgments translate, for students like Maya, into the rigid practices and beliefs about writing they adopted in high school to please teachers and pass tests.

Our pushback against industrial assessment began in our classrooms, where we have been developing pedagogies and curricula focusing on students' literate identities and their transition to college for the past several years. We use directed self-placement and offer credit-bearing parallel tracks for multilingual students. More recently, faculty in our program embraced antiracist grading practices, recognizing that traditional grades worked against linguistic diversity and justice (Crusan et al., 2016). Our equity-based classroom practices and pedagogies were tested in 2018 when our academic senate required us to recertify our writing courses (and ensure that they continued to meet campus general education requirements) and to conduct a direct assessment of student mastery of the learning outcomes in a generic rubric for written communication that teachers in our program had never used.

Such program assessment is often tricky terrain for writing program administrators and writing teachers. Of all the practices that encode reductive assumptions about "good writing," program assessment may be the most fraught. Traditional outcomes assessment that was a feature in the type of rubrics our university asked us to use inevitably assumes a static, universally agreed-upon notion of good writing. Such assessment presupposes a traditional banking model of education where teachers deposit writing skills into students, who then demonstrate those skills for grades or "show mastery" on a program assessment rubric. Perhaps because it seems to require that we adopt a view of literacy that we do not actually hold, program assessment also often feels disconnected from our work in the classroom, creating resentment and resistance among faculty and undermining faculty buy-in. In response to these problems, many scholars (e.g., Broad, 2003; Haswell, 2001; Lee, 2016) favor "organic" models of assessment over "industrial" approaches. An organic assessment is locally contextualized and symbiotic; assessment of "good writing" flows from teachers' judgments about what they value in their classrooms, assignments, and student work. Moreover, it means a symbiotic relationship between assessment and practice; the assessment has to loop back into meaningful changes in the classroom. These changes can only happen when, paraphrasing Broad et al. (2009), the assessment sparks conversation, learning, surprise, engagement, and insight from teachers, who translate those insights back into curricula and pedagogy.

## The First Year: Finding Out What Teachers Think "Good Writing" Is

Thus, rather than rely on the "powerfully conserving and stabilizing effect of traditional five-point rubrics" (Broad, 2003, p. 122), we began our program assessment with dynamic criteria mapping (DCM). This approach to assessment rejects the importation of evaluative methods or findings from outside current local contexts. Instead, it invites teachers to use ethnographic research methods to investigate and understand teaching and learning. As Broad (2003) argues, traditional assessment rubrics are "too simple and too generic to effectively portray the educational values of any specific classroom, department or program" (p. 4). DCM is thus a "rubric-free" method in which faculty "inquire into and document how we evaluate our students' texts" (p. 16). It is a form of qualitative— ethnographic—inquiry done over time that "yields a . . . useful portrait of any program's evaluative dynamics" (p. 13).

Our assessment team consisted of writing program tenure-track and lecturer faculty (including two who regularly teach multilingual students and have expertise in TESOL and multilingual writing), who met weekly. Our goal was to use DCM to build an assessment process that would give us a lens through which we could analyze the kinds of learning goals teachers in our program value and help us assess what we value. We began by reading student reflections collected from our classes and, from there, mapping the values we bring to our reading of them.

Criteria mapping revealed that teachers in our program place a high value on students' growth toward complexity and independence as writers. Teachers valued student reflections that articulated a departure or shift from reductive writing concepts to more complex perspectives. In addition, they celebrated students' growing independence and sense of ownership as writers.

Our criteria mapping also revealed that teachers in our self-study were sensitive to the nuances of students' growth. Teachers often pointed to developmental idiosyncrasies, to the way that students sometimes move backward before moving forward as they engage in the process of "unlearning" practices and beliefs from high school. Teachers noted the circuitous routes many students take in their first year as they encounter new literacy contexts and expectations. Assessment practices focused on judging "good writing" mask the ways that students can and do develop as literacy learners for their college years. To miss those milestones and development was to miss much of what teachers felt were some of the most critical aspects of their work.

Finally, faculty in our self-study emphasized "noncognitive" aspects of students' experiences in their classrooms. These noncognitive elements of the writing classroom include the U.S.-based National Writing Project's habits of mind. These are traits that scholars argue are more highly correlated with future success than are traditional measures of "cognitive" abilities or writing skills, as well as the identity work that scholars have long argued accompanies literacy development (Canagarajah, 2006; Casanave, 2005; Matsuda, 2001, 2015). We wanted an assessment process to help us improve students' experiences and growth in terms of habits of mind and understand more deeply the interconnections between literacy and identity for our students. For our self-study team, bringing these values to light was, in some ways, the easy part. As we noted earlier, teachers in our program manifest these values in many ways: their curricular choices, pedagogical approaches, use of contract grading, and commitment to eliminating deficit models and hierarchies between courses designed to meet "remediation" mandates or serve multilingual students. Nevertheless, when our self-study team turned to the work of analyzing student writing, these values seemed to disappear, and we fell back on the language of formal assessment, looking at easily identifiable (reductive) markers of skill acquisition or mastery, the low-hanging fruit. Articulating a new language for assessing student writing that reflected our pedagogical values and eschewed the language of skill mastery became the work of the second year of our self-study.

## The Second Year: Gathering Student Reflections and Creating Our Assessment Lens

The first step in creating a new assessment language for our program involved articulating key threshold concepts that reflected our pedagogical values. Threshold concepts are "portals" that students move through and signal identity shifts as they cross into new discourse communities. We articulated key threshold concepts encapsulating our teaching goals and values. From there, we created a map of student learning with detailed descriptions of typical milestones in students' journeys toward understanding each threshold concept. These descriptions emphasized the journey students undertake rather than mastery of skills, showing us the kinds of discoveries and struggles students encountered in our courses rather than attempting to determine whether students had arrived at a particular destination. In addition, we wanted to know how students viewed their progress and emerging identities as college students and writers. Thus, our descriptions aim at capturing students' growth over time (via their reflection) rather than on students' level at a particular moment.

Analyzing students' reflections rather than their written products allowed us to turn away from the question *What is good writing?* and instead to look solely toward what student writers do and know. We created a reflection assignment, and with student and teacher permission, we collected reflections from across sections. We gained approval from the Institutional Review Board to use the students' reflections in our analysis for this article. The anonymous student work we present here has not been altered or edited.

Assessing reflection made sense for our program because reflection is a central component of what we teach. Moreover, reflection is a foundational principle and process that underlies self-assessment theory in L2 writing classrooms. Students use reflection as an analytical tool to understand their learning and evaluate their progress against specified goals. To analyze students' reflections, we created a map describing a typical trajectory toward the portals represented in each threshold concept. Next, we plotted the trajectory and created a rubric-like map that we could use to guide our analysis. The map includes descriptions of students' growth along with five points in their journey toward the portal of each threshold concept.

## The Third Year: Analyzing Student Reflections

In the third year, we began a more formal process of analyzing student reflections collected from teachers across our program. Collaboratively, we identified the threshold concepts students grappled with and analyzed their journey toward the "portals" these concepts represented. A typical reflection from Minh, a multilingual writer who self-placed in our two-semester "stretch" course, illustrates our process:

> Being able to learn something aside from writing essay after essay constantly pleasing to me. I learned to build a system or rather a way of thinking that help me reflect after the end of each week. I would lay in bed every Sunday and look back at how my week had went. I would see how productive I was and how much time I have wasted from daily distraction. I would look back and see how I could have done things differently to produce better results.

Our self-study team analyzed Minh's reflection in terms of the two threshold concepts that were most salient in Minh's reflection: Threshold Concept #1 (*Writing requires engagement and agency; writers bring their voices, lived experiences, and identities to their work*), and Threshold Concept #5 (*Writers nurture academic habits of mind (metacognition, curiosity, openness, persistence, flexibility, engagement, creativity, responsibility) to strengthen their thinking and writing*). For Threshold Concept #1, we noted that Minh continues to view school writing negatively, describing the tedium of writing "essay after essay" and his pleasure in learning something "aside from" writing. Our self-study team noted how typical Minh's view is: Many students view writing for school as hoops to jump through to please a teacher. Confidence—what scholars often term "self-efficacy"—is essential to student achievement and literacy development. Our organic assessment approach showed us how and where students like Minh struggled with self-efficacy and which assignments and activities helped promote self-efficacy—insights that would not have been visible to us had we used a more traditional approach to assessment.

Similarly, our assessment tools helped us understand how international and immigrant students, in particular, struggle with self-efficacy. This is particularly true after years of schooling that require them to regurgitate or imitate what they have learned to achieve a specific score or earn a grade they need for advancement. For example, teachers noticed that students find it especially challenging when asked to reflect on and respond to a writer's idea or something presented in class. Similarly, such students may not have been encouraged to give their own opinions on a published writer's ideas or to challenge their instructor's points. Students who have come up through U.S. schools, in contrast, grapple with reflection for slightly different reasons, with the inculcation that school writing requires objectivity and evidence rather than experience, reflection, or opinion. These distinctions matter pedagogically; our assessment tools helped bring them into evident relief, leading to rich discussions among the self-study team about how best to support literacy development for different student populations.

Minh's reflection signaled movement toward Threshold Concept #5. Here the self-study team noted changes in Minh's practice as a writer, which manifested in a growing understanding of the importance of reflection for academic success and an improved sense of self-awareness and self-monitoring. Traditional assessment methods would have zeroed in on Minh's adherence to or deviations from academic language conventions, perhaps noting grammatical errors or difficulties with organization. This approach, however, blinds us to the effects of the actual curriculum in our courses. Instead, we focus on students' identities and purposes as college students and on their writing processes and metacognitive practices. In our program, these are widely held to be necessary precursors to students' mastery of formal rhetorical conventions.

Mateo's reflection also enabled meaningful discussion among teachers. In our analysis of Mateo's reflection, we saw a student moving closer to the threshold of agency as he considered how his experience in his writing class helped him develop rhetorical agency:

> I learned to write to what audience I was trying to get to and what language to use to make my writing easy to understand. I also learned to write in the way that works with me. I shouldn't be silenced by choosing a language that maybe isn't popular or liked by others.

As we did with Minh's, our self-study team analyzed Mateo's reflection in terms of Threshold Concept #1: *Writing requires engagement and agency;*

*writers bring their voices, lived experiences, and identities to their work.* However, unlike Minh, Mateo no longer writes merely to please his teacher or check a box on the rubric. Instead, Mateo has taken on a burgeoning writer identity and strives to communicate in a genuine way to an imagined reader. He resists following predetermined writing methods while seeking to bring his voice into the assignment and is moving toward an understanding of power relations in schooling:

> I have learned how there are different forms of English and how other cultures have impacted the language. Before this class I wasn't aware that there are many different ways to speak english but after the readings and other assignments I have really been interested in learning more about it. [I've learned] how some students did not recognize their own home language. It made me curious on why that was. I wasn't really aware of it, but schools try to force us to speak the same way.

Mateo, in this passage, captured the essence of Threshold Concept #2: *"Good" writing is not universal; writing is interrelated with identity, culture, and power.* In shifting the focus from the quality of Mateo's writing to interpreting what Mateo knows about writing, our self-study team could see aspects of students' learning and literacy that a traditional assessment approach would have obscured.

## From Product to Process: What We Learned about What Writers Do

Student reflections offered a window into students' writing behaviors and practices, focusing our attention on their struggles with the writing process rather than on the supposed gaps in their skills or deficits in their writing. In their reflections, students wrote about the "how of writing," noting difficulties with getting started and coming up with ideas. They wrote about their hesitations and false starts as they struggled with what to write and especially with how to revise their ideas once they had a draft. Audrey's reflection is typical:

> I personally had a lot of issues because whenever I would have a paper due, I would always skip doing outlines or brain storms for papers. In fact I would always treat my first draft as if it were the final draft. This would make it tough for me to know if what I wrote

is actually good enough. . . . I would take a long time to even start writing because I want to perfect my introduction and thesis. Once I actually finished my paper, I would look over what I just wrote and wonder what to change. I guess the problem there for me is that, normally for most people a lot of change happens between the first draft and final draft, but with my way of writing, I would get stuck on if there is anything I want to change. Cause I put so much effort into it to begin with, I wouldn't know if it is good enough to earn a good grade.

Reflections like Audrey's prompted discussions among the self-study team to contemplate strategies to improve how we teach the writing process. Scholars (Duff, 2010; Emig, 1971; Gallagher, 2016) have long understood that students' literacy performances are rooted in the writing process and behaviors as much as they are an artifact of their literacy "skills." As we are learning in our self-study, attention to students' practices reveals students' assumptions and struggles and helps us correct blind spots in our teaching. Students' struggles with the writing process would not have been visible using traditional assessment methods.

## From Product to Knowledge: What We Learned about What Writers Know

The reflections we collected focused heavily on what students know about writing. Our reflection assignment asked them to tell us about their understanding of five key aspects of writing. This allowed our self-study team of teachers to see the developmental journey many of our students complete in our courses. Focusing on students' development, in turn, has allowed us to design more effective scaffolding, assignments, and lessons, moving students more intentionally toward the Threshold Concepts and our larger learning goals.

We have also been able to identify areas where students struggle. For example, as we discussed students' reflections, we saw that many students seemed to reject or ignore our pedagogical emphasis on the complexities of literacy practice. Many students preferred the stability of a more straightforward concept or precept about writing. Here is a typical example: "[I learned] to make sure APA citations were clear and correct. This learning outcome will now help me in the future of the rest of my classes because I now feel more confident when it comes to writing and to cite sources." Teachers in our program view citation broadly, as a rhetorical tool that writers use to participate ethically in the conversation or to credit authors who expanded and deepened one's thinking. But for this student, "correct" citation became a central learning outcome, a way, perhaps, to reduce complexity into more familiar or manageable terms.

Another student, Ziai, wrote:

> When I use the quote from others' essays, it also pushes me to learn how paraphrasing author ideas, paraphrase is very important to us when we're writing an academic essay. Paraphrasing is a good way to learning English, because we need to learn some new words instead of the author's words, and learn how to make a new structure of the sentence, which is part of grammar. On the other hand, put the quote in the right place is very important when we need to citation.

Students focus on technical skills (introducing quotes, citing sources), perhaps because those lessons are easy to grasp and remember. However, our self-study team also saw reflections like these as an indication that the students struggled to understand academic literacy practices in the complex ways we aim for in our classes. This revelation prompted discussion among teachers about how we can improve. How do we teach source citation, for example, to promote not just technical skills but also a more complex understanding of citations as a way to participate in intellectual conversations? How do we scaffold students from relying on simple understandings of writing learned in high school to embracing the rhetorical complexities that academic writing entails? Discussing such questions has helped us change our classroom practices, in some cases slowing down to allow time for students to grapple with complexity.

## From Product to Reflection: What We Learned about Writing and Reflection

One of the themes that emerged from our self-study was that "good writing" equates with self-awareness, not skill. Teachers in our program value metacognition and reflection as pedagogical goals, and they celebrate meta-awareness and reflection as signs of successful student learning and growth. However, we also wrestled with complexities in defining and assessing reflection. Teachers wondered, for example, whether students might be more adept at reflecting on writing practices than they are at implementing these practices, good at "naming what they know" but unable to put that knowledge into practice in their writing. As one teacher in our self-study team put it: Many of my students can tell me what makes a good summary (i.e., important bibliographic information, the author's purpose, the main ideas, language for acknowledging the source, paraphrases, objectivity), but most of those students would probably not be able to write a summary of an article. Likewise, most of my students have heard about finding a focus (or deciding on a thesis) and including relevant details, but this does not mean that they are able to generate well-developed paragraphs.

Similarly, teachers worried that they were failing to prepare students for the challenges ahead by focusing on reflection and knowledge about writing. For example, one teacher, echoing what Horner (2015) calls the "discourse of need"—discourses that justify a skills-based approach to writing instruction—commented:

> In many ways, I still feel pressured to prepare students for gatekeeping beyond our classes. As a writing instructor, it's my responsibility to prepare my students for the academic writing they'll be expected to do in their other classes and graduate studies (if they should choose to pursue graduate work). Students are assigned to write lab reports, summaries, critical analyses, research papers, lit reviews, and annotated bibliographies. Good writing in these assignments requires students to have an understanding of the forms and the conventions of academic writing. . . . For these reasons, I feel a sense of responsibility to teach these conventions and assess students on how well they can apply them in their writing.

We note here the double vulnerability we face in our writing program: We serve students who are perched precariously on the margins of the university, and as lecturer faculty, most of whom are part-time, commuting as adjuncts around the Bay Area, we are often powerless to resist the pressure to align our teaching with more traditional understandings of literacy learning. As we noted in our introduction, our self-study was an act of resistance aimed in part at this vulnerability—an attempt to make visible and justify our values and to celebrate literacy learning that is invisible in more traditional assessments.

In analyzing reflection, we attempted to circumnavigate what Oleksiak (2020) calls "the improvement imperative." He writes, "Improvement is what writing teachers hope to find in student writing or thinking and, like all classroom practices, is shaped by an instructor's values regarding what counts as good writing" (Oleksiak, 2020, p. 308). An alternative conception of good writing, in Oleksiak's view, is that good writing is "messy, complicated, embodied, intimate, and aware of the matrices of oppression that complicate privilege and marginalization" (p. 307). To escape the improvement imperative, Oleksiak encourages us to see writing as a "worldmaking" activity, to go beyond the "legitimized and routinized" moves that teachers make and then to start to discover how students think about their own writing (p. 307). These became the steps we took to see how students started to see themselves as writers rather than producers of academic texts. Following Oleksiak, we encouraged teachers on our assessment team to embrace "slow reading" of students' reflections in order to see the worlds students create and inhabit. Letting go of the improvement imperative, embracing slow reading, and listening to students opened up vistas on teaching and learning that would not have been visible using traditional assessment practices.

## Changes in Judgment: Beyond "Good" Writing

What did we gain by jettisoning "good writing" in favor of analyzing what student writers do, what they know, and how they reflect? Our self-study uncovered areas for curricular improvement that would not have been visible via traditional assessment. It generated rich discussions of teaching and learning among the faculty who participated in the assessment and paved the way for new ways of understanding students' writing. Finally, this organic assessment allowed us to capture aspects of students' learning and literacy that are important but that do not always manifest in writing performances.

In the end, the most critical gains from altering how we define and assess "good writing" were the corresponding shifts in pedagogy, curricula, and feedback practices that participation in our self-study evoked. For example, here is one of the teachers in our self-study:

> The opportunity to . . . look closely at student experiences and thinking helped me renew my love of the craft of teaching. . . . If we want the classroom to be a site of authentic learning, there has to be a release from a conventional sense of small judgment—and a recognition and elevation of the thinking we see if we look for it. I take this lens more often to my student's essays and now essay

> grading is less odious and more enjoyable as I seek to celebrate accomplishments of shifts in thinking rather than get too bogged down in technical challenges.

Another teacher similarly commented:

> For me, the most meaningful takeaway from this semester has been the opportunity to see student work through the eyes of my colleagues and to grow my own thinking about what our students' writing might mean (both for us and for them). . . .

Redefining assessment to focus on writers rather than "good writing" helped us resist the discourse of need and the deficit models it sustains when reading students' work. Our program has always been oriented toward social justice; our teachers trained for many years in student-centered pedagogy; our program learning outcomes have a first-year experience overlay that privileges voice, belonging, and self-efficacy. Nevertheless, even in this context, teachers in our self-study labored initially to read student work through the broader lens we adopted. This challenge suggests that the discourse of need—that pressure teachers feel to arm students with skills and to clean up their prose—remains powerful.

Over time, we have strengthened our resistance to this discourse. Our self-study team analyzed Maya, Ziai, Aliza, Mateo, Minh, and Nathan as success stories in that they developed agency, adopted new literate practices, and began to form a more complex writer's identity. In capturing this growth, our program assessment shifted the emphasis from definitions of "good writing" toward understanding "good writers"—their practices, knowledge, development, struggles, and self-understanding.

## References

Adler-Kassner, L. (2017). 2017 CCCC Chair's Address. *College Composition and Communication, 69*(2), 317–340.

Broad, B. (2003). *What we really value: Beyond rubrics in teaching and assessing writing.* University Press of Colorado.

Broad, B., Adler-Kassner, L., Alford, B., & Detweiler, J. (2009). *Organic writing assessment: Dynamic criteria mapping in action.* University Press of Colorado.

Canagarajah, A. S. (2006). Negotiating the local in English as a lingua franca. *Annual Review of Applied Linguistics, 26,* 197–218.

Casanave, C. P. (2005). Uses of narrative in L2 writing research. In P. K. Matsuda & T. Silva (Eds.), *Second language writing research: Perspectives on the process of knowledge construction* (pp. 17–32). Lawrence Erlbaum.

Crusan, D., Plakans, L., & Gebril, A. (2016). Writing assessment literacy: Surveying second language teachers' knowledge, beliefs, and practices. *Assessing Writing, 28*, 43–56. https://doi/10.1016/j.asw.2016.03.001

Duff, P. (2010). Language socialization into academic discourses. *Annual Review of Applied Linguistics, 30*, 169–183.

Emig, J. (1971). *The composing processes of twelfth graders.* National Council of Teachers of English.

Gallagher, C. W. (2016). What writers do: Behaviors, behaviorism, and writing studies. *College Composition and Communication, 68*(2), 238–265.

Haswell, R. H. (Ed.). (2001). *Beyond outcomes: Assessment and instruction within a university writing program* (Vol. 5). Greenwood Publishing Group.

Horner, B. (2015). Rewriting composition: Moving beyond a discourse of need. *College English, 77*(5), 450–479. https://www.jstor.org/stable/44075076

Inoue, A. B. (2015). *Antiracist writing assessment ecologies: Teaching and assessing writing for a socially just future.* Parlor Press LLC. https://wac.colostate.edu/books/inoue/

Inoue, A. B. (2019). *Labor-based grading contracts: Building equity and inclusion in the compassionate writing classroom.* University Press of Colorado. https://doi.org/10.37514/PER-B.2019.0216.0

Lee, I. (2016). Putting students at the centre of classroom L2 writing assessment. *Canadian Modern Language Review, 72*(2), 258–280.

Matsuda, P. K. (2001). Voice in Japanese written discourse: Implications for second language writing. *Journal of Second Language Writing, 10*, 35–53. https://doi.org/10.1016/S1060-3743(00)00036-9

Matsuda, P. K. (2006). The myth of linguistic homogeneity in U.S. college composition. *College English, 68*(6), 637–651. https://doi/10.2307/25472180

Matsuda, P. K. (2012). Let's face it: Language issues and the writing program administrator. *Writing Program Administration, 36*(1), 141–164.

Matsuda, P. K. (2015). Identity in written discourse. *Annual Review of Applied Linguistics, 35*, 140–159. https://doi.org/10.1017/S0267190514000178

Oleksiak, T. (2020). A queer praxis for peer review. *College Composition and Communication, 72*(2), 306–332.

# Part II

# Mentoring, Supervising, and Publishing

Chapter 7

# Imagining Emotions, Relationships, and the Good Academic Writer

*Gary Barkhuizen*

## Introduction

I approach writing this chapter as someone who has much experience as an academic writer. I completed my doctoral dissertation many years ago and have been writing and publishing ever since. When I look back at my dissertation now, I'm somewhat surprised at the good quality of my writing. I produced coherent arguments and, what appears to me even now, highly acceptable "academic" written text well beyond what I should have been capable of at that early stage of my career. This is not to say that I'm a good writer. I'm often told by reviewers and other readers that my writing is "accessible." I'm never quite sure how to take this—how it makes me feel. Is it a compliment? I'm not aware of trying to be "accessible." What I always do, and perhaps this is what makes my writing accessible, is to imagine myself as one of my readers. How would they understand what I have just written? Would it make sense to them? Would it get across the meaning I am trying to convey? Satisfactory answers to these questions probably mean that I am on the right track.

Although I keep the responses of my potential readers in mind, I tend to pay far less attention to how my writing makes them *feel*, in other words to what their emotional responses are to what they read. For example, I can think of some possibilities based on my own emotional responses to reading other academic writers' work:

*Frustrated*: because I do not understand the writer's ideas and concepts.

*Vulnerable*: because I have had my lack of knowledge exposed in an area I am working in.

*Anxious*: because those gaps mean more reading and more work and not making progress.

*Fearful*: because grasping the content, the further reading, and application to my work might be too much for me to achieve.

*Confident*: because I've understood all the writer's ideas and can see how they can be used in my own work.

*Inspired*: because I have been energized with new focus and hope.

*Happy*: because I feel I have read something I understand and that is useful.

*Relieved*: because I can confirm that my own research is supported by the literature and so will likely make a contribution.

These examples signal a clear emotional connection between what is written and what is read, a connection between what a writer has written and a reader's emotional response to it (Benesch, 2020; Han & Hyland, 2019)—in other words, an emotional connection between the *writer* and the *reader* through the text. It is this type of connection I wish to explore in this chapter. But I want to take it back a few steps in the writing process, to the drafting stage—specifically, to the emotional *relationship* between the writer and the reviewer of drafts. Academic texts typically go through multiple drafts, with readers in the form of reviewers, editors, and graduate student supervisors, for example, providing feedback along the way. In this chapter, I focus on the graduate student as writer and (what I will call) a supervisor, typically a university academic, as reader and responder to the written drafts.

Han and Hyland (2019) remind us that "academic writing is an emotionally laden process" (p. 1), and this includes feelings associated with a reader's feedback. As Benesch (2020) cautions, the entire process of responding to student writing has the potential to be "emotionally charged" (p. 54) for both writer and reader. When they respond to students' writing, a common concern of teachers and supervisors is the "negative emotional consequences for students" (Han & Hyland, p. 1). Cameron, Nairn, and Higgins (2009), as research student supervisors, comment on the emotional effect their feedback might have on the quality of their relationships with their students and consequently on their writing:

> As supervisors who see the writing struggle of so many of our graduate students we are particularly interested in how the supervisor and graduate student relationship can impact on student writing. What do we say to graduate students about writing (and their writing in particular)? What do we not say? How do we say things about writing? (p. 274)

As a way to explore the connections between feedback provided to graduate research students about their writing and their emotional responses to that feedback, I examine how I imagine what they feel about their writing when they submit their drafts to me and how they will feel about their writing and the feedback (and me) when they receive my feedback. I pay attention not only to these specific "objects" that they focus their emotions on (Pekrun & Linnenbrink-Garcia, 2012) but also on how I imagine their emotional responses will affect both our student-supervisor relationship and their future academic writing, including its development. To do this, I have generated four composite research students with varying writing identities, and for each of these I have created a hypothetical scenario in which I discuss how I imagine the composite student will respond emotionally to a range of academic writing "objects" of focus. In the concluding section of the chapter, I examine a number of themes arising from the scenarios in relation to emotions, relationships, and the good academic writer.

## Emotions, Activity, and Learning

Before getting into the scenarios, I briefly provide some theoretical context that will help to explain the interconnections I make in the scenarios among writing, the emotional responses to feedback on that writing, the relationship between the writer and the reader, and the activity of further post-feedback writing. I draw on aspects of sociocultural theory. Long ago, Vygotsky (1986), commenting on the relationship between emotions and learning, said that the separation of intellect and affect "makes the thought processes appear as an autonomous flow of 'thoughts thinking themselves,' segregated from the fullness of life, from the personal needs and interests, the inclinations and impulses, of the thinker" (p. 10), and added that this position had been a major weakness of traditional psychology. More recently it is accepted that "emotions are integral to what people do and know. . . . What we do, how we do it, and how much we want to do it, are all part of how well we perform the tasks that we face" (Roth, 2007, p. 41). Roth goes on to say that emotions relate to practical actions in two ways. First, emotions shape both the way we think and our practical activity (e.g., academic writing), and second, our practical activity is directed toward the generation of positive emotions: "we act so that we are better off in the long run, even if it means we have to incur costs in the form of emotional hardship in the short term" (p. 44).

In terms of academic writing, this means that emotions are associated with what writers think about their writing—for example, what they think about the process of writing and the product—and also with how they act on their thoughts. The emotions may sometimes be hard to endure (such as when a student receives negative feedback from a supervisor on a draft of a chapter) and the activity resulting from those emotions may be challenging (having to revise the draft, possibly multiple times). But eventually the outcome of the revisions will be (1) a product that is acceptable to both writer and supervisor, and (2) associated positive emotions, such as relief and a sense of achievement. Yang (2019), also from a sociocultural theory perspective, explains this relationship between emotions and activity by pointing out that emotions have an *appraisal function*, reflecting the relationship between the motives or needs of a person and the outcomes of their actions. For example, a student writer may become angry after realizing that their first draft of a dissertation chapter is not up to standard. The anger may prompt the student to evaluate their needs or the writing outcomes more closely. Yang notes that emotions also have an *action-regulating function*, whereby a person changes their action-readiness, or what they do in response to the emotions. The student writer, for example, may decide to work hard on the revisions or to improve their academic writing by seeking support from a writing tutor.

In sum, Han and Hyland (2019) state that emotions elicited by feedback are important, as "they interact with cognitive and behavioral dimensions of engagement" (p. 3); that is, the feedback means the writer will think about their writing and will act on those thoughts, usually with the goal of improving their writing.

## The Object Focus of Academic Emotions

Academic emotions are emotions that are linked to learning, instruction, students' engagement with learning and achievement (Pekrun & Linnenbrink-Garcia, 2012). These are emotions relevant to academic settings and activities and would thus include emotions associated with academic writing. In other words, we have emotions about something—the *object focus* of our emotions. In academic writing, this could be the act of writing (writer's emotions), responding to the writing in order to provide feedback (reader's emotions), responding to the feedback (the writer again), and making revisions to the writing (the writer) for the reader to reassess (the reader). Emotions are associated with all these stages and to the relationship between writer and reader, all of which are potentially fraught with emotions. Pekrun and Linnenbrink-Garcia (2012) describe a number of object foci of academic emotions (what the emotions are focused on; what people react to), and I have adapted these for situations of students responding to feedback on their academic writing, particularly the four scenarios presented in the next section (see Table 1).

## Imagining Emotions: Four Composite Students and Four Scenarios

In what follows I describe four composite students. These do not represent any specific student—and certainly not any research student that I know or have worked with. Instead, each composite student represents a type of student writer, generated from the many students I have supervised over many years—from final-year undergraduate students to master's students to doctoral students. And by student I mean research students who are writing reports based on research projects they have carried out (I will call the writing "dissertations"). I am not talking about students of writing (L2 writing), and I do not identify the language background of the composite students.

Next, for each composite student I present a scenario that describes my imagined interaction with the student's writing. My role is that of supervisor, someone who provides guidance and support to the research student writer. In some contexts this role has other names, such as advisor

Table 1  Object focus of emotions in students responding to feedback on academic writing

| Object focus | Definition |
| --- | --- |
| *Prospective achievement emotions* | Emotions pertaining to the expected outcomes of the academic writing before receiving feedback from the supervisor as well as its accuracy and appropriate style, genre, and content. Emotions may include hope, anxiety, confidence, and hopelessness. |
| *Retrospective achievement emotions* | Emotions pertaining to the extant outcomes of the academic writing (the submitted draft) after receiving feedback from the supervisor. Emotions may include joy, contentment, shame, and sadness. New *prospective* achievement emotions will be evoked by the revised draft before it is submitted to the supervisor for further feedback. |
| *Cognitive emotions* | Emotions involved in cognitively processing the supervisor's feedback on the academic writing. Emotions may include curiosity, surprise, and self-doubt. |
| *Social emotions* | Emotions pertaining to the supervisor (as a person) who read the draft writing and provided feedback. Emotions may include contempt, admiration, gratitude, and fear. |
| *Topic emotions* | Emotions induced by the topic and content of the academic writing. Emotions may include boredom, excitement, indifference, and loyalty. |

or mentor. Again, these scenarios are hypothetical and thus are not based on any actual events. Each scenario addresses one or two of the object foci of emotions related to responding to student academic writing described above in Table 1. The scenarios also describe how I imagine the student will respond emotionally to my feedback.

I must also acknowledge here that the descriptions of the composite students and the scenarios have the potential to generate stereotypes related to, for example, gender, ethnicity, and even nationality. The descriptions and scenarios aim, instead, to be as specific as possible, even at the risk of being provocative, so that emotions and the quality of writing can be more precisely analyzed.

# Composite Student #1: The Struggling All-Rounder

## The Student

This student really struggles with writing. Their usage (grammar, vocabulary) is poor, and their academic writing style is underdeveloped. Their ideas lack coherence, and they find it hard to visualise what a completed dissertation section or chapter should conventionally look like. But they struggle with much else as well. They have limited research knowledge and skills, and they find it hard to nail down and stick to a topic and its accompanying research questions.

## The Scenario

Student #1 is working on his doctoral research proposal, a 20,000-word document that needs to be completed during his first year of doctoral study. This student has struggled to decide on a topic that is both interesting to him and feasible to research, which means that whatever he writes is tentative and "in note form." He has still not formulated satisfactory research questions and is nowhere near completing his proposal even though he is nearing the end of his first year of study. Student #1 has shown me bits and pieces of his writing over the year as well as a first draft of the proposal's introduction and literature review. From what I have seen so far, I have grave concerns about his progress as a writer and his future in the doctoral program.

Student #1 has submitted to me the second draft of his proposal's introduction and literature review—about 8,000 words. It is very difficult to read. Almost every sentence has usage problems such as a grammatical error, inappropriate academic vocabulary, and strings of words that simply do not make sense. It is extremely hard to find the ideas in much of the writing. As I read the draft, I feel very worried for the student. As an international student, the consequences of his not making it through the first year—and thus having to discontinue doctoral studies—are devastating. It is hard to decide what to focus on in my feedback, and the option of sending the student to the Writing Center crosses my mind.

In terms of Student #1's *prospective achievement emotions* (emotions pertaining to his written second draft before submitting it for my feedback), I imagine he would feel extremely anxious. Many of our consultations during the year were about his writing, and here he has again presented a substantial piece of writing for scrutiny. There was also the added stress of struggling to pin down a research topic; no research questions were included in draft two. I imagine *topic emotions* (academic emotions relating to the topic of the writing), therefore, are verging on hopelessness, desperation, and, more harmfully, disassociation for Student #1. I am also concerned about what my feedback will do to our developing relationship. In terms of *social emotions* (those pertaining to me as reader who provides feedback on his writing), I imagine he will continue to show me respect, but I also imagine he may be losing some patience with my constant criticism. I try to take into account his developing feelings of frustration as I write my notes on his second draft. I want Student #1 to learn from my feedback, I want him to take his writing seriously and to improve, and I also want our relationship to be good.

## Composite Student #2: The Struggling Writer

### The Student

This is a bright student, with good research ideas and skills. The student is well-read and knows relevant theory and how to apply it in their studies. They know how to structure a thesis or dissertation and can visualise the finished product, and within specific chapters and sections their organization of content is good. But their surface-level usage (grammar, vocabulary) and academic writing style are not good at all, and they know it.

### The Scenario

I have now received what appears to be the fourth draft of the first findings chapter of Student #2's doctoral dissertation—at least that is what the filename says. It is the second time I have seen this 10,000-word chapter, in fact. The first time I had a chance to read it, I did so quickly to get an overview of the chapter and to assess its organization. All was very good indeed. This student has designed an excellent study, collected and analyzed all the data, and has decided to write up the thesis starting with the findings (results) chapters. She knows what a thesis should look like—she is not having any problems with the content of the thesis or its organization. But Student #2 fears writing. She has told me many times that she is a poor writer and feels embarrassed giving me her writing to read. She once tried to employ a proofreader for a section of her proposal, but that process messed with her concepts and ideas in the writing, and she decided not to try it again.

I know as I begin reading this second-draft chapter that it is going to be hard work for me. I know that the ideas will be there, but how easily will I be able to access them in the student's written text? For this piece of writing I decide to focus primarily on her usage. I will read each sentence carefully and make corrections and revisions as best I can. This will be enormously time-consuming. I will become irritated and lose patience. But I believe that Student #2 will appreciate the feedback. In terms of the object focus of her emotions, I imagine her *retrospective achievement emotions* (the emotions pertaining to the writing after having received feedback on it) will include a level of embarrassment (matching her *prospective achievement emotions*) and annoyance at the number of errors, particularly those she recognizes and should have gotten right in the first place, and also feelings of hope, because Student #2 always aims to learn from these errors. I imagine that she will show determination in her future writing activity to keep improving. Since we have already worked together for three years, I doubt this particular piece of writing will affect her *social emotions* toward me as her reader and supervisor. We get along well together, and I don't see that changing.

## Composite Student #3: The Good Writer

### The Student

This student writes very well indeed. Their work is easy to read—in fact, it's a pleasure to read. It contains very few surface-level usage errors, and the academic style is mostly appropriate. But in contrast to Student #2, they are weak on the theoretical aspects, and they lack clear ideas about research design and methodology. Typically they have limited background in the relevant discipline. Their weakness is thus a matter of theoretical and methodological substance. Sometimes their good writing can even conceal this weakness.

## The Scenario

As part of the doctoral application process, applicants submit what is called a statement of research intent—a short research proposal of about three pages. When I first read Student #3's statement, I was most impressed. The writing was fluent, the ideas were coherently expressed, and it was error-free. I thought that some of the ideas for the study needed developing, and it was theoretically thin, but I believed there was plenty of time for development in these areas once the student started the doctoral program.

He was accepted and began his studies. I like to get my students writing as soon as possible—notes, memos, ideas, syntheses of readings, for example—and to let me read these prior to meetings as a stimulus for our discussions. Student #3 has submitted a 10-page overview of the proposed study with a statement of its aims, the description of the geopolitical context of the study, a summary of a few key studies, and a list of provisional research questions. I read it without stopping—there are no distractions such as grammatical or annoying spelling errors, and the ideas are very easy to follow. However, what is immediately apparent is that the writing lacks the appropriate academic discourse for the discipline. It is almost as if Student #3 has no background in applied linguistics or TESOL at all. I feel that someone from a completely different discipline has come up with a good idea for a research topic in language learning and teaching and has decided to do a study on it. Concepts in applied linguistics are virtually absent, and when Student #3 attempts to use them, they are vague or inaccurately used. Further, it greatly resembles non-academic writing; it is informal and literary in style.

My own emotions while reading the text include feelings of pleasure at being able to sail through the document with such ease. However, I also feel some unease, since the student is now enrolled in a high-level research degree program, and it is now evident that he lacks substantial background knowledge in the field. What feedback am I going to give him when we meet to talk about his 10-page overview? In terms of his *cognitive emotions* (emotions related to his cognitively processing my feedback on his writing) I imagine he will initially be surprised about my perceptions of his lack of academic and disciplinary discourse, but in the short time I have known Student #3 I also imagine that he will be intrigued to find out exactly what I mean. He will spend time with his writing, reviewing it closely. He will enthusiastically take up my advice to read more widely (I will suggest relevant, topic-related readings). I imagine he will be motivated to take up the reading challenge, feeling confident that his good writing will always be there to support him. He is excited about the topic of his study, and so I imagine his *topic emotions* (emotions induced by the content of what he writes about) are unlikely to change at such an early stage of his research journey, no matter what I say about his academic writing.

# Composite Student #4: The Strong All-Rounder

## The Student

This is a student who writes very well, has a strong theoretical background, and has clear ideas about their research project. They probably have experience in a related academic field and have some academic writing experience. They are aware of dissertation writing conventions or can easily and independently find out what they are. Their writing is readable and engaging.

## The Scenario

Student #4 is more than halfway through writing her dissertation. She started at the beginning, with the introduction chapter, and has just submitted to me her discussion, a chapter that follows a series of findings chapters. Writing the discussion is the first time in the entire dissertation writing process that she feels like she has stumbled. The student is an experienced English language teacher and teacher-educator and is completing her doctorate part-time while continuing to work at the same university where I work, with a slightly reduced workload. She teaches classes to pre-service teachers and also mentors their action research projects. She has been a confident doctoral student right from the start, having read widely, with a sound knowledge of the field and plenty of experience writing academic reports.

She really is a good academic writer. My feedback on her writing has almost always been exclusively about content—about her research ideas and related theory—which means that our conversations have been engaging and productive for both of us. I learn a lot from her. Along with the discussion chapter, she has sent me an accompanying note saying she didn't quite know how to organize it and how to integrate the theoretical concepts she wrote about long ago in the literature review chapter. She knows what she is supposed to do, but she can't seem to actually do it.

I imagine when she wrote the note and contemplated her finished draft chapter, she was feeling somewhat confused and, for the first time, probably a little anxious (these being *prospective achievement emotions* pertaining to her writing in the draft chapter she submitted to me). When I anticipate my feedback I know it will not be about the quality of the writing—the usage—or about the ideas themselves, since I am confident that Student #4 has these under control. Her note has warned me it would be about the organization of the ideas and their relation to theory; my feedback is going to be specifically about this. Imagining her emotional response to this feedback (her *retrospective achievement emotions* relating to her draft chapter) I expect she will be appreciative and will be motivated, enthusiastic even, to immediately begin doing the revisions. Cognitively (*cognitive emotions*), she is aware that revising is a typical activity in the process of academic writing, and she is expecting to do so after my feedback. She may feel some self-doubt about getting it right, but in the past, such doubts in her writing have been resolved with further revision and further conversations with me.

## Good Writing as Good Relationships

Cameron, Nairn, and Higgins (2009) state that emotions are both individual and relational. They refer to the "betweenness of writing relationships" (p. 274), such as those between graduate students and their dissertation supervisors. Individual writers experience emotions associated with their writing, and their readers experience emotions when they read and respond to the writing. And when readers provide feedback to the writer, further emotions are evoked. This all has an effect on the relationship between the writer and the reader. Sometimes these relationships are fairly distant and relatively unimportant, such as that between the writer of a journal article and the reviewer of that article. But for graduate research students and their supervisors, the relationship is vitally important. They work together for a number of years and work through multiple drafts of multiple chapters. A lot of writing and reading goes on, and a lot of conversations take place. There is also over time a variety of emotions focused on the various "objects" of the entire academic writing situation.

In this chapter, I presented four hypothetical scenarios that revealed how research students with different writing identities (the four composite students) responded emotionally to a number of object foci associated with their writing, including me as their supervisor (*social emotions*). In the scenarios, I described how I imagined the students would respond emotionally to my feedback. I was able to do this because of my knowledge of who the students were—what kinds of writers they were, what kinds of graduate students, what kinds of people. I believe that knowing who one's students are (particularly their writer identity) enables supervisors to more accurately anticipate how they will respond to their feedback, and how their mindsets (Powell & Driscoll, 2020) will impact their ability to act in the future, as they process the feedback and their emotions and revise accordingly. I would therefore suggest that supervisors strive to develop a close, productive "writing relationship" with their students early on in the research and dissertation writing process. Benesch (2020) cites Brannon and Knoblauch (2006), who suggest that rather than agonizing over which types of feedback are most effective for producing better writing, the concern should be with "the impact of commentary on the quality of the relationship between teacher and student" (p. 12).

When a good relationship is in place, it is far easier to have conversations about emotions—to address the emotions (whatever their valence) rather than dismissing or ignoring them. Saying "don't worry" or "don't be anxious" is not helpful. Instead, it makes sense to examine the emotions—where they come from, what they mean, and what can be done about them. As Cameron, Nairn, and Higgins (2009) say, "the point is not to erase difficult emotions from writing but to find in them their productive potential rather than paralysis." If having good relationships means having good conversations about emotions, then I would argue that open and honest conversations about emotions makes it possible to have good conversations about writing. These conversations between a student and a supervisor can focus on, for example, what bad writing is (perhaps based on the student's actual writing), what good writing is (what the student is not yet producing), and the student's writing dilemmas (the choices that need to be made to improve their writing in the future). A student and their supervisor can decide together what good writing is *for that student*—at the stage they are at in their development as a writer, how they perceive their identity as an academic writer, where they are in the production of their dissertation, what they desire to produce, and how they envisage their future writing selves. Good writing, then, is relational. However, within changing and emotional relationships it is also important to take into consideration the preferences of the students, who may not be too concerned about their relationship with their supervisor and instead just want to get the writing right and finish their dissertation!

## References


Benesch, S. (2020). Theorising emotions from a critical perspective: English language teachers' emotion labour when responding to student writing. In C. Gkonou, J.-M. Dewaele, & J. King (Eds.), *The emotional rollercoaster of language teaching* (pp. 53–69). Multilingual Matters.

Brannon, L. & Knoblauch, C. (2006). Introduction: The emperor still has no clothes: Revisiting the myth of improvement. In R. Straub (Ed.), *Keywords on teacher response: An anthology* (pp. 1–15). Boynton/Cook.

Cameron, J., Nairn, K., & Higgins, J. (2009). Demystifying academic writing: Reflections on emotions, know-how and academic identity. *Journal of Geography in Higher Education, 33*(2), 269–284.

Han, Y., & Hyland, F. (2019). Academic emotions in written corrective feedback situations. *Journal of English for Academic Purposes, 38*, 1–13.

Pekrun, R., & Linnenbrink-Garcia, L. (2012). Academic emotions and student engagement. In S. L. Christenson, A. L. Reschly, & C. Wylie (Eds.), *The handbook of research on student engagement* (pp. 259–282). Springer.

Powell, R. L., & Driscoll, D. L. (2020). How mindsets shape response and learning transfer: A case of two graduate writers. *Journal of Response to Writing, 6*(2), 42–68.

Roth, W.-M. (2007). Emotion at work: A contribution to third-generation cultural-historical activity theory. *Mind, Culture, and Activity, 14*(1–2), 40–63.

Vygotsky, L. S. (1986). *Thought and language* (E. Hanfmann and G. Vakar, Trans.). MIT Press.

Yang, H. (2019). The nexus between pre-service teachers' emotional experience and cognition during professional experience. *The Australian Educational Researcher, 46*, 799–825.

# Chapter 8

# What Is "Good Writing"? Pre-service Teachers Prepare for the College Writing Classroom

*Robert Kohls, Katelyn Endow, Kimani Lincoln, Mona Shaath, Rachael Tupper-Eoff, and Monique Ubungen*

"What do you believe about how we learn how to write?" I ask a room full of pre-service writing teachers. "And what are those beliefs based on?" I scan the gallery of faces on my Zoom screen, our virtual classroom during Spring 2021. "Feel free to unmute yourselves or write in the chat," I add with anticipation. This is the first day of a graduate seminar I am teaching on the sociolinguistics of academic literacy. It's a class I have been eager to teach for a long time, and I waste no time getting the students to talk about their own experiences with writing. I notice a few nervous smiles and one or two puzzled looks from this class of preservice writing teachers. After a few moments, hands slowly rise, students unmute themselves, and answers pop up in the chat. Comments, reactions, and interactions soon volley from student to student as we share our beliefs, hash out our ideas, and challenge one another's assumptions about what we know about writers, writing, and the writing process. Amidst muting and unmuting our microphones, navigating our awkward interruptions and overlaps, and reacting with emojis of raised hands, thumbs up, and grinning faces, I smile and think to myself, *This is going to be an amazing class.*

Ontological and epistemological questions about the nature of writing push us to consider how our own beliefs about writing have been shaped by social, cultural, and institutional expectations passed down from one generation to the next, delivered through literature, style guides, and curricula and conveyed most notably through our teachers' comments on our essays. As the instructor, I hoped that after taking this course the students would be able to read sociolinguistic scholarship with an eye to challenging their own assumptions about writing, the writing process, and their own classroom pedagogy. I believe that before students set foot as new teachers in a first-year writing course, assign their first essay, or give feedback on a piece of writing, they need to examine their own assumptions about writing and have some idea of what writing and language mean to them and the role it plays in their lives and in the lives of their own students. These two fundamental questions about our own ideas about writing structured our coursework together, helped us to read the scholarship more critically, and allowed us to write this chapter with a clear purpose.

Except for a few, most students in this seminar were fairly new to teaching. At the outset of the course, I introduced the "Good Writing Project" and invited the students to collaborate with me voluntarily on writing this chapter. "The course readings, discussion, and assignments will serve as preparation," I said. Smiles popped up on my Zoom screen. I stressed the importance of sharing their ideas, experiences, and struggles with a wider audience of graduate students, teachers, and scholars beyond our seminar. Over the course of the semester, we investigated language, ideology, and power in educational settings in the United States and around the world. We examined mono- and multilingual written communication including differences between oral and written speech, global attitudes toward language standardization and codification, cross-cultural views on academic writing and rhetoric, and perspectives on authorial voice, stance, and identity around domestic, immigrant, and resident writers. Theresa Lillis's (2013) book, *The Sociolinguistics of Writing*, served as our core text. We built upon her discussions of rhetoric, literacy, and writing as everyday practice with scholarship by Samy Alim, Deborah Cameron, Hilary Janks, Shirley Brice Heath, April Baker-Bell, Paul Matsuda, Ilona Leki, Melinda Reichelt, Ryuko Kubota, and many others. The readings reflected theoretical, empirical, and ideological perspectives on academic language socialization, antiracist writing pedagogies, and critical discourse analysis. In addition to reading, responding to, and discussing the scholarship, these students also completed several projects including fieldwork involving surveying and interviewing people about their beliefs about good writing, a genre analysis project, and a reflection essay on the characteristics of good writing.

The real work on this chapter began after the course was over and once we started to meet to flesh out what we wanted to say. This was no longer a navel-gazing, intellectual classroom exercise confined to weekly conversations; we now had to flesh out those ideas and put them down on paper. Among the original nine students, five agreed to co-author this book chapter with me—Katelyn, Kimani, Mona, Rachael, and Monique. The collaborative process got underway with students first reading each other's final reflection essay on what good writing was to them and then identifying common patterns, points of disagreement, or insightful perspectives. We met every other week over the course of six months to write, read, respond, and discuss. Our chapter is by no means a mandate on what good writing is but rather serves as a class record of our conversations, thoughts, and reactions to this complex question. In the next three sections, I step back and let the students take over and share what they learned about good writing from the course, what they learned from each other about good writing, and what they want to teach their future students about good writing. In the final remarks, I return to summarize our reflections and together we offer suggestions for preparing pre-service writing teachers.

## What We Learned about Good Writing from Our Course

So then, what is good writing? As writing teacher candidates, we wrestled with this question on a weekly basis in our readings, online posts, and in-class conversations. We felt that a logical place to start this discussion was with Leki's (1995) well-known study "Good Writing: I Know It When I See It." She taught us that coming to any consensus about what constitutes good writing among students, writing teachers, and content area faculty is messy. ESL students reported that good writing was interesting, relatable, detailed, and showed some rhetorical skill. We agreed. However, based on the feedback that students in Leki's study received from their teachers, they gleaned that good writing depended upon whether their essays were being read by a writing teacher or a content professor. We were intrigued. Much to their frustration, students learned that good writing was not a priori good; that is, it is not universal and applicable in all contexts regardless of the teacher. They believed their content-area teachers preferred good ideas and examples, whereas they believed their writing teachers were less interested in content and more interested in organization, grammar, style, and engaging essay topics. In comparison, the writing teachers and content-area teachers Leki interviewed saw the importance of a clear introduction, organization, ideas, and overall argument, but content-area faculty often went further, commenting on the strength of the argument. We agreed with both sets of teachers that good writing teaches us and leaves us better informed about the world.

If Leki taught us that good writing is largely subjective, Nauman, Stirling, and Borthwick (2011) reminded us that as future writing teachers we need to examine how we may unwittingly pass our beliefs about good writing on to our students through our assessment practices. They reported that one-third of participants saw good writing reflecting "good thinking," awareness of the audience, and some uniqueness of voice. Another one-third saw structure and clarity as key, and the last third saw purpose, voice, and correctness as essential. Lastly, we sought to get a "cross-cultural" view of good writing. Reichelt's (2003) study of English and German teachers' views of good writing taught us that the notion of good writing also varies across cultures. This insight challenged us to reconsider the traditional American preference for academic writing to be reader-centered with a thesis statement and distinct topic sentences. We agreed with Reichelt that focusing on formal concerns can interfere with writing development and we appreciated her insight into having conversations with our students about good writing. As teachers, we realize that conversations about good writing are grounded in how we scaffold, model, and sequence writing assignments, facilitate in-class discussions, ensure that students write with a purpose, and assess their writing. Although it is impossible to distill what we learned in class into a simple soundbite, we agreed that our conversations focused broadly on the role of literacy, voice, and genre in writing.

## Literacy

We couldn't have a meaningful conversation about writing without considering the role of literacy and linguistic diversity in our students' lives both in and outside of school. We saw literacy as more than just the ability to read and write but as knowing and navigating the "dominant discourse" and coming to terms with the complex role that "academic literacy" and "Standard American English" play in maintaining power structures within society and the education system (Alim, 2010; Gee, 2005; Heath, 1982; Kucer, 2009). Rachael eloquently summed up these limited views on literacy in her response to Snow and Ucelli (2009) in our class's online forum, stating, "It seems that we as a society have collectively decided that 'academic language' somehow equates to good writing." The idea that there is such a thing as "academic language" has been the subject of some debate (see Rosa & Flores, 2017).

With the help of Alim (2010), our conversations about literacy evolved into conversations about linguistic diversity, the importance of inclusivity in the writing classroom, and critical language awareness. Alim pushed us to consider the person behind the language. In our conversations, we reflected on funds of knowledge (Moll et al., 1992) and the importance of incorporating students' lived experiences into the writing classroom. If we are not careful, warns Janks (2004), blindly teaching the dominant discourse will only continue to privilege certain forms of writing over others. Home literacies, especially those that do not align with the dominant discourse, are often invisible at school and considered a hindrance (Pahl, 2014). We gathered that the relationship between language use and student identity is an unbreakable bond and therefore must always be acknowledged and respected in academic spaces. (Unfortunately, this is an issue that is much more easily discussed than one that can be resolved!)

## Voice

It seems that no conversation about writing in a first-year writing course in the United States can exclude voice. We agreed that voice acts as a way to assist the development of producing good writers. But why? Literacy scholars have examined a writer's voice in K–12 contexts (Sperling & Appleman, 2011) and L2 writing scholars have examined different cultures and linguistic backgrounds to adapt, resist, and modify their writer's voice in English (see Atkinson, 2001; Tardy, 2012). Scholars such as April Baker-Bell (2020) remind us of the frustrations that many writers who identify as Black, Indigenous, and People of Color (BIPOC) face when attempting to adapt their voice to Standard Academic English (SAE). In the United States, a culturally and linguistically diverse country, writing instructors often promote practices that otherwise deny both mono- and multilingual students the ability to express themselves as freely as they would in their own culture or local communities. Baker-Bell's work problematized for us the potential harm of a singular voice as an academic standard among L1 writers and showed us how the promise of embracing the idea of "multiple voices" can boost the confidence of marginalized students. Among multilingual writers, Matsuda (2001) argued that constructing a voice in any discourse can be challenging. Students are deprived of the discursive options they know from their L1 but also have not yet mastered the discursive options available to construct a voice in English. Matsuda suggested that multilingual writers will therefore greatly benefit from exposure to "multiple sites of discursive practices in English" (p. 51), which will in turn facilitate their understanding of how they can diverge from normative discursive practices in ways that will be understood by their intended audience.

## Genre

Along with literacy and voice, we explored the role of genre in good writing. In examining written genres, we found that Clark (2019) echoed Matsuda's argument, noting that the challenges her doctoral students experienced when attempting to write publishable articles in English were not due to their language skills but rather their "unfamiliar[ity] with the 'genre' of scholarship in the social sciences" (p. 159). Therefore, she suggested that helping students develop genre awareness is a key element in teaching multilingual students (for similar advice, see Tardy, 2019). As Clark noted, the term *genre* in the field of writing studies is better understood in reference to the function, purpose, and action of a particular text as opposed to its form. However, she highlighted the disagreement among scholars as to whether it is possible to explicitly teach genre to students. Freedman (1995) argued for an "implicit pedagogical model" in which students acquire genre knowledge through the experience of attempting to write and read within a particular genre. Students then receive feedback that confirms or modifies their understanding of that genre. Williams and Colomb (1993) and Swales (1990) contended that student writers do benefit from explicit instruction in genre in that it allows them to understand the characteristic features of a genre and how to then use those features to guide their own writing. As a class, we believe these positions suggest that students benefit most from both direct instruction around specific genres and sustained writing practice with feedback in these genres, which would also grant them exposure to the multiple sites of discursive practices that Matsuda recommends. Genre awareness is clearly part of what both teachers and students need to think about when considering good writing.

# What We Believe about Good Writing

For our final assignment of the semester, we each reflected on our own evolving beliefs about good writing in a short essay that we posted to the course's online forum. We read our classmates' essays and identified common themes that surfaced across our essays, including the frequency of words we used to talk about writing, our use of metaphors, and the emphasis we placed on the writer's voice.

## Words We Used to Describe Writing

As our writing group began to meet to collaborate on this paper, our classmate Mona analyzed all of our good writing reflection papers and compiled a quantitative list that captured the most frequently occurring themes. Mona's findings fueled our subsequent group discussions and inspired us to investigate which individual words occurred the most frequently across our reflection papers.

We created a corpus from among our ten papers (8,726 total words) by using the software *AntConc* (Anthony, 2021). Table 1 lists the words that occurred the most frequently among all of our reflection papers.

Examining our findings, we expected words such as *writing* and *student* to be prevalent given the prompt of the assignment. What was intriguing, however, were the words that we found at the bottom of our frequency list. Table 2 documents some of the terms that were important to our class discussions about good writing but were either hardly used or completely absent in our papers.

Surprisingly, we wrote very little about thesis statements and grammar. How could we, aspiring college writing instructors, ignore these topics, which are so central to academic writing and English language

Table 1

| Token | Frequency | Percent of Papers in which Token Appears |
|---|---|---|
| writing / writer | 333 | 100% |
| student(s) | 102 | 100% |
| purpose | 31 | 70% |
| academic | 23 | 70% |
| ideas | 22 | 80% |

Table 2

| Token | Frequency | Percent of Papers in which Token Appears |
|---|---|---|
| voice | 14 | 40% |
| thesis | 5 | 40% |
| grammar | 4 | 30% |
| punctuation | 0 | 0% |
| spelling | 0 | 0% |
| errors | 0 | 0% |

learners? Grammar and language issues were definitely a substantial part of our class discussions, but the way we talked about them in our papers was dispassionate. In our papers, we believed voice to be important to good writing, yet we struggled to define it in our own reflections and thus avoided writing about it. It quickly became clear that our struggle to conceptualize "voice" paralleled the struggle that many novice writers face in finding their voice as writers. Interestingly, we found ourselves using metaphors to capture the elusive concept of voice and as a nuanced way to articulate our own complex understanding of "good writing."

## Visualizing Voice Through Metaphors

The act of characterizing "good writing" creates complications and difficulty, even for the most seasoned writers, thinkers, and teachers. Similar to finding ourselves in dinner party debates over the meaning of beauty or responding "What's so funny?" to missed punchlines, providing a complete answer to "What is good writing?" is a sticky business. If it really is true that "we know [good writing] when we see it" (Leki, 1995, p. 24), then we have to work to define what it looks like and how it is created in words, images, and actions that we use and understand in our everyday lives.

The use of metaphor grants us the ability to tease out our beliefs on good writing and make our intangible thought processes real. Lakoff and Johnson (2003) highlighted the fundamental presence of metaphors in our regular language use and how "metaphorical expressions in everyday language . . . give us insight into the metaphorical nature of the concepts that structure our everyday activities" (p. 8). Similar to the act of show and tell, these metaphors allow us to create visual elements to map out what exactly is going on in our heads. In this case, the "mind" and its ability to think, create, and dream can be seen as an ontological metaphor for a symbolic, physical space or container of knowledge, beliefs, and ideas. Metaphors are ingrained in our communication system to create a sense of realness and clarity for what only seems to exist in our heads. This simple yet complex act of comparison paints a picture of our humanity and our desire to have both physical and cognitive understanding of a concept, and this is because "[o]nce we can identify our experiences as entities or substances, we can refer to them, categorize them, group them, and quantify them—and, by this means, reason about them" (Lakoff & Johnson, 2003, p. 26).

In this conversation, we drew upon four metaphors developed by three colleagues that connected the concept of "good writing" to treasure troves, jazz music, glass slippers, and magically fitted pants. Although these metaphors seem to mesh together fantastical and romantic ideas regarding the qualities that constitute good writing, they actually signify that "good writing" is defined by a sense of *aesthetics*. Concepts such as purpose and context play fundamental roles in determining writing quality, but there are certain intrinsic and unquantifiable elements present in writing that greatly influence its ability to be regarded as "good." These (often invisible) elements are tailored to the individual, and in the case of our metaphors, they determine what makes good writing *shine* (like a gem) and what sets the writing standard between treasure and "fool's gold."

In our metaphors, we also illustrated that good writing can be worn like a ring, a shoe, and even a pair of pants. This presents a sense of belonging within our writing and demonstrates how closely we associate our thoughts and ideas to our physical being. Ede (1989) connects this sense of ownership over writing to the concept of voice, explaining, "Just as you dress differently on different occasions, as a writer you assume different voices in different situations. . . . Whatever the situation, the choices you make as you write and revise . . . will determine how readers interpret and respond to your presence in the text" (p. 158). We wear our words like clothes, and in the case of determining what good writing is, we assess writing quality on an individual level through how well the language fits us.

Even though we can use metaphors to help describe what good writing is, the terms we use are somewhat abstract. In discussions with our class, voice was used to identify qualities of good writing. Mona expressed her understanding of voice as "straying from the common way of saying something, breaching the border to express yourself in an individual way. It is convention breaking." And she concluded that "good writing, then, must stray from what has been done. It cannot mimic. It must diverge to be distinct." Katelyn raised the questions of what normative and divergent features we should focus on when teaching students and how we might accomplish this. She asked whether we should focus on a specific genre like the traditional academic essay or first look at real-world examples, such as the one examined by Matsuda. We continued to ponder these questions as we considered their intersection with written genres.

Elbow (1981) first described voice as something that most people have in their speech but often lack in their writing. In the same way a parent can recognize the sound of their child in a group, voice allows the writer to be distinguished to the point where you can feel the author's presence as if they were speaking directly to the reader. Voice captures the essence of the writer on the page, and for this reason it's very difficult to describe the strength of voice as an indication of good writing. Voice is not something you can point to, yet it is extremely essential to developing strong and high-quality writing skills and requires more of personal understanding by the learner rather than an instructor's feedback.

Traditionally in the United States, multilingual writers have often been expected to leave their L1 writing identities behind as they adopt "American" rhetorical conventions such as voice. For many multilingual writers, the concept of writing with an individual voice may be new because different rhetorical systems convey voice in different ways. Consequently, multilingual writers might display voice in a style that conflicts with the expectations of their American teachers. We believe that writing teachers need to develop their own awareness of how multilingual writers might convey voice in their writing.

If we want to cultivate good writers in our classrooms, we need to provide multilingual students the time, space, and opportunity to grapple with voice without imposing our values on them or stifling the students' ability to find their voice. Awareness of their voice empowers students to become strong, confident writers who have the tools to produce good writing. Although voice and metaphor offer ways for us to understand the concept of good writing, they alone are not enough. The question we have to ask is, "How can we teach students—especially multilingual writers—to create good writing?"

# How We Can Encourage Good Writing in a Multilingual Classroom?

So now what? After reading, thinking, and writing about various perspectives on good writing, literacy, voice, and genre and hammering out our beliefs as a group, we were eager to consider what a classroom approach to developing good writing among multilingual writers might look like. How do we put what we have learned into practice? In this final section we have identified some approaches and activities that we plan to bring with us into the classroom. We spotlight the role of student choice and student voice in good writing. Although multilingual students frequently deviate from English-language writing conventions, it is often without intention. When we encourage their deliberate choices, we believe we strengthen their voices and lay the foundation for good writing. As we describe below, we can do this by engaging our students in explicit instruction, collaborative discovery, and engaging in activities that we have captured in the mnemonic term PRACTICE.

## Explicit Instruction

Writing in an unfamiliar language is not easy. As teachers, we can acknowledge this vulnerable undertaking with our classes, which can ease the transition to academic writing in English. Because multilingual learners are neither experts in English nor fully aware of all cultural and rhetorical expectations in college writing courses, it is key that their writing classes introduce them to writing conventions and give them room to explore, take risks, and learn from mistakes. We believe that explicit instruction in written genres is an excellent way to tap into writers' funds of knowledge and to teach them about the importance of rhetorical analysis and how to prioritize process over product. Below, we introduce a genre analysis project that shows teachers how to promote deliberate student writing choices. By analyzing sample texts, breaking down components of good writing, and giving them plenty of opportunities to practice, students can bring their thoughts and experiences to academic writing.

## Collaborative Discovery

The second key component of helping multilingual writers develop good writing is through collaborative discovery. We believe that when we have students collaborate as they practice writing conventions, we invite individual differences and elicit their voices. Rather than imposing standards to mimic, student-centered group work can invite students to bring themselves to their work.

## PRACTICE

As a checklist of priorities to guide us as we plan to teach multilingual writers, we have created a mnemonic: PRACTICE. The first four letters, which represent "purpose," "reader," "assumptions," and "context," remind us to highlight the rhetorical situation. The second half of the mnemonic, which stands for "time," "ideas," "collaboration," and "evaluation," acts as a prompt for us to focus on the writing process and to give students time to develop their work. The suggested guiding questions can be used to focus conversations about rhetoric and process. In collaboration with their peers, students can draw on their existing knowledge and bring themselves to their work.

| | Priority | Guiding Questions |
|---|---|---|
| P | Purpose | What is the author trying to accomplish? |
| R | Reader | Who is the intended audience? |
| A | Assumptions | What are the expectations of this genre? |
| C | Context | When and where was this written? |
| T | Time | Where in the drafting process are you? |
| I | Ideas | What do you want to say? |
| C | Collaboration | How has your writing changed since the peer review? |
| E | Evaluation | What is your assessment of your work? |

The PRACTICE mnemonic bundles our recommendations for teaching good writing. With these considerations, we can continue to check our teaching strategies for encouraging good writing.

## Putting It into PRACTICE: Genre Analysis Project

So how do we put this all together? Although multilingual students may be beginners in academic English, writing teachers cannot assume that they are novices everywhere. Students bring a lot to the classroom and to their assignments: their cultural perspectives, individual expertise, and personal motivations. Writing expectations in English may not necessarily overlap with written genres in other languages. Genre conventions might be unfamiliar, and this provides an opportunity for explicit instruction. What kinds of antecedent genres do students bring to their classes? A student's prior experiences can inform their learning. Their voice is pulled into the class when writing teachers draw on their fund of knowledge (Moll, Amanti, Neff, & Gonzalez, 1992). Students' cultural and linguistic diversity creates opportunities for fresh forms of writing. Engaging in a genre analysis project gives students space to practice and reflect on deliberate writing choices together through collaborative discovery.

We believe that one way teachers can help multilingual writers understand what makes writing "good" is by having them analyze sample texts and apply what they have learned. Using the concepts of "purpose," "reader," "assumptions," and "context," as prompted by the mnemonic PRACTICE, students can become more aware of expectations and the rhetorical choices and moves we make as writers by making their own strategic writing decisions. Discussing existing texts helps students consider their choices when they write. A group genre analysis project serves multiple functions: It makes genre transparent, it allows students to draw on their funds of knowledge, it provides opportunities to work in multiple modalities, and it offers chances for students to build their language skills as they work together. Establishing genre conventions allows students to identify how their writing decisions will satisfy their purposes.

## Part One: Scaffolding

Scaffolding gives students time to explore, assess and reassess, and ultimately interrogate some of their initial assumptions about genre expectations and what constitutes "good writing." The first part of the assignment consists of examining sample texts from a particular genre. The teacher can select a few different texts within a genre such as poems, social media posts, or advertisements. Instructors elicit an initial description of the genre from the class. Next, the students analyze one text together as a class. The instructor facilitates this by posing questions for students to consider, such as *Who is the intended audience?* or *What makes you think so?* Next, in small groups, students examine another sample. Each group examines the same example, revealing multiple interpretations. By scaffolding these steps, writing teachers help generate discussion about purpose, audience, context, and genre.

By generating multiple interpretations of genre in the small groups, writing instructors are encouraging students to assess and revise their initial definitions.

## Part Two: Analyzing

Building upon the previous activities, teachers engage students in a genre analysis of their own choosing, working in groups. With this activity, teachers should think about how to draw out students' voices and prior knowledge. Instructors have student groups start by selecting a genre to analyze and providing a brief definition of that genre. Next, students collect sample texts to examine and analyze. Teachers can encourage students to draw from a wide range of texts in order to help them discover the rules that bind each of the texts into that specific genre. At the end of the data collection and analysis, teachers ask students to revisit their initial genre definition and reassess. In providing opportunities for reflection and analysis, instructors empower students' voices. By encouraging students to articulate to each other how these texts have upheld their original definition and met their assumptions about the genre and how they have diverged, instructors facilitate a collaborative negotiation of meaning that draws on students' funds of knowledge. Finally, students build upon their collective knowledge when they are able to articulate the purpose, context, and audience for the sample texts they have collected.

## Part Three: Composing

The final element of this assignment is the culmination of critical thinking, practice, and exploration. Teachers can draw out students' new and prior knowledge and experiences by having them create their own text within the genre they have analyzed. We see this next step as an opportunity for instructors to encourage students' engagement with writing as both a process and a product and to bring in the second half of our PRACTICE mnemonic: "Time," "Ideas," "Collaboration," and "Evaluation." To facilitate this iterative process, teachers have students begin with an idea draft. Next, in small groups, students review each other's drafts, and reviewers are asked to identify the author's purpose, audience, and context. Finally, as students present their text to the class, they describe how their text meets their purpose, addresses their audience, and represents "good writing." With these steps, instructors emphasize the process of writing to students through developing content, working with their peers, and receiving feedback about their own "good writing."

Following our discussions and analysis of what makes writing "good," we offer these suggestions to writing instructors so that they can promote good writing in multilingual classrooms. Each of these related activities asks students to articulate their initial assumptions and then question and reassess those assumptions about genre. Reading and writing are integrated through reviewing, analyzing, and reflecting on examples of the genre. As students discover the rhetorical conventions and reader expectations of various genres, including the academic genre associated with college writing, they learn not to elevate one genre over another but see each as appropriate to a purpose, audience, and context.

Students then engage in their own writing practice as they work to craft a text of their own—learning by doing. With classroom projects like these, writing instructors prioritize the empowerment of budding writers and encourage students to develop a rhetorical awareness that can inform their own writing. Multilingual students who can analyze their own rhetorical choices with PRACTICE can be better positioned to produce good writing.

## Closing Remarks

Writing is hard work. It takes practice. Writers must read widely to develop a deep appreciation of how authors make writing work. Good writing means different things to different people and differs according to genre, field, medium, and rhetorical exigence. As usage changes over time, so do societal attitudes about the qualities of good writing. Although the students agreed that there is no universal definition of good writing, they still felt that what makes good writing is its ability to spark an emotional response within us. I agreed with them. We connect. We become invested. We don't get bored. Prose can produce sensations of excitement and pleasure and admiration for how good the authors make us feel or how they spark our intellect through their use of imagery, metaphor, structure, and language. We want to read on. We seek out opportunities to read more of that author's work. Although we recognize that the idea of a writer's voice is a cultural construct, it offers the promise of resonance to the writing and can help us to remember how that piece made us feel and remember what the author taught us.

Our conversations about good writing and our own reactions to the scholarship on literacy and writing kept us focused on two central questions: *As writing teachers in linguistically heterogeneous classrooms, what do we want our students to learn? If writing involves creating meaning with language, what do we want them to be able to do with language?* Our experience writing this chapter together brought us again and again to questioning our own assumptions, beliefs, and values about writing and gave us a deeper appreciation of the struggles that all writers and most especially multilingual writers go through when learning to write in an additional language. We agreed that the first step to raising student awareness about writing begins with teachers reflecting on their own ideas about what makes good writing and good writers. Being aware of and questioning our assumptions and values about writing helps to ensure that our feedback is meaningful and that our curricula, syllabi, and assignments engage students in their intellectual development and encourage them to reflect meaningfully about the power of writing to shape their lives.

## References


Alim, S. A. (2010). Critical language awareness. In N. Hornberger & S. L. McKay (Eds.), *Sociolinguistics and language education* (pp. 205–231). Multilingual Matters.

Anthony, L. (2021). AntConc (Version 4.0.0) [Computer software]. Waseda University. https://www.laurenceanthony.net/software

Atkinson, D. (2001). Reflections and refractions on the JSLW special issue on voice. *Journal of Second Language Writing, 10*(1–2), 107–124. https://doi.org/10.1016/S1060-3743(01)00035-2

Baker-Bell, A. (2020). *Linguistic justice: Black language, literacy, identity, and pedagogy.* Routledge.

Clark, I. (2019). Genre, transfer, and related issues. In I. Clark (Ed.), *Concepts in composition: Theory and practice in the teaching of composition* (3rd ed.), (pp. 159–204). Routledge.

Elbow, P. (1981). *Writing with power: Techniques for mastering the writing process.* Oxford University Press.

Ede, L. (1989). *Work in progress: A guide to academic writing and revising.* Bedford.

Freedman, A. (1995). The what, where, when, why, and how of classroom genres. In J. Petraglia (Ed.), *Reconceiving writing, rethinking writing instruction* (pp. 121–144). Lawrence Erlbaum.

Gee, J. P. (2005). What is literacy? In P. Vandenberg, S. Hum, & J. Clary-Lemon (Eds.), *Relations, locations, positions: Composition theory for writing teachers* (pp. 29–39). National Council of Teachers of English.

Heath, S. B. (1982). What no bedtime story means: Narrative skills at home and school. *Language and Society, 11*, 49–76. DOI: 10.1017/S0047404500009039

Janks, H. (2004). The access paradox. *English in Australia, 139*, 33–42. DOI:10.3316/aeipt.133630

Kucer, S. B. (2009). *Dimensions of literacy: A conceptual base for teaching reading and writing in school settings.* Routledge.

Lakoff, G., & Johnson, M. (2003). *Metaphors we live by.* University of Chicago Press.

Leki, I. (1995). Good writing: I know it when I see it. In D. Belcher & G. Braine (Eds.), *Academic writing in a second language: Essays on research and pedagogy* (pp. 23–46). Ablex Publishing.

Lillis, T. (2013). *The sociolinguistics of writing.* Edinburgh University Press.

Matsuda, P. (2001). Voice in Japanese written discourse: Implications for academic writing. *Journal of Second Language Writing, 10*, 35–53. https://doi.org/10.1016/S1060-3743(00)00036-9

Moll, L. C., Amanti, C., Neff, D., & Gonzalez, N. (1992). Funds of knowledge for teaching: Using a qualitative approach to connect homes and classrooms. *Theory Into Practice, 31*(2), 132–141. http://www.jstor.org/stable/1476399

Nauman, A., Stirling, T., & Borthwick, A. (2011). What makes writing good? An essential question for teachers. *The Reading Teacher, 64*(5), 318–328. DOI:10.1598/RT.64.5.2

Pahl, S. (2014). The aesthetics of everyday literacies: Home writing practices in a British Asian household. *Anthropology and Education Quarterly, 45*(3), 293–311. DOI: 10.1111/aeq.12069

Reichelt, M. (2003). Defining writing: A cross cultural perspective. *Composition Studies, 31*(1), 99–126.

Rosa, J., & Flores, N. (2017). Unsettling race and language: Toward a raciolinguistic perspective. *Language and Society, 46*, 621–647. https://doi.org/10.1017/S0047404517000562

Snow, C., & P. Uccelli. (2009). The challenge of academic language. In D. R. Olson and N. Torrance. (Eds.), *The Cambridge handbook of literacy* (pp. 112–133). Cambridge University Press.

Sperling, M., & Appleman, D. (2011). Voice in the context of literacy studies. *Reading Research Quarterly, 46*(1), 70–84. DOI: 10.1598/RRQ.46.1.4

Swales, J. (1990). *Genre analysis: English in academic and research settings.* Cambridge University Press.

Tardy, C. (2012). Current conceptions of voice. In K. Hyland & C. Sancho Guinda (Eds.), *Stance and voice in written academic discourse* (pp. 34–48). Palgrave Macmillan.

Tardy, C. (2019). *Genre-based writing: What every ESL teacher needs to know.* University of Michigan Press.

Williams, J. M., & Colomb, G. G. (1993). The case for explicit teaching: Why what you don't know won't help you. *Research in the Teaching of English, 27*(3), 252–264. http://www.jstor.org/stable/40171226

## Acknowledgments

We would like to extend a special thanks to our colleagues Andy Alvarez, Ilana Baer, Christopher Pascua, Lindsey De Genova, Melissa Ledesma, and Erica Salas for their intellectual contributions, which deeply enriched our classroom conversations and helped to make this chapter possible.

# Chapter 9

# Five Mentors, or, My Earliest Muses Will Always Be with Me

*Martha Clark Cummings*

## The Beginning

If I am going to write about good writing, I must begin with my father, the first person who taught me how to write with clarity. In my mind, there is always a glowing, heartwarming scene taking place on the screen porch of the house on Linden Avenue in a leafy suburb of New York City. My father and I sit together in two comfortable chairs, my mother and sister occupied elsewhere in the house. Outside the robins are singing and I listen to them as I wait while he reads what I have written for school, making notes on the pages. I don't know how long or how often this happened, but I imagine it happened a lot. I was somewhere between the ages of 10 and 15, when I went through whatever it is teenagers go through that makes them wish their parents dead. I remember clearly sitting like this with my father, talking about what makes a piece of writing good, his telling me, for example, that it was simple, clear, and direct, that it had a purpose and an intended audience, not just the teacher, but whoever I imagined would appreciate what I wrote. That was when I began to pay attention to what good writing was. I consider myself very lucky to have had a father who cared about such things and was willing to share what he knew with me.

Finally, he turned to me, ready to talk. I was not anxious, as I always was at school when the teacher called on me, but eager to hear what he had to say. In these moments he was kind, which often he was not in the rest of what passed for family life in our household. He began by telling me what I did well. I don't know where he learned to do this. He was a lawyer, and as far as I knew then, most of his writing was legal briefs. (Concise statements summarizing a client's case.) Possibly in college or law school he had had a mentor who helped him with his writing the way he was helping me. No one talked about writing as process or drafting and revising back then, even though he did it himself, but he knew editing, and this is what he taught me: how to transform what I had written into simple, direct, clear prose with no unnecessary words and nothing that would confuse the reader. I came away from those sessions feeling grateful and confident. If my father thought my writing was good, then I had nothing to fear from my teachers.

One Christmas, he gave me a copy of *The Elements of Style* (1920) by William Strunk Jr. (This was before E. B. White came into the picture.) I read the book from cover to cover on Christmas Day, lying on the sofa in the library, and again many times over the following years. I also spent many hours perusing my father's other books on style and rhetoric, including H. W. Fowler's *A Dictionary of Modern English Usage* (1965) and Eric Partridge's *Usage and Abusage* (1942). After my father died in 1983, I learned that in 1955 he had published an article called "The Language of Horse Racing" in *American Speech*, a respected peer-reviewed journal, and that he was an amateur linguist when I was very young, presumably before he was consumed by the practice of law. I read it for the first time quite recently and found it beautifully written and extremely insightful. I also found one error, which I know if he were alive, not only would he be delighted to learn that I could answer a question he and his readers had been pondering sixty-five years ago, but also, he would have written to the editor to correct the error since no one else seemed to have found it.

I knew that my father and I did not discuss everything we needed to know to produce good writing, but I could not articulate what that was. I did not talk to my father about this because I didn't want to hurt his feelings, but all of his reference books seemed to me to skate on the surface of something much deeper that wasn't taught in school either. I knew that reading helped but didn't understand how. I was extremely quiet all through high school and college, but I had a lot of questions and ideas, so I wrote a lot and I did notice that the more I wrote, the better my writing became.

I do not remember receiving any writing instruction in elementary or high school, although we must have, since we were required to write research papers in 8th and in 12th grade. I asked my current Facebook friends who attended elementary and high school with me, but none of them could remember much either. One said we were taught about topic sentences. Another, that we learned that each paragraph was supposed to be about one thing. We all remembered our peculiar and humiliating experiences during those years. My particular humiliating memory was of our 7th grade English teacher, Mr. Curtis, a portly, gray-haired man with a malicious smile, mocking me for writing about winning a blue ribbon at a horse show. "Our blue ribbon gal," he would say when he called on me in his sardonic tone, or "Let's hear from the girl who won the blue ribbon." That certainly taught me to keep my achievements to myself, which I guess was a lesson about appropriate and inappropriate writing topics. But life was hard enough with all of my classmates already thinking I was stuck-up and rich because my sister and I were the only ones in town who owned horses. Mr. Curtis chiming in only made it that much worse.

## Lucy Calkins and Gay Brookes

Lucy Calkins's arrival at Teachers College was Shakespearean. Looking back, I realize that when I met her in 1983, she was a beginner, teaching graduate courses for only her second semester, but she quickly became an example of how, in the American educational system, "a single char-ismatic thinker, backed by universities and publishing houses, can wield massive power over how and what children learn" (Goldstein, 2022). Now, so many years later, she is the founding director of the Teachers College Reading and Writing Project, her "Units of Study" curriculum mandated in public elementary schools in New York City and many other states (not without a great deal of controversy, most recently with her own admission that it was an error to exclude phonics from her read-ing curriculum for beginners), featured in a lead article in *The New York Times* (2022).

As soon as I arrived to start the master's program in TESOL in the fall of 1982, walking down the creaky wooden floors of the hall-ways, standing in line at the cafeteria to go into the austere Tudor Dining Room with its dark wooden beamed ceilings, heavy wooden tables and chairs, and large high heavily draped windows, I heard the excited talk of students taking her course. Up to that point, I had always been able to keep my writing and teaching lives separate. I was writing fiction and thought that my writing might become muddied or at least muddled by the writing of my English language learners (ELLs). Actually, I did go through a period when any preposition after any other word sounded fine to me. At that time, TESOL (Teaching English to Speakers of Other Languages) was still focused on oral/aural skills, using the audiolingual approach, an offshoot of behaviorism in psychology. "Let me teach listening and speaking," I thought, "and leave the teaching of writing to someone else." How selfish this seems to me now.

The master's program in TESOL was very practical; one of its important components was having to teach particular skills using particular methods as part of the curriculum. People grumbled about this, of course. We were paying to teach instead of teaching for pay. We also had to participate in learning another language in what later became known as a "designer method" but at the time was regarded as groundbreaking, life-changing, revolutionary. None of them involved writing. When I arrived to register for courses, jet-lagged and disoriented, returning to New York from two years in France, I was staying with a French friend and continuing to speak French because my subtenant had not yet moved out of my apartment. My advisor was John Fanselow, who taught the more practical aspects of the program, including observation and supervision. He was one of the two full-time faculty members in the program at the time, the other being Leslie Beebe, who was in charge of the more theoretical side: SLA, grammar, and sociolinguistics. John suggested in an offhand way that I begin my first semester with an experience in learning a new language, Japanese, using the Silent Way, in an extended weekend retreat scheduled to start the following evening. (The teacher was his wife. He did not mention that.) At the time I had no interest in learning Japanese and no idea what this "Silent Way" was. I am sorry to say that I do not remember one word of Japanese from that 15-hour experience. I do remember that it was fun and empowering to try to guess what the teacher was trying to encourage us to say by tapping on various colored rectangles with her pointer.

All around me, for the rest of that semester, I continued hearing people talk about Lucy Calkins as if she were a rock star. Wondering at the enthusiasm, I cast aside my principles about separate teaching/writing lives by registering for her course. Ironically, the only available practicum in the master's program in TESOL in the spring semester was Teaching Writing, taught by Gay Brookes, who was a doctoral student at the time. In the spring semester, then, in addition to six hours per week of supervised teaching of writing, I had an hour and a half seminar learning the value of Controlled Composition, where students were given short paragraphs with easy vocabulary and asked to change them from singular to plural or present to past, for example (Brookes & Withrow, 1985). Another evening every week, I was packed into a room with sixty or so other students, including Gay, my practicum supervisor, waiting with bated breath for Lucy to enter the room like a whirlwind and stand erect behind her lectern—she was a small woman but had the presence of a giant—delivering her message about writing as process with evangelical zeal. Sometimes I imagined that in her passion for the subject she was standing on her toes for the entire ninety minutes of the class, except for the times when she stopped short and said, "Turn to the person next to you and talk about. . . ." In only one semester, she completely changed the way I thought about helping my English language learners (ELLs) become good writers. It was such a relief to think that we could have a room full of writers writing, that each day instead of laboriously working through grammatical changes to prewritten paragraphs we could begin with a 10-minute-long mini-lesson about a relevant important feature of good writing and link the lesson to the writing students were working on, and through this repeated process: brainstorm ideas, draft, receive feedback from classmates/instructor, revise, and finally edit. As I saw it, Lucy was giving me permission to teach writing the way I wrote.

I noticed that as the semester progressed, Gay Brookes's writing practicum seminar began to take on more features of the kind of writing workshop advocated in Lucy's class. This framework has remained with me for all the teaching of writing I have done since. And if I am completely honest, controlled composition has too. Nowadays, most of my students do not read books or articles or essays or stories in English—or in their own languages, for that matter. They do not have the language of good writing available to them. One thing I know for sure is that if I am not actively reading something well written in English, my own writing deteriorates, begins to sound more and more like what I am reading in the newspaper or, worse, something a character on TV might say. The activities in books like *10 Steps* require students to pay attention to basic sentence patterns and grammatical structures without the added burden of unfamiliar vocabulary. Clearly, they are more helpful in editing than in generating text. In the mixed-level classes I have been teaching for the last fifteen years, some students find these exercises very useful, even relaxing. There is no multi-tasking involved.

So, in one way or another, Gay Brookes and Lucy Calkins are always in the classroom with me, reminding me of what I know and that I know how to do it.

# Ann Raimes

I don't think I have ever been happier than when I was teaching my first college ESL writing class at Hunter College. I was filled with hope and new ideas about how I might actually be able to teach writing to these students in similar ways to how I approached the task of writing myself. The students were mature young adults with strong reading and writing skills in their native languages. They were all fairly recent immigrants and refugees. Many were highly educated in their own fields—a woman doctor from China who read my ears and told me I had a thyroid condition— she was, of course, correct—a lawyer from Argentina, an engineer from Cambodia. They had all internalized the value of school and knew how to motivate themselves. I was lucky that I had been assigned to teach the second of three levels in the ESL program, in which I could address comfort, confidence, and fluency in the expression of their ideas rather than the standardized academic essay with its introduction, three points, and conclusion. The students enjoyed the tasks I gave them, suggested ways to make them more engaging, and believed that everything we did in class would help them to become better writers. They found every new activity I introduced to them fascinating. Freewriting, for example, as a way to get started: They had never had an instructor who wrote with them, had never shared their writing with a classmate, reading aloud. They asked me to read what I had written, and I obliged them, reminding them to give me the same kind of feedback they were giving each other, that is, to tell me what they understood, what they liked, and what they wanted to hear more about. I asked them to remember Donald M. Murray's advice, as I paraphrased it: The goal of feedback was to make the writer want to get back to her desk and continue writing.

At the time I joined the part-time faculty at Hunter, Ann Raimes was coordinator of the Developmental English Program (1,500 students), which included the ESL program. Both were housed in the English Department. I almost never crossed paths with her, but when I did, she always stopped to ask me to describe how the class was going. She had pure white hair (although she couldn't have been older than 40) and a razor-sharp intelligence quite visible in her eyes. She had already published many textbooks and articles and continued to do so in spite of her administrative duties and her frequent one-to-one meetings with students. During one of our brief conversations she told me her perspective on teaching ESL writing, a version of which I found later in one of her many articles:

> There are, unfortunately, no neat formulas for getting to an exquisite
> final product, one step at time. Giving instruction in writing is not . . .
> simply a question of getting the right tools and following directions.
> If it were, more people would be good writers, and more teachers and
> textbook writers would be rich. We must accept the chaotic and messy
> nature of writing—but teachers do not like chaos, so they have sought
> to impose order on it by focusing on grammar, rhetorical modes,
> and models of academic discourse, to provide themselves with neat
> systems to teach. (Raimes, 1983a, p. 260)

Because I was working with Ann, I thought the least I could do was familiarize myself with her published writing, just in case there was a moment when I could ask her about it, or if any of my classmates at Teachers College were to ask me if she was really the big deal people said she was. And how glad I was that I did. Her writing exemplified my definition of good academic writing, most importantly to me, for having a clear distinctive writer's voice, humor, and metaphors. No one could pick up one of her articles and imagine it had been written by anyone else. Very often she used an extended metaphor that worked through the entire piece. For example, in her article "Tradition and Revolution in ESL Teaching" (1983b), the first sentence reads, "You are sitting in a room with an experimenter who shows you playing cards quickly" (p. 535). She continues with this very effective hook, pulling the reader into the challenging topic of the theory of paradigm shifts, demonstrating that we in the field of ESL writing were still in the middle of one and that we might do better to disentangle ourselves from conflicts and controversies rather than claim that we, like L1 writing professionals, had succeeded in making the shift already.

In the article she invites the reader to engage with her in this ongoing conversation, rather than implying that the context might be too difficult for non-specialists, as so many academic writers do. She defines difficult concepts, either parenthetically or by an added sentence beginning with "That is. . . ." or with comprehensible quotations from other authors. She gives crystal clear, lively examples to illustrate concepts without including one unnecessary word. She often begins paragraphs with questions, reminding the reader of where we are headed: "And what of our own field, teaching English to speakers of other languages?" (p. 537). At the end of a section of conscientious examination of the traditional ways of teaching ESL writing, the final paragraph begins, "Perhaps some of you are by now muttering, 'Yes, we know all that. That's old hat. Nobody subscribes to that stuff anymore'" (p. 539). How reassuring it is for us, her readers, to be acknowledged, directly addressed in this way. And, of course, we stay with her to find out what she will say next.

At the end of the article, she reminds us of where we are—in a place she has clearly described to us as the middle of a paradigm shift—and neatly ends her essay with a reference to an anomalous playing card that turned up in the first paragraph of the essay. Not only did I learn valuable knowledge from her work, but I also learned subtle but effective ways to break down the barriers between personal and academic writing.

## Rebecca Mlynarczyk

Another teacher, author, and scholar who helped me to better understand my position on academic discourse versus personal writing was Rebecca Mlynarczyk, who was my colleague at Hunter when I started there and again many years later at Kingsborough Community College, where I currently teach. Rebecca has spent much of her career dispelling the myth that there is no place for personal or narrative writing in academic discourse. Even though the argument has changed since the 1980s, when scholars argued that the divide was as impenetrable as the Berlin Wall, it has not been settled. It didn't help matters one bit when Jerome Bruner, in his 1986 book, *Actual Minds, Possible Worlds*, clearly distinguished between the "narrative mode" and the "logico-scientific or paradigmatic" mode, two terms that were bandied about for decades after he described them. Either the thinking and writing was academic or, if it was narrative, it wasn't. With the onset of the Common Core Curriculum, emphasizing the need for more informational and less literary reading, starting in kindergarten, the divide grew stronger. For me, Mlynarczyk's (2014) citation of Bourdieu and Passeron (1986), "The divorce between the language of the family and the language of school only serves to reinforce the feeling that the education system belongs to another world" (pp. 10–11) called to mind Mina Shaughnessy's (1977) words at the start of open admissions at the City University of New York (CUNY): "Cut off from the impulse to say something, or from the sense that anything he (the student) might say is important to anyone else, he is automatically cut off from the grammatical intuitions that would serve him in a truly communicative situation" (p. 86).

Rebecca and I spoke together often about the need for academic writing teachers to allow their students to write in their own personal voices, even in the middle of an academic essay, to feel that they are expressing what they have to say. At the end of an article published in 2006, she wrote: "I believe that students cannot write a strong and convincing argument unless they have first grappled with their subject in a deeply personal way" (p. 7). Slowly, the world of academic writing took a turn, helped by Bruner's 2003 book, *Making Stories: Law, Literature, Life,* in which he asserts that "it's essential to use storytelling—narrative—*along with* academic discourse and cautions, 'it is when we lose sight of the two in league that our lives narrow'" (Mlynarczyk, 2014, p. 102). Good writing, then, must include storytelling.

Each time Rebecca and I spoke about what makes writing good, I understood why it was that so many people told me my writing was good even though I never followed the conventions of academic discourse; it was that readers are drawn into a story. This phenomenon has followed me all my life, surely thanks to my early mentors and my own quest to find out what good writing is. At the TESOL convention in 1997, a well-known academic writer came up to me at the president's reception and whispered, "I loved 'Sardo Revisited,'" a chapter I had contributed to Bailey and Nunan's (1996) *Voices from the Language Classroom.* I wondered why she was whispering. There was nothing risqué in what I had written. Possibly it was because I had broken the rules of academic writing and had followed instead the rules of good narrative writing and poetry. I paid attention to small, specific details, used my senses, retained my sense of humor. My writing was accessible, welcoming the reader in and inviting her to come up with her own theories about how to teach ELLs to produce good writing. I wrote in a clear, comprehensible voice. I wrote from my heart. I never pretended to know what I thought before I had written it, making my writing speculative.

## The World We Live in Now

The world has changed. Every day the news is worse than we could have imagined the day before. There are days when all I can think to do is find a quiet place—or the closest I can get to one—and write about how I feel, then try to write something that will transport me from the real to the imagined, even if only for a moment. Poet Billy Collins would call this good writing because it contains "the light-handed feel of the hypothetical, the mode of wonder, the tone of an open investigation" (2005, p. 4).

One thing I learned very quickly was that if the students I was teaching had to pass the dreaded standardized CUNY writing test at the end of the semester, anything I tried to teach them that did not seem related to the test they ignored. I caved in immediately, having learned from Gay Brookes at Teachers College that if students perceive that you have the information they need but for some reason are withholding it, they will resent you bitterly and evaluate you poorly at the end of the semester. It's worth adding that these student evaluations are particularly important for new and untenured instructors. OK, then! Once I had made sure they had read and understood the instructions—often the most challenging part of the test—every week we spent 90 minutes writing responses to the prompts. I wrote with them, as I always did. One thing I noticed was that in all of my own 90-minute essays, my longest example to support my thesis was always in the form of a story: specific, concrete, heartfelt. I began combing through the sample student essays that were handed out to us with each prompt to illustrate with the holistic scores from 1 (lowest) to 6 (highest), with 4 being passing, that the essays with the highest scores often included stories. I decided that if I could teach them how to write a good story that carried the reader away from examining sentence-level or even discourse-level errors too closely, then they would pass the test, allowing them to take courses in their majors, as well as one or two semesters of first-year composition, where they would have plenty of time to learn the fundamentals of hard-core academic writing. I was aware that I was experimenting on them and that the experiment might fail, but I was confident that if I got through to them, if they believed me, their writing would change dramatically once they cast off the leaden cloak of the rules of academic writing as their previous instructors had defined them.

In my classroom, Lucy Calkins is ever present, reminding me to "teach the writer, not the writing," and to get to know my students as well as I possibly can, so I understand their passions and struggles. I teach them about drafting and revising. At first some of them object vehemently. "I have to write this *again?*" they grumble. I am ready for this reaction with a video clip of a Q&A with Amy Bloom. First, we read two paragraphs from "Silver Water," one of Bloom's short stories. (See excerpt at the end of the chapter.) As a critic in *The New Yorker* put it on the inside flap of the front dust jacket of *A Blind Man Can See How Much I Love You: Stories* (Bloom, 2001), "Amy Bloom gets more meaning into individual sentences than most authors manage in whole books."

The students and I talk about what makes these paragraphs examples of good writing, and I ask them how many times they think she revised them. Some say none. She is a writer, born that way. She has a gift. Others say maybe once or twice. Then I show them a member of the audience in the video—Bloom has just finished reading a story—asking "How many times do you revise your stories?" Amy Bloom pauses, thinking. "Usually I revise each sentence about seventeen times," she says. I turn off the video. The classroom explodes. "She's crazy!" they exclaim. "That's too much work!" "Who would do that?" "Someone who loves language and cares deeply about good writing," I reply. "So no more complaining about revision. OK?" They reluctantly agree.

Unfortunately, when I teach on Zoom, which I am doing for the fifth semester, I feel disabled, as described so eloquently by Floyd Skloot, in his 2005 essay about living with brain damage: "I face a kind of ongoing mental vertigo in which thoughts teeter and topple. . . . I lose my way . . . my concentration fragments and my focus dissolves" (p. 291).

Sometimes it feels dangerous, as if I were trying to juggle hand grenades. One wrong move and the students could disappear from the screen, or worse, we could be accidentally blown through some mysterious black hole to the pages I write and wish to share with no one. My anxiety over not being able to find, let alone click on, the tab that would allow me to access the material I was planning to share with them on my screen makes my heart pound wildly. This is when, on good days, my five earliest mentors, or "muses" as I prefer to call them now, step forward and help me. My father tells me, as he often did, to review and practice the procedures between classes. Then make connections. Make checklists of what needs to be done in what order. There is no shame in not being able to remember. Gay Brookes reminds me of all the activities we came up with when, with Jean Withrow, we wrote our two reading/writing textbooks, *Changes* and *Inspired to Write*. Look at the teacher's manual, she says. Surely there are things you can do online as well as in the classroom that do not involve all this clicking. Use one of those. And many times I do, on days when I feel I have forgotten how to teach. Lucy Calkins tells me again that the key to helping students become good writers is to ask them questions about what they are writing so that they internalize these questions and ask them of themselves when they read their drafts. Ann Raimes reminds me that the most important reading the students do is the comments we write on their drafts. Rebecca Mlynarczyk reminds me to calm myself and them by having something engaging and accessible to read and respond to available and easy to find during a crisis on the screen. I listen. Slowly, I get better at this.

At some point in every semester, I give my students what I have come to realize is my personal definition of good writing. I tell them to ask themselves if they have written a good enough essay that if they printed it on paper and left it on the train, or the bus, or in the cafeteria, does it begin with an image or idea so compelling that the person who picks it up is so immediately engaged that she looks away from her cell phone to continue reading? Does she clearly understand the writer's main idea, gently presented at first before diving into a story that illustrates in concrete, specific ways that the writer cannot be wrong, and then, even though the reader has reached her stop or might be late for class, she must get to the end of this essay, written in such a clear, distinctive voice, to find out if the short conclusion expresses hope or despair? Will the reader smile or wish she could cry? Either way, she knows that reading this brief essay has altered her, not just for a moment but forever.

Excerpts from "Silver Water," short story by Amy Bloom (1993, pp. 87–88)

Paragraph #1:

> "My sister's voice was like mountain water in a silver pitcher; the clear blue beauty of it cools you and lifts you up beyond your heat, beyond your body. After we went to see *La Traviata,* when she was fourteen and I was twelve, she elbowed me in the parking lot and said, 'Check this out.' And she opened her mouth unnaturally wide and her voice came out, so crystalline and bright that all the departing operagoers stood frozen by their cars, unable to take out their keys or open their doors until she had finished, and then they cheered like hell.
>
> That's what I like to remember, and that's the story I told to all of her therapists."

Paragraph #2:

> "The worst family therapist we ever had sat in a pale green room with us, visibly taking stock of my mother's ethereal beauty and her faded blue t-shirt and girl-sized jeans, my father's rumpled suit and stained tie, and my own unreadable seventeen-year-old fashion statement. Rose was beyond fashion that year, in one of her dancing teddybear smocks and extra-extra-large Celtics sweatpants. Mr. Walker read Rose's file in front of us and then watched in alarm as Rose began crooning, beautifully, and slowly massaging her breasts. My mother and I laughed, and even my father started to smile. This was Rose's usual opening salvo for new therapists."

## References


Bailey, K. M., & Nunan, D. (Eds.). (1996). *Voices from the language classroom: Qualitative research in language education.* Cambridge University Press.

Bloom, A. (1993). Silver water. In A. Bloom, *Come to me: Stories.* HarperCollins.

Bloom, A. (2001). *A blind man can see how much I love you: Stories.* HarperCollins.

Bourdieu, P., & Passeron, J-C. (1986). Introduction: Language and relationship to language in the teaching situation. In P. Bourdieu, J-C. Passeron, & M. de Saint Martin. *Academic discourse: Linguistic misunderstanding and professional power* (pp. 1–34). Stanford University Press.

Brookes, G., & Withrow, J. (1985). *Ten steps: Controlled composition for beginning and intermediate language development.* Alemany Press.

Bruner, J. (1986). *Actual minds, possible worlds.* Harvard University Press.

Bruner, J. (2003). *Making stories: Law, literature, life.* Harvard University Press.

Collins, B. (2005). *Billy Collins teaches reading and writing poetry: Complete workbook from Masterclass.* National Public Broadcasting.

Cummings, G. C. (1955). The language of horse racing. *American Speech, 30*(1), 17–29.

Cummings, M. C. (1996). Sardo revisited: Voice, faith, and multiple repeaters. In K. Bailey & D. Nunan (Eds.), *Voices from the language classroom: Qualitative research in second language education* (pp. 224–235). Cambridge University Press.

Fowler, H. W. (1965). *A dictionary of modern English usage.* Oxford University Press.

Goldstein, D. (2022, May 22). In the fight over how to teach reading: This guru makes a major retreat. *The New York Times.* https://www.nytimes.com/2022/05/22/us/reading-teaching-curriculum-phonics.html

Mlynarczyk, R. W. (2006). Personal and academic writing: Revisiting the debate. *Journal of Basic Writing, 25*(1), 4–25. http://www.jstor.org/stable/43444074

Mlynarczyk, R. W. (2014). Storytelling and academic discourse: Including more voices in the conversation. *Journal of Basic Writing, 33*(1), 4–22. http://www.jstor.org/stable/43858445

The New Yorker (2001). A blind man can see how much I love you: Stories. [Excerpt from a review on the inside flap of the front dust jacket of *A blind man can see how much I love you: Stories* by Amy Bloom] Vintage.

Partridge, E. (1942). *Usage and abusage: A guide to good English.* H. Hamilton Press.

Raimes, A. (1983a). Anguish as a second language? Remedies for composition teachers. In A. Freedman, I. Pringle, & J. Yalden (Eds.), *Learning to write: First language/Second language* (pp. 258–272). Routledge.

Raimes, A. (1983b). Tradition and revolution in ESL reaching. *TESOL Quarterly, 17*(4), 535–552. https://doi.org/10.2307/3586612

Shaughnessy, M. (1977). *Errors and expectations.* Oxford University Press.

Skloot, F. (2005). Gray area: Thinking with a damaged brain. In L. Gutkind (Ed.), *In fact: The best of creative nonfiction* (pp. 288–306). Norton.

Strunk, W. (1920). *The elements of style.* Harcourt, Brace & Howe.

Withrow, J., Brookes, G., & Cummings, M. (1990). *Changes: Readings for writers.* St Martin's Press.

Withrow, J., Brookes, G., & Cummings, M. (2004). *Inspired to write: Readings and tasks to develop writing skills.* Cambridge.

**Chapter 10**

# Good Writing in Book Reviews

*Christine Pearson Casanave, with Yongyan Li*

> Competent writing has all the needed components of a genre.
> Good writing is "competent writing + [plus]" (Yongyan Li, personal communication, August 7, 2020)

As dull as they might seem to a ladder-climbing academic—and even to those who have already made the climb—book reviews are a common and important academic genre in TESOL and applied linguistics. They serve the useful functions of acquainting readers with books they might not be familiar with and of providing novice and established scholars with opportunities to publish something small and manageable and to get their voices heard about topics they feel strongly about. In a larger sense, they help construct, disseminate, and evaluate disciplinary knowledge (Groom, 2009, pp. 124–125). Many journals in applied linguistics and language education feature book review sections with their own special editors assigned to handle reviews of single books. We should note from the start that a review of a single book, the topic of this chapter, differs from a book review article, which is usually longer than a book review and discusses how several books treat a related topic (see Diani, 2009).

The conventional book review genre, although informative, is potentially dreadfully boring, partly because it is so predictable in structure and content. We don't usually look to book reviews for models of what we are calling "good" or "stylish" writing of the sort discussed by writing experts such as Joseph Williams (Williams & Bizup, 2015), William Zinsser (2006), or Helen Sword (2009, 2012). A book review typically introduces a book, summarizes the chapters one by one (ho hum), then comments briefly on the content, and ends with a praise-critique-praise move (Brienza, 2015; Hyland, 2000/2004). It may also contain other elements, such as identification of the intended audience and the book's relationship to a discipline or field (Hatcher & McDonald, 2011; USC Libraries Research Guides, 2020). In the conventional book review, the moves and steps are easily plotted out (Hatcher & McDonald, 2011; Swales, 1990). Concerning content, we expect the book review to provide information and evaluation (Nodoushan & Montazeran, 2012) but not much more. The conventional book review genre thus does its job. Readers learn of the existence of a particular book, who it was written for, something about its content and structure, and the reviewer's assessment of how successful the author was in achieving the book's purpose. This basic information allows readers to update their knowledge of the topic of a book and to decide whether they want to read the book themselves or use it as part of their teaching materials.

However, we do not often find guidelines for writing book reviews (but see Lewis, 2020) or hear about the quality of writing in book reviews, even though we might learn something about other aspects of reviews. For instance, in writing about the links between phraseology and epistemology in book reviews, Groom (2009) does not discuss quality of writing, but he is quite sanguine about the contributions that book reviews can make. The best reviews, he points out, disseminate and evaluate recent knowledge contributions to a field and help move that knowledge forward, what he calls the "discursive construction of disciplinary knowledge" (p. 124).

Although the book review genre can be quite predictable, cultural and disciplinary conventions differ to some extent in what is expected in a book review (e.g., Moreno & Suárez, 2009). For instance, there may be differences in the balance of summary and evaluation and the type of critique (see some of the chapters in Hyland and Diani, 2009), in the balance of praise and criticism (Hyland, 2000/2004), or in the extent to which a review comments on a book author's knowledge of a topic or on an author's lexical and rhetorical strategies for establishing voice and identity. Book reviews also differ in how or whether they convey the authority of the reviewer. For example, do reviewers reveal openly whether they are established scholars or graduate students? Do their reviews radiate confidence in themselves as scholars or timidity and subservience to the published authors they are reviewing? Are the reviews written in the first person and do they openly reveal the reviewer's stance, or does the reviewer avoid all use of personal pronouns and personal opinions? Do the reviews mainly summarize and praise a book or do they contain substantive analytical, critical, and even personal commentary? Or do they only critique a book without emphasizing a book's strengths? Are they engagingly written, and do they reveal the reviewer to be an accomplished writer and, importantly, a reader of related works?

Having worked for some years as book review editors for a major applied linguistics journal (*Journal of Second Language Writing*), Yongyan Li and I became interested in how reviews of books on second language writing (our specialty) can be written in ways that bend the stereotypical book review genre. We sought reviews that demonstrate not only a reviewer's knowledge and evaluation of a book but that also go beyond information about the book itself, including being written in a way that sparks readers' interest and engagement in the review itself as well as in the book. We found that a book review is usually competently written, giving us a sense of what a book is about and the reviewer's scholarly opinions about it but without necessarily drawing readers of the review into meatier, more interesting or controversial discussions of it, without revealing much about the reviewer as a writer and scholar, and without being a model of good writing. Reviews that go beyond summaries and a bit of commentary include discussions of how a book relates to other books on similar topics, how a book fits into or does justice to larger discussions of issues brought up in the book, what the reviewer's own experiences with the book are, including how the reviewer uses it or might use it in the future in classes or in scholarly work, and what the reviewer's views are of the book's writing quality and even of the author.

But in general, from our work both as book review editors and as readers of book reviews, we found that most book reviews, although competently done, do not stand out as particularly engaging pieces of writing. In addition to their predictability of structure and content, they are too often bland, impersonal, and humorless. Of course, one might ask whether humor of any kind belongs in an academic book review, but we would ask "why not"? In spite of its reputation, academic writing does not need to be boring or humorless (Billig, 2013; Caulley, 2008; Pinker, 2014; Sword, 2009, 2012, 2017; Warchal, 2019). But most important for this chapter, most readers probably don't look to book reviews for models of good writing, whatever they understand by this slippery concept.

One possible reason that book reviews don't jump out at us as venues for reviewers to display writing that is engaging, eloquent, and personal is that they generally don't add much to a scholar's career. Authors thus have little incentive to showcase their creative linguistic and intellectual talents in the book review genre. As Yongyan wrote me in a personal communication (August 8, 2020): "After all, how many would care to work to produce such 'good writing' when a book review is not counted in performance assessment?" When academic writers' performance assessments are generated from ratings of different kinds of scholarly writing, with book reviews low on the rating scale, Yongyan's point makes complete sense. Book reviews don't count for much in such a system.

Graduate students might be more likely to embrace book reviews as an early publication effort. In the first place, reviews do not involve original research. Instead, they require careful reading and critique of someone else's work—tasks that graduate students might do as a normal part of their graduate program. Reviews might thus be written in a book-report style by students as an assignment for a class or as one of their first publications, even though they count for very little on their CVs (Brienza, 2014). However, a question for the student or novice scholar who wishes to publish a book review will be how much background experience and knowledge it takes to do a credible and insightful job of reviewing and how much attention needs to be paid to the quality of writing. We believe it takes quite a bit of both.

In the remainder of this chapter, we exemplify some of the interactions we have had with book review authors over several years in order to highlight our efforts to encourage them to go beyond the stereotypical book review genre in their writing and to attend to good writing, in addition to merely describing and commenting on a book. Our main points for the purpose of this chapter have to do with clarity of several kinds, as well as with balance and personal connections, including how reviewers might have used the book themselves and responded to the book at a personal level. These points are drawn from the communications we had with authors as they were drafting and revising their book reviews. We were not always successful—the genre tradition of the book review is very entrenched—but we tried. We also tried whenever possible to invite established scholars who are themselves good writers to review a book that seemed to fit their interests and expertise.

## Clarity

We consider clarity to be a hallmark of good academic writing, even when the writing deals with complex or abstract topics. In other words, clarity of writing does not equate with simplicity of topic or treatment, nor does it refer exclusively to linguistic clarity, which focuses mainly on the extent to which words and sentences are comprehensible to readers. Of course individual words and sentences need to be clear and accessible to readers, but good writing in book reviews, as in all kinds of academic writing, requires more than this kind of clarity. Many of the feedback comments we provided on drafts of book reviews concerned the need for reviewers to clarify other aspects of their reviews, from general readability ("We both found the review very hard to follow") to specific aspects of clarity, such as audience and context, including how a book connects with a field, points being made, and—to be sure—language and terminology. Some examples follow, taken from our email communication with reviewers and with each other.

## Asking Reviewers to Clarify a Book's Audience and Context

A book review is not written for the self but for readers. In the first place, the well-written book review will inform readers of the intended audience and context for a book. General or specialist scholars? Graduate students? Teachers? Researchers? We sometimes asked a reviewer specific questions about this. For a book on teacher education, for example, Yongyan asked a reviewer from Turkey the following:

> YL: Would anyone in a teacher education program in Turkey, for example, find this book useful? Does the book suit teacher educators in the U.S. who deal mainly with international students rather than U.S. public school students?

Other examples of our suggestions and questions to reviewers about audience and context include the following comments:

> **CPC:** I think a bit more clarification would help on how this book is relevant to students, researchers, and teachers of L2 writing.
>
> **CPC:** State audience and context here. Who is the book primarily aimed for? Novice teachers? People in MA programs and in training?
>
> **YL:** Pls make this context clear from the early part of the review!

In other words, a perceptive and experienced reviewer will know what the audience in a field is interested in and needs and will comment in a prominent place in the review on how well a book meets, or does not meet, those needs.

In conjunction with comments that clarify the audience and context, a well-written book review will situate the book being reviewed within discussions taking place in the larger field. For example, Yongyan asked a reviewer, "So in what ways does this book contribute to the wider discussions?" Without such connections, the book review will stand alone as an uncontextualized commentary.

## Asking Reviewers to Clarify Points, Language, and Voice

Many of our comments to book reviewers concerned clarity of points, language, and voice—some of the hallmarks of good writing in book reviews as in other kinds of academic writing. As a relatively short piece of writing, a book review needs to be easy to follow and to express points clearly and succinctly without making readers struggle to search for or parse meanings. In particular, we sometimes asked reviewers to adjust language or syntax so as to clarify logic in long or convoluted sentences or to make sure that the topic or point of a book was clearly stated. Both of these kinds of clarifications seem basic to good academic writing:

> **CPC:** What does "which" refer to?
> **CPC:** I did not understand this sentence. Can you just delete it?
> **YL:** I also find it hard to understand.
> **YL:** Change "<u>rather simplified</u>" to "highly accessible"?
> **CPC:** Yes, good idea.
> **CPC:** Maybe be much clearer about this? I was not sure what this phrase meant.
> **CPC:** I wonder if there is any way to adjust this first paragraph so that it starts out with a clearer statement about the topic of this particular book.

Further, as often happens in academic writing, reviewers use comparative linguistic structures in a variety of ways. However, we found that sometimes when a comparative word or phrase was used, no clear comparison was made: "more" what? "greater" what? In such cases, we asked what was being compared.

Another kind of clarity at the level of language concerns clarity of terminology and language use—essential for good writing in a book review. Reviewers will understandably pick up pertinent terminology (field-, discipline-, and topic-specific words and phrases) from a book they are reviewing but might use it without defining it for readers who are not specialists in a field. They might even use their own specialized terminology to describe, analyze, or critique a book, again without defining terms, which to them have become second nature. In looking through our comments to reviewers, we found many instances in which we asked reviewers to clarify terms for readers who might be unfamiliar with them. Such clarification of specialized uses of language seems to us to be a hallmark of good writing in academic book reviews:

> **CPC:** I have been a bit confused about the term "graduate communication" (as opposed to, say, graduate education).
>
> **YL:** It may be better to define briefly what is meant by "curricular issues" with reference to the scope covered in the book.

We also asked reviewers to clarify how they were using nonspecialist words and phrases in their reviews:

> **YL:** Can you indicate "controversial" in what sense?
>
> **CPC:** Methods (as in techniques) or methodologies (theories and assumptions underlying methods)? Please distinguish.
>
> **YL:** So the meaning of this part of the sentence is not clear to me.
>
> **CPC:** I, too, could not figure out what this long commentary was about. Cut, or cut way back.

We often asked for clarifications of other kinds, too. For example, a well-written book review will specify whose views are being presented—those of the reviewer or of the book author and cited works. For example:

> **YL:** The book reviewer needs to distinguish between the views in the book, her own view, and the citations more clearly.
>
> **CPC:** Here, too, I am losing track of whose voice these statements are in. Distinguish the author's view carefully from your own commentary.
>
> **YL:** Pls make it clear if this is your view or Zhang's view of the contribution of his study.
>
> **YL:** Is this a point made by Zhao or is this your view?

We also asked reviewers to avoid or spell out all but the most widely used abbreviations, acronyms, and initials, again in the interest of clarity and readability for readers outside narrow and specialist subfields. We felt that initialisms such as L2, ESL, EFL, EAP, and the acronym TESOL did not need to be spelled out, but we actually overlooked a few of these that in retrospect I wish we had asked the author to clarify (". . . conferences such as WRAB, AAAL, AILA, PRISEAL"; Burgess, 2018). This aspect of good writing in book reviews constitutes a courtesy to readers.

In general, such basic clarifications can be conveyed in a writing style that is clear but routine and standard or in a style that is more elegant and engaging. The writing style will thus help distinguish a competent book review from one that we might consider well or engagingly written. Good writing in book reviews, as we state in our epigraph, is "competent writing + [plus]" (Yongyan Li, personal communication, August 8, 2020).

This goal of clarity does not mean that reviewers should avoid flair and pizzazz. It just means that they need to consider what their readers know and don't know about a specialized topic and associated terminology and then what they can learn about that topic from the book being reviewed. It is fine for reviewers to display erudition in a book review but not to needlessly obfuscate.

## Asking Reviewers to Add Details and Examples

Clear academic writing inevitably includes details and examples that make concrete any points that the author wishes to make. Good writing in book reviews is no different. Specific details from the book being reviewed will give readers a concrete idea of what a book is about as well as its style:

> **CPC:** I think readers will appreciate more detail here and in the next paragraph on the content of these chapters. . . . I was having trouble picturing the book.
>
> **CPC:** Both YL and I hope you can be more specific, e.g., "Issues such as . . . can also be. . . ." Also, the relevance or not, to non-U.S. contexts and readers will be important to discuss in a bit more detail.
>
> **YL:** Again, I wonder what kinds of research-based findings are presented in relation to what issues. Can an example or two be provided for an illustration?
>
> **CPC:** In general, we both feel you can be more concrete in the commentary section, including a specific evaluation as to how well you think this book applies to EFL (non-U.S.) contexts.

In sum, in a short piece of writing like a book review, clarity of many kinds seems fundamental to good writing. Clarity can efficiently and engagingly provide readers with the information they need to update their knowledge on recent topics in a field and to decide whether to read the book being reviewed themselves. Although clarity seems central to good writing in book reviews, several other aspects of good writing in book reviews are revealed in our comments to reviewers' drafts. We briefly comment on two of those—balance and personal experience—in the remainder of this chapter.

## Asking Reviewers to Balance their Reviews

A basic characteristic of good writing is that it is organized and balanced in a way that makes sense to readers of a particular genre. Although book reviews are often conventionally structured, as we have already mentioned, the placement, organization, and balance of paragraphs in a review need to work together as a whole as well as individually:

> **CPC:** This paragraph seems out of place here. Place at the end somewhere?
> **CPC:** Divide this long paragraph into at least 2.

Likewise, the description of chapters in a book being reviewed might be presented by reviewers in the order in which they appear in the book (this is conventional) or in a less conventional, more thematic, and potentially more interesting way. In either case, the description of chapters needs to be sensibly organized, even if reviewers choose not to describe each one:

> **YL:** I believe the description of the chapters needs to be presented in a better organized way.

Our comments to reviewers on restructuring their drafts asked them to balance the summaries and commentary differently:

> **YL:** If you condense the chapter summaries somewhat, you may expand on what the authors suggested regarding future research.
> **CPC:** The review is a good first draft, but long on summary and short on discussion and on links to related work. See if you can adjust the balance a bit in a second draft.
> **CPC:** I think the previous sentences can be pruned way back. Include only what is essential for readers to know.

Likewise, we paid attention to the balance of different kinds of comments, such as praise, criticism, and personal commentary. All book reviews routinely display both praise and criticism of a book, often in a predictably structured way, as already noted. The balance of praise and criticism might shift, depending on the reviewer's take on the book, but both are routinely included (praise, then criticism, then ending with praise). Here, too, praise and criticism can be written in a competent but routine way or in a way that displays what we are calling "good writing"—language and phrasing that show a reviewer's facility with language and appreciation of how words and sentences sound and how they fit together.

## Asking Reviewers to Discuss their Personal Experience in Relation to a Book

One of the features of good academic writing that we espouse in this book on good writing in TESOL and applied linguistics is a clear link between a piece of writing and the author of that writing. In the case of book reviews, Yongyan and I hoped that reviewers would avoid vacuous if common passive structures such as "It should be noted that. . ." and instead front their authority as reviewers: "I should note that. . . ." Overuse of hedging, too, can weaken a reviewer's authority, just as assertions that are made too strongly can overstate that authority. Such statements, weak or strong, tell us something about the reviewer, whose identity, as in all academic writing, is revealed or constructed in the discourse (Hyland, 2012).

In other words, in a well-written book review, we learn something not just about a book being reviewed but also about the reviewer—a human being who is writing about something written by another human being. Who is the reviewer? Why is the reviewer interested in a particular book—its topics, author, style? What is it about the book that sparked a reviewer's intellectual and emotional responses? How does the reviewer use or plan to use that book in teaching or professional development, or did the reviewer read the book for pure pleasure? And how can the content and evaluative comments of the book review be conveyed in an engaging style of writing?

For example, in going through our collection of email correspondence with reviewers we found cases where we responded to a traditional impersonal first draft with requests to make the draft more personal by using the first person rather than the passive voice. We also commented positively on reviews that had a personal flavor and requested that reviewers connect a book to themselves personally:

> **YL:** I like this personal note. I believe many writing teachers will echo this.
>
> **YL:** It would also be useful for readers if you could include a discussion that perhaps first comments on how you, or colleagues, have used this text with your own students and if it worked for you.

In short, we encouraged authors to write book reviews that were clear at many levels; were balanced in praise, criticism, and commentary; and included personal connections that reviewers had with the book they were reviewing.

## To Conclude

In an email to me, Yongyan wrote that "to what extent one can produce 'good writing' in this [book review] context perhaps depends on many factors: talent, expertise, experience, motivation, time, mood/the right mentality, etc." (personal communication, August 7, 2020). For our purposes, we hoped that reviewers with such talents, expertise, and motivation would be interested in contributing book reviews to the journal, even though the book review is a humble and probably underappreciated genre that does little to further the careers of either novice or established scholars. However, it is precisely because established scholars don't need to further their careers that they are in an ideal position to use their talents and creativity to go beyond the perfunctory genre that is designed only to give basic information about books in a field. They can invest their talents as readers, writers, and thinkers to explore and innovate in their reviews and to draw readers into interesting discussions inspired by a book.

As some published examples demonstrate (e.g., Edwards, 2020; Hedgcock, 2019; Hirvela, 2016; Vandrick, 2018), in the hands of an experienced scholar the book review genre has the potential to add substance, interest, and personal connection to a disciplinary field. It can go beyond examining a book's linguistic and rhetorical features (see the several language-oriented chapters on reviews in Hyland and Diani, 2009) and beyond an uncontextualized treatment of a book's content. Coming from an accomplished writer, a well-written book review not only provides summaries and critiques of books but also serves as a model of good academic writing, displays perceptive and creative thinking, and conveys personal responses and connections to a field and to related work. For this reason, book reviewing probably should not be used primarily as exercises in publication for novice scholars, who lack the experience to approach a review from all these perspectives. We believe that book reviews are best done by "experienced teachers-researchers-writers in a field" (Yongyan Li, personal communication, August 8, 2020). Of course, some reviews by graduate students are nonetheless quite good, managing to break with the stereotypical form even if lacking the personal-experiential connections (see, for example, PhD student Fawzia Mazanderani's 2017 blog review of Helen Sword's book *Air & Light & Time & Space: How Successful Academics Write*).

In other words, with some exceptions, it is usually the experienced and well-read scholar who is in a position to write a meaningful review and to model good writing or to help graduate students write such a review. Such a reviewer situates a discussion of a book within relevant issues and literature in a field and includes the reviewer's personal connections to those issues and literature. A good book review, in other words, is more like a well-crafted essay with both a purpose and a point of view than a summary and critique of a single text. It critically evaluates not just the book itself but also the issues brought up in the book and links them to other literature, to readers, and to the reviewer's own experience as well. It does this in a way that not only makes readers want to read the book being reviewed but also makes them want to read the review itself carefully, from start to finish. And the really good book review is a model of good writing. It makes readers say to themselves: "I want to read this book being reviewed, but I also want to be able to write the way this review is written."

## Afterthought

It occurred to me after I finished the draft of this chapter that there might indeed be an important purpose for a routine, boring book review: It could be a great soporific for stressed-out academics with insomnia. . . .

## References

Billig, M. (2013). *Learn to write badly: How to succeed in the social sciences.* Cambridge University Press.

Brienza, C. (2014). Why you (yes you!) should write book reviews. *Inside Higher Education*, December 5.

Brienza, C. (2015). Writing academic book reviews. *Inside Higher Education*, March 27.

Burgess, S. (2018). Review of the book *Global academic publishing: Policies perspectives and pedagogies*, edited by M. J. Curry & T. Lillis. *Journal of Second Language Writing, 41*, 74–76.

Caulley, D. N. (2008). Making qualitative research reports less boring: The techniques of writing creative nonfiction. *Qualitative Inquiry, 14*(3), 424–449.

Diani, G. (2009). Reporting and evaluation in English book review articles: A cross-disciplinary study. In K. Hyland & G. Diani (Eds.), *Academic evaluation: Review genres in university settings* (pp. 87–104). Palgrave Macmillan.

Edwards, T. (2020). Review of the book *Academic writing and identity construction: Performativity, space, and territory in academic workplaces*, edited by L. M. Thomas & A. B. Reinertsen. *Journal of English for Academic Purposes, 43*, 100806.

Groom, N. (2009). Phraseology and epistemology in academic book reviews: A corpus-driven analysis of two humanities disciplines. In K. Hyland & G. Diani (Eds.), *Academic evaluation: Review genres in university settings* (pp. 122–139). Palgrave Macmillan.

Hatcher, T., & McDonald, K. S. (2011). Creating and publishing nonrefereed manuscripts: How to write editorials and book reviews. In T. S. Rocco, T. Hatcher, & J. W. Creswell (Eds.), *The handbook of scholarly writing and publishing* (pp. 222–235). Jossey-Bass/Wiley.

Hedgcock, J. S. (2019). Review of the book *The discourse of peer review: Reviewing submissions to academic journals*, by Brian Paltridge. *Journal of Second Language Writing, 43*, 88–90.

Hirvela, A. (2016). Review of the book *Teaching and researching writing* (3rd ed.), by Ken Hyland. *Journal of Second Language Writing, 33*, 1–2.

Hyland, K. (2000/2004). *Disciplinary discourses: Social interactions in academic writing.* University of Michigan Press.

Hyland, K. (2012). *Disciplinary identities: Individuality and community in academic discourse.* Cambridge University Press.

Hyland, K., & Diani, G. (Eds.). (2009). *Academic evaluation: Review genres in university settings.* Palgrave Macmillan.

Lewis, M. N. (2020). Here's a good book: Hints on writing a book review for academic journals. *RELC Journal, 53(1)*, 1–8.

Mazanderani, F. H. (2017). Review of the book *Air & light & time & space: How successful academics write*, by Helen Sword. https://blogs.lse.ac.uk/lsereviewofbooks/2017/06/16/book-review-air-light-time-space-how-successful-academics-write-by-helen-sword/

Moreno, A. I. & Suárez, L. (2009). Academic book reviews in English and Spanish: Critical comments and rhetorical structure. In K. Hyland & G. Diani (Eds.), *Academic evaluation: Review genres in university settings* (pp. 161–178). Palgrave Macmillan.

Nodoushan, M. A. S., & Montazeran, H. (2012). The book review genre: A structural move analysis. *International Journal of Language Studies, 6*, 1–30.

Pinker, S. (2014). Why academics stink at writing. *The Chronicle of Higher Education.* September 26. http://chronicle.com/article/Why-Academics-Writing-Stinks/148989/

Swales, J. M. (1990). *Genre analysis: English in academic and research settings.* Cambridge University Press.

Sword, H. (2009). Writing higher education differently: A manifesto on style. *Studies in Higher Education, 34*(3), 319–336.

Sword, H. (2012). *Stylish academic writing.* Harvard University Press.

Sword, H. (2017). *Air & light & time & space: How successful academics write.* Harvard University Press.

USC Libraries Research Guides. (2020). Writing academic book reviews. https://libguides.usc.edu/c.php?g=235208&p=1560694.

Vandrick, S. (2018). Review of the book *Second language creative writers: Identities and writing processes,* by Yan Zhao. *Journal of Second Language Writing, 40*, 84–86.

Williams, J. M., & Bizup, J. (2015). *Style: The basics of clarity and grace* (11th ed.). Pearson Education.

Warchal, K. (2019). Humour in professional academic writing. *Theory and Practice of Second Language Acquisition, 5*(1), 43–54. https://doi/10.31261/TAPSLA.2019.05.03

Zinsser, W. (2006). *On writing well: The classic guide to writing nonfiction* (30th Anniversary Edition). HarperCollins.

# Part III

# Personal Perspectives

# Chapter 11

# I'm a Good Writer, but I'm Boring

*Melinda Reichelt*

I'm a good writer, but I'm boring. My writing doesn't have panache, but it's informative. Getting started is hard, so I usually rely on tried-and-true templates and safe strategies, like using straightforward sentences, basic vocabulary, and traditional organizational schemes. This helps me get started and work quickly. I aim for a concise, accessible style. You know the spiel: introduction, review of literature, blah, blah, blah. Just get it written and over with, then revise for clarity. I haven't savored the creative process, nor aimed for beauty. Until recently, I hadn't thought much about making my writing *interesting*—because, frankly, I don't usually find the writing in our field creative, beautiful, or interesting. It just communicates.

But now I'm at a career point where I can publish more slowly, lingering on the labor of writing. And as I draft this piece during the quaronavirus (quarantine + Corona + virus) crisis, writing is providing me with a constructive enterprise. I'm lucky: My loved ones and I have remained healthy so far, and my spouse and I are still employed. I'm troubled only by minor annoyances, such as not seeing friends in person, missing out on professional conferences, having to forgo our usual summer camping and holiday travel to visit loved ones, and having to teach online. (Okay, that last annoyance is beyond "minor.") Writing adds variety to the other Coronahobbies I'm cycling through, like exercising in an effort to offset the delicious sourdough bread and macarons my daughter keeps baking, doomscrolling through the news on my phone, trying to achieve inner peace through yoga, and watching movies that appeal to my family. (I'm beginning to seriously question their taste in film.) Writing is a respite, time I can spend alone in a full house, with a reason to bar everyone from my workspace and take extra pleasure in my endeavors.

Writing has always been pleasurable for me because I think I'm decent at it and because getting words on the page, another page written, and another piece submitted each provides a sense of accomplishment. So *I* enjoy writing, but is my writing enjoyable for readers? Is it good writing? Maybe I should be less selfish and try to make my work not only a nice experience for me but entertaining, provocative, and compelling for others. In the last year or so, I've started to wonder whether I can go beyond utilitarian goals and give readers a more stimulating experience. Recently, in attempts at making various pieces of writing less lifeless, I've included an attention-getting anecdote, revealed my values, disclosed a professional weakness, and even tried humor. I've also experimented with other methods of keeping my readers awake: making dazzling word choices (and sometimes even including a little alliteration, but without creating purple prose); being more personal, hopefully without seeming self-absorbed; and adding asides. In this chapter, I write about my attempts to be less dreary. I also describe the worries that have kept me from taking risks that might have jazzed my writing up. And I explore how this urge to become a livelier writer makes me question how I teach writing, including ESL writing. Should I try to help students write with flair? Or should I teach them to play it safe, given their status as students and as novice writers, often of a second language? What will help them the most to become "good writers"?

## Recent Attempts at Being Less Lackluster

### Sarcasm, Singular "They," and a Sabbatical Proposal

Around a year ago, I wrote a sabbatical proposal about singular *they*. In it, I explored the use of singular *they* in sentences like *Someone left their coat in the room, and I hope they come to get it*; I described prescriptive attempts to eliminate the use of singular *they*; and I described more recent usages of singular *they* (and some new pronouns) to refer to people who are not gender-binary. I knew that I needed to make readers take me and my project seriously, but I also wanted to stand out, so I took some risks. I included a personal anecdote, one that identified me as a mother— which in academia is not always a terribly strategic move. The anecdote alluded to mammary glands, which could make readers uncomfortable.

And although I worried that my readers might interpret me as being flip, I tried to be funny when I commented on the anecdote (see the phrase I've now bolded in the excerpt below):

> Besides these uses of singular *they* [outlined in preceding paragraphs], I have also noticed an additional use of the pronoun *they*, one that surprised me when I first saw it. In 2008, I read the following sentence, included in a bulletin-board note posted at my child's daycare:
>
> 9. *If a breastfeeding mother wants to feed their child, they can use the teacher's lounge.*
>
> Since *mother* is singular, I was taken aback that the singular, feminine pronoun *she* was not employed, **since all the breastfeeding mothers I had encountered had been female**. I surmised that *their* and *they* were used in example 9 because the mother in question was any general mother, not a specific mother. (Although the daycare was quite progressive, I am certain this use of singular *their/they* was not intended to be gender-inclusive or respectful of the pronouns of mothers who are not gender-conforming.)

My sabbatical proposal was successful, but I don't know if it was in part because of the personal anecdote and cheeky tone I aimed for in this passage. Other than a long series of endorsement signatures, I didn't get any feedback except that my chair told me she thought my topic was very interesting and she hoped that I would eventually share my research with the university community. Because of my success, I was emboldened and decided to write more personally, perhaps even glibly, in the future. I think doing so will help me become a better, less boring writer.

## P-stranding, Matrix Complementizers, Prosodic Asymmetries, and ESL Writing

Recently, I've been finishing up a chapter called "Linguistic Bias against ESL Writing?" (Reichelt, 2021). The chapter is to be included in a volume about linguistic bias on the U.S. university campus. It's based on a presentation I gave as part of a panel at the Annual Meeting of the Linguistic Society of America (LSA) (Reichelt, 2019).

When I drafted the chapter, I avoided writing about my teaching experiences because I didn't want to seem self-absorbed or reliant on anecdotal evidence. Good writers supposedly aren't self-absorbed, nor do they rely on anecdotes, right? Later, I realized that I'd made a mistake with the approach I'd taken. At the time, though, I thought I could make the piece lively simply by choosing and using snazzy vocabulary. For example, I explained that in the United States, the field of second language writing had "coalesced" particularly around the *Journal of Second Language Writing* and the Symposium on Second Language Writing. I wrote that Truscott (1996) had "decried" the widespread but unexamined practice of error correction, thus creating a "flurry" of research about written corrective feedback. Regarding the much-discussed notion of translingualism (see Atkinson & Tardy, 2018; Canagarajah, 2015; Casanave, 2017; Gevers, 2018; Horner, NeCamp, & Donahue, 2011; Matsuda, 2014), I wrote the following: "Despite questions about the nuts and bolts of implementing a translingual pedagogy, the notion of translingualism in L2 writing provides a strongly contrasting viewpoint to the focus on error correction" (Reichelt, 2021). This sentence garnered a "Love it" comment in the margin from one of the editors, one of very few specific positive comments. I'm not sure if they were simply agreeing with the sentiment, but I have to think that the phrase "nuts and bolts" had something to do with this response. I firmly believe that part of good writing is using first-rate (but not necessarily formal) vocabulary.

As I was about to submit a final draft of the chapter, I read it through once more, this time to see if I could do anything more to add some pep. In my re-reading, I realized the chapter was bland despite my sparkling word choices. As an aside: Reading through the draft with an eye toward the liveliness of the piece reminded me of an experience several years ago, when co-authoring a piece entitled " 'A Table and Two Chairs': Starting a Writing Center in Łódź, Poland" (Reichelt et al., 2013). I was impressed and inspired by my seven co-authors' use of narrative and vivid vocabulary. I especially appreciated the creativity, humor, and use of dialogue in the introduction, written by Łukasz Salski. Reading my co-authors' work, I realized my talents lay in the area of handling the logistics of a paper co-authored by eight people rather than in writing with spirit. In that piece, my co-authors were good writers, but I was boring. I'm trying to change.

So back to the linguistic bias chapter. I decided I wanted to enliven the piece. But I had reservations. I was writing for an audience of linguists who present at the LSA on topics like P-stranding, matrix complementizers, and prosodic asymmetries. Serious stuff, and serious people, ones who might question the credibility of an applied linguist writing about lowly pedagogical issues. If there were ever a time not to be myself, this was it. Based on the audience I had conjured for myself and on my perception of what their perception of me might be, I felt pressure to achieve credibility by maintaining a distanced, objective, scholarly tone. I thought I was employing features of good writing, but I was just being defensive. And my writing had suffered for it.

So in my eleventh-hour revision, I began by making a change in the first paragraph. I had originally used stuffy phrases like "this chapter reviews the literature on. . ." and "this chapter also explores. . ." and "Finally, this chapter provides suggestions for. . . ." To add energy, instead of having the chapter doing these things, "I" did them. This set the stage for me to pop up as a character throughout the chapter. I added eight short passages about my teaching and administrative roles at my university; my opinion about protocols suggested in the L2 writing literature for treating error; conversations I've had with ESL students about their NES peers' treatment of them; and my teaching practices, including those related to peer review and grading ESL student papers. After making these changes, I read the resulting revision. The additions didn't make me look weaker; they demonstrated confidence that my opinions mattered, as they should, given my more than thirty years of teaching experience. These personal asides will probably be useful for readers who are not ESL writing specialists. I hope my revisions invigorated the piece and made it more informative.

## Teaching Writing: Risky Behavior, Gamification, and Soliloquies of Joy?

My attempts to make my writing livelier will likely make it better. So I wonder: Besides trying to add dash to my own writing, should I try to teach students in my courses (in a U.S. university) to be better writers by writing with flair? This would mean encouraging them to take more risks. As a tenured full professor with a decent publication record, I can afford to take risks. But they are novice writers, and some are non-native English speakers to boot. Can they afford such gambles?

I asked a novice (native-English-speaking), almost-college-age writer in my household if she would want to be taught to undertake academic writing with flair and if she thought I should teach my students to write with flair. With a very serious face, she replied, "No." I asked why not, and she told me that writing with flair could undermine their credibility. They could be seen as not being objective and as using "loaded" language. Writing with flair was for *creative* writing, she said. She didn't seem to think that good academic writing should be written with élan.

She has done a good job of absorbing her teachers' lessons about academic writing. And student writers certainly need to understand that they must establish credibility with readers. But can students include lively lexis, perhaps even wordplay, humor, and/or discussion of their personal experiences, values, and attitudes without undermining their credibility—even as novice writers? I wonder. What would happen if I encouraged my students in this direction? Would I get some weird writing? Maybe. Might that writing be more interesting than the usual fare from my students? No doubt. I know some instructors might object to teaching students to write with flair, especially if they think it will have negative consequences for students. This could be especially salient for graduate student writers, whose committee members might look unfavorably upon experimentation, or for students pursuing publication, who could be penalized if their work doesn't conform to the traditional (usually boring) expectations of academic writing. If I were teaching those writers, I might be reluctant to ask them to take risks. Although I would discuss with them the possible consequences of experimentation, I might still encourage them to push the envelope a bit—if they wanted to. I would definitely ask them what they saw as the definition of "good writing."

But I'm considering this in terms of the master's students, upper-level undergrads, and first-year ESL students I teach. Should I encourage them to try some of the following suggestions for making your writing better, inspired by Sword (2012) and Zinsser (2006)?

1. Use "I"—and maybe even "you."

2. Write interesting, perhaps even funny titles, headings, and subheadings.

3. Write an attention-getting first sentence and a memorable last sentence.

4. Tell a relevant story, maybe one about yourself.

5. Draw in something you've read or know about that at first may seem unrelated to your topic, then relate it to your topic.

6.  Present your own experience, values, or attitude toward your topic.

7.  Be funny.

8.  Do something that makes the writing fun for you; your enjoyment will probably come through to the reader.

9.  Be yourself; as Zinsser (2006) writes, let your writing convey "humanity and warmth" (p. 5).

10. Experiment with word choice. You might get it wrong, but that's okay! Have fun looking for just the right word.

I could ask students to take at least one risk in each piece of writing and to identify it to their classmates during peer review and to me when they submit their work. I might assign extra credit for risk-taking, awarding a small number of points for risky behavior in and of itself, and more points when the riskiness results in effective writing. Of course, I wouldn't have to be the sole arbiter. Class members could be involved in the process. We could even have a silly awards ceremony at the end of the semester. Such gamification of writing would probably enhance students' motivation and interest in the class and help them understand that they have power as writers to resist genre conventions, even as they learn about them. I would, of course, weave in conversations with them about audiences and the possible consequences of risky writing. I would hope all this would help them become better writers.

As a modest test run of these ideas, I recently gave the above list of ten ways to make writing more interesting to students in my course "Issues in ESL Writing." Most of the students are pursuing a master's in English with a concentration in writing studies, and this course is required for them. I asked students to use the list when writing a two-page introduction to their final project, an annotated bibliography about a topic within L2 writing. I was entertained by the outcome. Their introductions were more engaging than those of previous cohorts, mostly because they connected their own encounters with writing (and teaching writing) to information in their annotated bibliographies. Everyone used "I" and wrote about their experiences and attitudes. Out of six students, three were brave enough to use "you"—but one avoided it by using "one" where "you" would have worked well. Old habits (and admonitions) die hard.

A few students included stories (all students' names are used with permission). Rin Baatz wrote about the impact of COVID-19 on her job as a writing center consultant. She had to move from in-person to online tutoring, which caused her anxiety about her ability to help ESL students without a whiteboard, props, or the opportunity to "decipher students' facial expressions and body language" (since most students kept their computer's camera off during the tutorials). Rin explained how her research and experience over time helped her become more confident about working with ESL students online.

I think my students worked extra hard at finding all-star vocabulary in order to make their writing better. Some of my favorite words and phrases were *dizzying* (Rin Baatz's description of the multitudinous approaches to online tutoring), *guttural sigh* (the response given by Angelica Leeds to the mere mention of peer review when she was in high school and college) and *fawning* as well as *abyss of their backpack* (see Ryan Feroni's introduction below). I also liked student Layne Polen's *persuasive prose*, probably because I admire alliteration, and Scott Peterson's *unlocking the literacy*, which likewise seems a little alliterative to me.

In 1954, American psychiatrist Fredric Wertham published a book called *Seduction of the Innocent*. Scott Peterson referenced this book in his introduction, even though at first it seemed unrelated to his annotated bibliography topic, using comic books in the ESL writing classroom. It turns out that in the book, Wertham claimed that reading comic books leads to juvenile delinquency. Scott explains that Wertham's work "created a stigma around the industry that still stands today" and that this may be why teachers have been reluctant to use comics in their classrooms. Scott was the only student who attempted to follow piece of advice #5, which suggests students draw in something that may at first seem unrelated to their topic.

Students weren't very good at writing interesting first and last sentences, and no one used a funny heading, much to my disappointment. But a few of them used humor. For example, Layne Polen wrote the following about overcoming the difficulty of writing:

> "Simple solution," you may be saying, though probably not—"just stick to your native language if you're writing." And though that sounds like a nice, lazy plan, if you want to maximize your ability to share your writing with others, you have to consider that it will be most accessible if it is published in English.

I liked Layne's cheeky tone.

Some of the humor was self-deprecating, as in Ryan Feroni's work, below. Another student, Angelica Leeds, used self-deprecating humor in a story of her "love-hate relationship" with peer review. Angelica wrote that she'd had mostly bad experiences with it in high school and college, and then wrote of her experiences teaching Composition I and II as a TA: "Although I have long questioned the effectiveness of peer review," she writes, "I implemented it in my classroom because it's the norm and what we are 'supposed' to do it (terrible rationale—I know.)" I thought this was not only honest but also funny, especially coming from someone I see as a top-notch student and teacher.

I was particularly fond of one of the introductions, written by Ryan Feroni. The first three of its four paragraphs are reproduced below. When Ryan emailed me to grant me permission to use his work, he wrote that he had reviewed the list of suggestions I gave the class before drafting his introduction. "Holistically," he wrote, "they all suggested to me that I should write something using my personality and voice." And he sure did:

*For as long as I've been in school, I've received written feedback from teachers on assignments I've turned in. And despite my awful handwriting (I'm left-handed, which apparently explains it), the only teacher to write a comment about having a hard time reading my writing was my Algebra teacher in High School. Everyone that has been in school has received written feedback from teachers on assignments, but most of us look right through the written feedback and zero in on the grade. This essentially renders the written teacher feedback meaningless, as students have been trained by parents and institutions that grades are the only thing of value. Maybe it was the conceited and arrogant part of me, but I always enjoyed reading the notes of praise that teachers wrote on my assignments. I guess that's because I've always been such a model student.*

*For most English classes I have taken in my life (both in High School and college), teacher feedback has been somewhat similar. You turn in a paper or assignment, the teacher reads through it and marks it up (which I have discovered is called "corrective feedback"), and then the teacher would write a few sentences at the end of the paper regarding their thoughts on your writing. Oh, and how could I forget—the grade was almost always written on the front page and circled in colored pen. As I mentioned, I would always read through the teacher comments regardless of the grade. I loved English, and even more so, I loved my teachers fawning over my writing. But I came to realize that for most other students, they would take a quick look at the grade on the first page and shove the paper into the abyss of their backpack without ever reading what the teacher had to say about their writing.*

*The first time I had an instructor who strayed from this norm was at the University of Michigan-Dearborn. We would submit hard copies of papers, and our teacher, Dr. B., would grade them. However, he refused to write the grade on the papers. Papers would still be marked up and contain comments in the margin, but the only way he allowed you to discover your grade was to listen to an MP3 file he recorded and posted to Canvas (similar to Blackboard, but a million times better). In the MP3 file, Dr. B. would discuss his thoughts on your paper for 2–3 minutes, and finally reveal the grade at the end of the clip. I came to love this method of giving feedback, as it ultimately felt much more personal hearing my professor's voice in discussing my work.*

I appreciated Ryan's humor, his relaxed, warm tone, and his personal examples. I was intrigued by his sentence "I guess that's because I've always been such a model student." I actually do think he's a model student, but he's also humble. Ryan told me that this sentence was meant to be sarcastic.

I had fun reading all my students' introductions, and I hope they had fun writing them. Their writing definitely conveyed "humanity and warmth" (Zinsser, 2006, p. 5). Reading (and grading) their work became a much more meaningful experience because I felt more connected to each student author. This made the overwhelming task of end-of-semester grading much more endurable—even pleasurable. After I read the first annotated bibliography, complete with lively introduction, I began to see grading these assignments as a treat. I doled out the annotated bibliographies to myself one by one, each a little reward for myself after I'd graded five papers from another class. I concluded that when students took up one or more of the ten suggestions I'd offered them for making their writing better, it led to better writing. I can't wait to encourage students in my future classes to take risks and make their writing more engaging.

If writers can connect with their readers by being personal, maybe I should get a little more personal with my students as a way of helping them become better writers. I frequently talk to them about my experiences as an L2 learner and L2 writer. (I've studied German, Spanish, French, Sanskrit, and Greek formally, and I've dabbled in Polish, Portuguese, Chinese, Ukrainian, Bulgarian, Māori, Italian, and Swedish for fun and travel purposes, with various levels of communicative success.) But I never talk to them about my writing joy. Should I tell them that when I write, I feel a sense of accomplishment and pride, especially when I rework a passage until it actually works or when I nail it with just the right word choice? That I feel more centered when I'm writing than when I'm doing just about anything else? Maybe I could be one of those *inspiring* teachers they make movies about, instead of just practical ol' Dr. Reichelt, who dutifully helps them plod along through the tedious steps of writing their final research project. But would waxing on about my joy actually improve their writing, or would it just be self-indulgent? Would it encourage them as writers, or would it put more distance between us: me, the experienced, native-English-speaking lover of writing, and them, the novice readers of writing, who are, in some cases, L2 writers? Would it help them become good writers? I don't know. I'll have to think about this more and talk to colleagues about it. Maybe we can all think about this. I might start by asking my students mid-semester, after they've been taking some risks and writing weirdly, whether they're experiencing any writing joy.

## A Concise Conclusion, Related by the Author Herself, Consisting of an Attempt (by Means of Entreaty) to Convince the Reader to Be Less Boring in Their Own Writing, to Which Is Added a Sincere and Heartfelt Promise from the Author to Do Likewise

I end with a plea: If you are a writer of academic articles, books, or book chapters that I might read, please up your game and try to be less boring. I promise to do the same.

## References

Atkinson, D., & Tardy, C. (2018). Disciplinary dialogues: SLW at the crossroads: Finding a way in the field. *Journal of Second Language Writing, 42,* 86–93. https://doi.org/10.1016/j.jslw.2018.10.011

Canagarajah, A. S. (2015). Clarifying the relationship between translingual practice and L2 writing: Addressing learner identities. *Applied Linguistics Review, 6*(4), 415–440. https://doi.org/10.1515/applirev-2015-0020

Casanave, C. P. (2017). *Controversies in second language writing: Dilemmas and decisions in research and instruction* (2nd ed.). University of Michigan Press.

Gevers, J. (2018). Translingualism revisited: Language difference and hybridity in L2 writing. *Journal of Second Language Writing, 40,* 73–83. https://doi.org/10.1016/j.jslw.2018.04.003

Horner, B., NeCamp, S., & Donahue, C. (2011). Toward a multilingual composition scholarship: From English only to a translingual norm. *College Composition and Communication, 63,* 269–300. https://www.jstor.org/stable/25790477

Matsuda, P. K. (2014). The lure of translingual writing. *PMLA, 129,* 478–483. https://doi.org/10.1632/pmla.2014.129.3.478

Reichelt, M. (2019, January 3). Dialect bias in feedback on L2 writing. In G. Clements (Chair), Linguistic discrimination on the University Campus. Panel Presentation at the Linguistics Society of America, New York.

Reichelt, M. (2021). Linguistic bias against ESL writing? In G. Clements & M. Petray (Eds.), *Linguistic discrimination in U.S. higher education: Power, prejudice, impacts, and remedies* (pp. 20–37). Routledge.

Reichelt, M., Salski, Ł., Andres, J., Lowczowski, E., Majchrzak, O., Molenda, M., Parr-Modrzejewska, A., Reddington, E., & Wiśniewska-Steciuk, E. (2013). "A table and two chairs": Starting a writing center in Łódź, Poland. *Journal of Second Language Writing, 3*(22), 277–285.

Sword, H. (2012). *Stylish academic writing.* Harvard University Press.

Truscott, J. (1996). The case against grammar correction in L2 writing classes. *Language Learning, 46*(2), 327–369. https://doi.org/10.1111/j.1467-1770.1996.tb01238.x

Wertham, F. (1954). *Seduction of the innocent.* Rinehart.

Zinsser, W. (2006). *On writing well: The classic guide to writing nonfiction.* Harper Perennial.

**Chapter 12**

# Taking an Insider's ELF Perspective on "Good" Academic Writing in a Global Context

*Selahattin Yilmaz and Diane Belcher*

## Introduction

Focusing primarily on the use of English in communicative settings where the majority involved are second language users of English from different linguistic and sociocultural backgrounds, English as a Lingua Franca (ELF) research has long advocated for the need to move away from monolingual native speaker norms that do not suffice to explain the complexities of how English is used internationally (Hynninen & Solin, 2017; Jenkins, 2017; Seidlhofer, 2021). Whereas the early ELF literature predominantly tackled issues regarding spoken language, the relatively recent expansion into the inquiry of writing has led to a proliferation of research efforts at the intersection of the two areas of research. Mauranen (2018), for instance, argues that "[i]t is the wish to communicate across boundaries that drives the use of lingua francas. For this we need to understand what good texts are like in a *global* context" (p. 5). Mauranen's call for such a global awareness acknowledges the reality of today's written scientific communication, which, as Turner (2018) observes, despite the myriad of regulating mechanisms in place, is constantly evolving to accommodate the diversity of global academic communities. The accumulating evidence from the analyses of English texts written by multilingual scholars is also in line with these claims, as the

**167**

findings point to a rather complex and varied discursive phenomenon influenced by numerous individual, social, and contextual factors (e.g., Carey, 2013; Lorés-Sanz, 2016; Martinez, 2018; Mauranen, 2012, 2018).

More recently, a globally informed ELF view of written academic communication is also echoed in discussions of pedagogy for second language learners and their teachers. Proponents of this perspective have increasingly promoted pedagogical practices that equip students with the knowledge and skills necessary to examine their views, appreciate the dynamism inherent in written academic English, and develop a critical understanding of the "good" textual practices for their own purposes and contexts (Horner, 2011, 2018; Jenkins, 2011; Solin & Hynninen, 2018; Yilmaz, 2021). These principles, of course, apply to all novice writers, no matter their first language, who are in the process of learning to write academically. It is plausible to suggest, however, that those writing in an additional language face added challenges due to the multilayered process of learning, evaluating, and appropriating local and global discursive practices to arrive at their own hybrid voice(s) (Canagarajah, 2013; Mauranen, Pérez-Llantada, & Swales, 2010). In support of such efforts, writing instructors play a crucial role in encouraging and facilitating students' investigations into their linguistic repertoires, literacy practices, and academic English in use.

In this chapter, we discuss the ELF perspective through email exchanges in which Diane interviews Selahattin in order to identify the dynamics that have contributed to the evolution of his views on "good" writing throughout his years of education and professional practice in two countries. To conduct the interview, Diane first sent a list of guiding questions to Selahattin, whose responses led Diane to ask follow-up questions. After several more rounds of emails, we decided that the interview had reached a natural end.

We consider our decision to do the interview via email rather than in person to have benefited us in several ways. The asynchronous email interview, as Hawkins (2018) argues, affords the participants "more control over their level of participation" (p. 494), which was certainly the case for this study. The flexibility to revisit and reflect on both the questions and answers helped us in constructing the narrative we wanted to present in this chapter "in [our] own space, at [our] own pace and at the time of [our] choosing" (James, 2016, p. 159).

Through Selahattin's reflections on the guiding questions, prepared by Diane in light of her own years as a teacher, researcher, and editor of L2 (and L1) writing, complex insights are brought to light into the dynamics that shape a second language user's views on "good" writing and the role ELF can play in conceptualizing English academic writing in a truly global context. The interview concludes by considering some implications of adopting an ELF perspective on providing support for, and continually rethinking, L2 academic writing, especially outside the so-called, and indeed still privileged, English-language "center" or "inner circle" (Kachru, 1985).

## Interview

**Diane:** *Did you grow up speaking Arabic and Turkish? I'm assuming all your early education was in Turkish, correct?*

**Selahattin:** Coming from a family of Alawite origin, I grew up in a Turkish-Arabic bilingual household. Older generations, including my parents, are generally fluent in both languages. However, in line with the Turkish-only ideologies in Turkey, Arabic is neither a commonly heard language in public life nor a language of instruction in schools. With Turkish becoming even more prevalent in the community, I was also not encouraged to speak Arabic. Thus, today I am a receptive bilingual; that is, my primary language is Turkish, and I am only able to understand the Arabic spoken in the community.

**D:** *How much writing in Turkish did you do in school, and how did you learn what "good" Turkish writing was? Through reading? For instance, were there exemplar or classic texts, examples of "beautiful" writing? Did you receive teacher feedback (maybe mainly in the form of grades)?*

**S:** I received a somewhat dedicated writing instruction first in secondary school, which involved writing short compositions on general statements such as famous proverbs. In high school, writing instruction involved exploring different genres through discussions and exemplar texts as part of the newly introduced Language and Expression (L&E) course. L&E was the outcome of the constructivist curricular change introduced by the Ministry of National Education (2005). In theory, it was a positive development as the focus of writing instruction shifted from the acquisition of knowledge to skills, and the textbooks aimed to encourage students to learn by doing. However, in my case, it seemed that my teachers were not comfortable with this newly adopted student-centered curriculum. In addition, the nationwide multiple-choice exams at the end of both middle and high school further decreased the already-scarce opportunities to practice writing. Throughout these years, I received feedback on my writing mainly in the form of grades. Occasionally, teachers left textual comments on structure, mechanics, and content.

When I think about my overall experience, I do not remember developing a clear understanding of what constituted "good" writing in Turkish. One particularly confusing experience I had was my teachers' mysterious and seemingly arbitrary search for literary quality in our writing, which was most evident in high school. Although this could be partly related to the exemplar texts in our books, the assumptions underlying my teachers' expectations were rather implicit and varied. The methods and learning outcomes of the writing instruction did not seem to be centered on these expectations, either.

**D:** *How did you feel about your own Turkish writing over the years, and how do you feel about it now?*

**S:** I generally felt that my Turkish writing skills were adequate for my needs. I use Turkish writing mainly for daily interactions such as text messaging and e-mail exchanges. Ever since I graduated from high school, I have not received any Turkish writing instruction, and I have generally been required to write in English for most of my educational and professional experiences, with two exceptions. One is the writing for assessment purposes in the several Turkish-medium undergraduate courses I took. The other is my more recent professional experience of writing abstracts and preparing slides for presentations. Although I remember the former as a relatively smooth experience, the latter has understandably been somewhat challenging, given my limited training and experience in Turkish academic writing. As a matter of fact, I have just purchased a dictionary of linguistic terms in Turkish, and I occasionally use corpora for help with certain expressions. I am still not expected to produce much Turkish writing as English is "the high language of academic communication and promotion" in Turkey (Doğançay-Aktuna & Kiziltepe, 2005, p. 258). However, I do wish I had better Turkish writing skills to handle the occasional Turkish writing tasks with ease.

**D:** *Has English affected how you view writing in Turkish?*

**S:** Due to my multifaceted involvement in English academic writing as a user, teacher, teacher trainer, and researcher, as well as not having ever developed a strong sense of Turkish writing, my view of academic writing in particular has become rather English-centric. Previous research reporting Turkish scholars' views on their English writing also documented similar findings (e.g., Buckingham, 2008; Uysal, 2008). In addition, with the undisputed role of English in both global and Turkish academic circles with which I am associated, I naturally do not feel the need to take immediate action to overcome my perceived challenges in Turkish academic writing.

**D:** *When did you start studying English and start writing in English?*

**S:** I started studying English when I was in the fourth grade. I had two lessons a week during which I remember learning basic grammar, vocabulary, and phrases through repetition and translation. Although the chances to write in English were greater in high school, they were designed to be writing-to-learn-language activities (Manchón, 2011). My first encounter with English academic writing was in the first two semesters of my undergraduate studies in English Language Teaching (ELT) at a public university in Turkey, when I was enrolled in my first two primarily learning-to-write courses. Throughout these courses, I was introduced to written academic English through general and discipline-specific texts that we analyzed in terms of topic and genre characteristics, and then we were assigned to write similar essays and a final research paper. The writing process involved at least one round of peer or teacher feedback, after which we revised and submitted our papers. Despite limited resources and crowded classes, it was a rather effective and comprehensive training that helped me not only learn how to write but also develop an understanding of L2 writing instruction. In the following semesters, I started taking courses in linguistics and on ELT methodology, which involved English writing for assessment purposes, and topics such as how to teach L2 writing.

**D:** *How did you develop a sense of "good" writing in English in your earlier years of English study?*

**S:** I think I started to develop a clear sense of "good" writing starting from my first year in college when I took the two writing courses I mentioned in my answer to the previous question. At the time, as far as I remember, my sense of "good" writing was still based largely on my pre-college experiences in which sentence-level structural accuracy was valued over macrostructure. The discipline-specific readings assigned in these courses, and the feedback I received on drafts of my writing, however, started to change my perspective gradually.

**D:** *Did you try to emulate certain writers or texts you read?*

**S:** The discipline-specific texts assigned as course readings, such as published research papers by the department faculty, were my primary sources of input. Although these texts were not introduced mainly as models to be emulated, I, like many of my friends, saw them that way for several possible reasons. First, I had limited prior English writing experience, and I was not familiar with how exemplar texts are exploited in the process and genre approaches, after which the course was designed. Besides, the course readings were easily accessible, and finding additional texts was not necessary until I started working on the final research paper. Lastly, I did not exactly know where and how to look for reliable academic sources that would diversify my exposure to academic English and guide my composing process. With no planned introduction and encouragement to develop library research skills, I rarely consulted the resources at the university library. Consequently, the few assigned texts served as convenient and trusted models for my writing.

**D:** *How did your sense of "good" writing in English evolve as you progressed through your years of English study? Or were you not aware of this sort of evolution?*

**S:** Ever since I started my undergraduate studies, my sense of "good writing" has continued to evolve. However, my awareness was relatively limited before I started working on academic writing in my master's thesis, which was when I discovered the vast literature on L2 academic writing in the disciplines largely from a corpus-linguistic perspective. In my doctoral dissertation (Yilmaz, 2020), I narrowed my focus and studied the common multi-word items with paired formal and functional characteristics in ELF academic writing. Bringing together different research strands, I found that the ELF research questioning the long-held beliefs and practices in academic writing is rather consistent with how academics write these days. This realization helped me develop a more informed and detailed sense of "good" writing that values the diversity of writers' backgrounds as well as contexts and purposes of use.

**D:** *Was there a specific point at which you shifted from studying English to studying in English (English-medium education)? If so, when did this happen and did you find yourself then producing much more writing in English? Did your sense of yourself as an English writer then change?*

**S:** Yes, I think the shift was the clearest in the second year of my undergraduate studies when I actually started to take linguistics and TESOL courses in English. I do not remember feeling a great change at the time, but now that I think about it, it was definitely a new experience. For the first time in my life, there was an authentically academic purpose for which I had to produce English writing. That was when I started to see English as not only a subject but also a valuable medium of professional communication.

**D:** *Did you feel that you went through a kind of maturation process as an English writer, e.g., from high school to undergraduate to MA, then PhD levels of education and life experiences (e.g., moving to the U.S.)?*

**S:** I do feel that I have matured over the years as a writer. During my undergraduate studies, being a novice writer, I was heavily reliant on the textual models I read, which started to change during my MA studies. As I began to present, publish, and work on my master's thesis, the role of the audience and my authorial voice in the discipline became more important. The maturation process was at its height, especially toward the end of my PhD studies. By that time, my experiences had become rather diversified, and my academic identity had largely been formed.

**D:** *Have you done, and do you still do, personal (or interpersonal, e.g., social media) writing in English as well as academic writing in English? If so, do you see any relationship between your more personal and academic writing? Do you think they need to be entirely different?*

**S:** During the nearly five years I had spent in the U.S., I primarily used English for personal as well as professional purposes, which also included face-to-face and online communication, posting on social media, and producing several academic writing genres such as reviews, articles, and reports. As a second language user who acquired English mainly in instructed settings, however, I started to feel comfortable doing personal writing in English only after my first year in the U.S. I needed some time to familiarize myself

with the informal and involved nature of personal writing. It
was also interesting to experience firsthand one of the findings
I reported in my master's thesis, that L1 Turkish graduate students
employed a remarkably more formal writing style than their native
counterparts (Yilmaz, 2016). I observed this difference widely in
my students' writing as well, which might be related to the strong
pedagogical focus on teaching second language users an outdated
view of "good" academic writing, the rules of which must be
strictly followed. I believe there are certainly important differences
between personal and academic writing, but discursive conventions
are bound to evolve over time and across settings (Casanave, 2010),
and academic writing is no exception (Horner, 2018). Besides, a
more informal and personally involved academic writing style is
on the rise (e.g., Biber & Gray, 2016; Hundt, Schneider, & Seoane,
2016; Hyland & Jiang, 2019).

**D:**  *What are your thoughts now on the role that Turkish plays, or should play, in
your life as a writer now that you are back in a Turkish-dominant setting but
also an academic context where English is still often privileged?*

**S:**  I do sincerely wish I had better Turkish writing skills that I could
utilize for a wider variety of purposes. However, after the limited
writing instruction I received during my K–12 education, I went
to English-medium schools and used English for professional
purposes. Therefore, I did not have the chance or the need to
improve my Turkish writing. Even though I, of course, write in
Turkish for daily personal and professional purposes, I have never
written a manuscript fully in Turkish. Being a first-generation
college student and not having received quality writing instruction
in my first language, I often think I am disadvantaged. When
teaching applied linguistics in the U.S., I used to experience the joy
of helping undergraduate students, mostly native speakers, uncover
interesting aspects of their first language. However, I do not
have the necessary expertise to do so if I were to teach a class on
Turkish linguistics. Considering how my metalinguistic awareness
in English facilitates my understanding of its use, I feel that I am
not as well-equipped when it comes to Turkish.

**D:**  *What audiences do you most want to reach as a writer, and how do those
audiences affect your sense of what "good" writing is? Would some of these
audiences be better reached in Turkish rather than English?*

**S:** As an early-career researcher, I first and foremost aim to reach wider audiences of disciplinary experts on international platforms, which, of course, is possible mainly through English-medium communication. Although Turkish is required in certain grant applications reviewed by committees with members outside the field, successful completion of certain projects depends on publishing results in international journals that are likely to be in English. Therefore, the emphasis on international recognition, often through English-medium research outlets and even by local gatekeeping mechanisms, also reinforces my English-centric sense of "good" writing.

**D:** *Do you think that your notions of "good" writing in English over the years could have hindered your ability to say the things you really wanted to say in the ways you really wanted to say them?*

**S:** My notions of "good" writing over the years have evolved alongside my understanding of and experience in using, teaching, and studying written English. Thus, it is hard to consider the role of one factor independently of the others. However, the increasing diversity of contexts, purposes, and conventions of usage inevitably shaped my writing, and I believe I became a more skilled writer eventually. Comparing my experiences of writing a paper during my master's studies and writing my doctoral dissertation, I easily identify the increased confidence I had in expressing myself in the latter. Not only was I encouraged to contribute to the field, but I also had a considerably broader knowledge base regarding disciplinary and genre conventions, as well as research in the field. Ever since I became involved in ELF research myself, I have also had a heightened awareness of the complexities of academic writing. For instance, now I know through ELF research that the difference in academic texts written by second language and native users of English is not merely about sentence-level structural accuracy but rather a combination of many factors such as the blending of local and global rhetoric, reliance on conventional language, and a highly explicit style (e.g., Carey, 2013; Murillo, 2018; Wu, Mauranen, & Lei, 2020; Yilmaz & Römer, 2020). In sum, to answer your question, I believe I was more restricted when I had much less experience as a writer and researcher than I do now.

**D:** *What do you tell your own students in Turkey about "good" writing in English? Do you worry that they hold themselves to a sometimes harmfully "native-like" standard?*

**S:** Although I do not explicitly discuss with my students the nature of "good" writing in general, we often have conversations about the widely held beliefs on academic writing conventions that they have also been previously taught. Especially those who have been introduced to a set of rules deeming English academic writing as uniform, static, and impersonal tend to get confused when I ask them to have a clearer personal stance or highlight the differences across disciplines and genres. I try to highlight the complexity of factors that shape "good" academic writing. I try to show them sample texts by writers of different backgrounds to exemplify the variation in the way different authors construct their texts.

**D:** *You have a strong commitment to ELF. How has this affected you as a writer, as a teacher of English or of future teachers of English? Has your own research on ELF been liberating in a sense for you as a writer and teacher? Is acceptance of ELF something you feel you need to educate others about?*

**S:** I think I can safely say that it has indeed been a liberating experience considering the conceptions that shaped my perceptions and practices of academic writing. However, it would be plausible to suggest that my stance on ELF is a moving target for several reasons. First, ELF research is fast evolving, and the progress made in the field affects my understanding of it as well. Second, the switch to adopting an ELF perspective on my English language use, research, and teaching has been rather slow and gradual. Every institution has established regulations shaping expectations and actions of everyone involved, and ELF is definitely not a tenet central to the mainstream disciplinary practice in our field. Besides, I try my best not to impose my ideological agenda, as I have needed a considerable amount of time to embrace my current perspective.

Nevertheless, I still argue that the commitment of ELF to effective communication over accuracy and conformity is essential in using and teaching English academic writing today, which necessitates certain changes in one's practices. This is why I try to adapt my teaching to include awareness-raising and investigative activities where students discuss and experience the sociolinguistic realities of English-language communication around the world.

For instance, covering topics such as dynamics of effective communication, domain-specificity, power, ideologies, and attitudes can help students equip themselves with a skillset for navigating through not only English academic writing but also any complex linguistic phenomena in their lives.

**D:** *Do you feel the world is making progress toward greater tolerance of ELF and broader notions of "good" writing? How would you like "good" writing to be conceptualized or viewed in your own immediate and in global context?*

**S:** It definitely is. Today most people participating in academic communication worldwide are second language users, which makes academia a truly authentic ELF setting. Thus, I argue that it is about time that the ELF perspective on "good" writing that embraces this lingua-cultural diversity and prioritizes effective rather than an idealized "nativelike" communication became more mainstream. As Mauranen (2020) argues, the ELF perspective, by approaching academic writing as a dynamic phenomenon shaped by the successful textual practices in disciplinary discourse communities, regardless of their conformity to nativelike norms, can lead to more efficient and productive use of time and resources in the L2 writing classroom. Our task, as language professionals, Mauranen further observes, should be to move away "from teaching and controlling correctness to teaching effective, competitive rhetoric" while striving for "a deeper understanding of what good texts consist of" (p. 77).

## Conclusion

The experience of the interview process, the outcome of which we have provided above, has been enlightening for both of us. Diane, as Selahattin's former instructor, PhD dissertation committee member, and now admirer of his work as a published scholar, learned much about Selahattin as a multiliteracy learner and ELF advocate and exemplar teacher and researcher. Selahattin feels that the experience of addressing Diane's questions, guided by her research on L2 writing, helped him reflect on and articulate his experiences and thoughts that contributed to his current ELF-informed view of "good" academic writing. Zooming in on his trajectory also enabled him to develop a deeper understanding as to how his view of "good" writing changed gradually from the somewhat

arbitrary emphasis on correctness and literary quality in his early education to his current research-informed ELF perspective valuing functional-
ity and situatedness of academic writing practices.

The interview has aimed to offer the reader a comprehensive overview of how Selahattin's current views of "good" writing evolved at
the intersection of major influences such as his background and educational and professional experiences, skills, and needs throughout his
journey as a second language user. With the ever-increasing diversity of
writers across the world, most of whom are second language users like
Selahattin, we believe that the ELF perspective on "good" writing carries
important implications for L2 writing pedagogy. The insights we gained
while writing this chapter have led us to emphasize particularly the role
of reflection and awareness in adopting an ELF perspective on L2 academic writing.

Effective ELF communication involves utilizing one's own multilingual resources adaptively according to the different contexts of English
language use and to users with varying resources (Jenkins, 2015). Thus,
an ELF-informed L2 writing pedagogy could start with helping learners develop a heightened awareness of their resources in English as well
as other languages through reflection on their journeys, which can also
facilitate their understanding of the complexities in written academic
English today.

Another implication is concerned with the pedagogical approach to
introducing written academic English. Following Horner's (2011) idea of
"collaborative investigation," we suggest that learners and teachers can
"serve as mutual resources for analyzing and transforming language practices" (p. 301). For instance, they can work together to explore different
academic texts and identify the linguistic and rhetorical variation across
genres, writers, and settings. It is our hope that such an ELF-informed
collaborative and exploratory instructional approach can embolden
learners to adopt a view of "good" English texts that they can comfort-
ably adapt to in light of their encounters with different textual practices.

## References

Buckingham, L. (2008). Development of English academic writing competence by
Turkish scholars. *International Journal of Doctoral Studies, 3,* 1–18.

Canagarajah, A. S. (2013). *Critical academic writing and multilingual students.* University of
Michigan Press.

Carey, R. (2013). On the other side: Formulaic organizing chunks in spoken and written academic ELF. *Journal of English as a Lingua Franca, 2*(2), 207–228.

Casanave, C. P. (2010). Taking risks? A case study of three doctoral students writing qualitative dissertations at an American university in Japan. *Journal of Second Language Writing, 19*(1), 1–16.

Doğançay-Aktuna, S., & Kiziltepe, Z. (2005). English in Turkey. *World Englishes, 24*(2), 253–265.

Hawkins, J. E. (2018). The practical utility and suitability of email interviews in qualitative research. *The Qualitative Report, 23*(2), 493–501.

Horner, B. (2011). Writing English as a Lingua Franca. In A. Archibald, A. Cogo, & J. Jenkins (Eds.), *Latest trends in ELF research* (pp. 299–311). Cambridge Scholars Publishing.

Horner, B. (2018). Written academic English as a Lingua Franca. In J. Jenkins, W. Baker, & M. Dewey (Eds.), *The Routledge handbook of English as a Lingua Franca* (pp. 413–426). Routledge.

Hundt, M., Schneider, G., & Seoane, E. (2016). The use of the *be*-passive in academic Englishes: Local vs global usage in an international language. *Corpora, 11*(1), 29–61.

Hyland, K., & Jiang, K. (2019). *Academic discourse and global publishing: Disciplinary persuasion in changing times.* Routledge.

Hynninen, N., & Solin, A. (2017). Language norms in ELF. In J. Jenkins, W. Baker, & M. Dewey (Eds.), *The Routledge Handbook of English as a Lingua Franca* (pp. 267–278). Routledge.

James, N. (2016). Using email interviews in qualitative educational research: Creating space to think and time to talk. *International Journal of Qualitative Studies in Education, 29*(2), 150–163.

Jenkins, J. (2011). Accommodating (to) ELF in the international university. *Journal of Pragmatics, 43*(4), 926–936.

Jenkins, J. (2015). Repositioning English and multilingualism in English as a Lingua Franca. *Englishes in Practice, 2*(3), 49–85.

Jenkins, J. (2017). Not English but English-within-multilingualism. In S. Coffey, & U. Wingate (Eds.), *New directions for research in foreign language education* (pp. 63–78). Routledge.

Kachru, B. (1985). Standards, codification and sociolinguistic realism: English language in the outer circle. In R. Quirk & H. Widdowson (Eds.), *English in the world: Teaching and learning the language and literatures* (pp. 11–36). Cambridge University Press.

Lorés-Sanz, R. (2016). ELF in the making? Simplification and hybridity in abstract writing. *Journal of English as a Lingua Franca, 5*(1), 53–81.

Manchón, R. M. (2011). Situating the learning-to-write and writing-to-learn dimensions of L2 writing. In M. R. Manchón (Ed.), *Learning-to-write and writing-to-learn in an additional language* (pp. 3–14), John Benjamins.

Martinez, R. (2018). "Specially in the last years. . .": Evidence of ELF and non-native English forms in international journals. *Journal of English for Academic Purposes*, *33*, 40–52.

Mauranen, A. (2012). *Exploring ELF: Academic English shaped by non-native speakers.* Cambridge University Press.

Mauranen, A. (2018). English as a Lingua Franca in written discourse. In J. I. Liontas & M. DelliCarpini (Eds.), *The TESOL encyclopedia of English language teaching* (pp. 1–7). John Wiley & Sons, Inc.

Mauranen, A. (2020). Good texts in non-standard English: ELF and academic writing. In K. Murata (Ed.), *ELF research methods and approaches to data and analyses: Theoretical and methodological underpinnings* (pp. 57–80). Routledge.

Mauranen, A., Pérez-Llantada, C., & Swales, J. (2010). Academic Englishes—A standardized knowledge? In A. Kirkpatrick (Ed.), *The Routledge handbook of World Englishes* (pp. 656–674). Routledge.

Ministry of National Education. (2005), Orta öğretim Dil ve Anlatım dersi 9, 10, 11, 12. sınıflar öğretim programı. [Secondary-level Language and Expression course curriculum for grades 9, 10, 11, 12.]

Murillo, S. (2018). Not the same, but how different? Comparing the use of reformulation markers in ELF and in ENL research articles. In P. Mur-Dueñas & J. Šinkūıenė (Eds.), *Intercultural perspectives on research writing* (pp. 237–253). John Benjamins.

Seidlhofer, B. (2021). Discourse and English as a Lingua Franca. In K. Hyland, B. Paltridge, & L. Wong (Eds.), *The Bloomsbury handbook of discourse analysis* (pp. 267–280). Bloomsbury.

Solin, A., & Hynninen, N. (2018). Regulating the language of research writing: Disciplinary and institutional mechanisms. *Language and Education*, *32*(6), 494–510.

Turner, J. (2018). *On writtenness: The cultural politics of academic writing.* Bloomsbury Publishing.

Uysal, H. H. (2008). Tracing the culture behind writing: Rhetorical patterns and bidirectional transfer in L1 and L2 essays of Turkish writers in relation to educational context. *Journal of Second Language Writing*, *17*(3), 183–207.

Wu, X., Mauranen, A., & Lei, L. (2020). Syntactic complexity in English as a Lingua Franca academic writing. *Journal of English for Academic Purposes*, *43*, 100798. https://doi.org/10.1016/j.jeap.2019.100798

Yilmaz, S. (2016). *A corpus-based investigation of the effect of nativeness and expertise on reporting practices in academic writing* [Unpublished master's thesis]. Bogazici University.

Yilmaz, S. (2020). *A constructional analysis of written academic English as a Lingua Franca: The case of unedited and edited research writing* [Doctoral dissertation, Georgia State University]. https://scholarworks.gsu.edu/alesl_diss/57.

Yilmaz, S. (2021). A plurilithic approach to English for Academic Purposes (EAP) writing instruction: Insights from English as a Lingua Franca (ELF) research. In A. F. Selvi & B. Yazan (Eds.), *Language teacher education for Global Englishes: A practical resource book* (pp. 125–131). Taylor & Francis Ltd.

Yilmaz, S., & Römer, U. (2020). A corpus-based exploration of constructions in written academic English as a Lingua Franca. In U. Römer, V. Cortes, & E. Friginal (Eds.), *Advances in corpus-based research on academic writing: Effects of discipline, register, and writer expertise* (pp. 59–88). John Benjamins.

# Chapter 13

# Putting *Self* Back into Academic Writing as a Liberatory Practice: Journeying through Personal to Academic

*Lisya Seloni*

## Introduction

This chapter focuses on the situatedness of good writing and the productive ways academics could link personal and scholarly discussions humanizing what it means to create knowledge through writing and other modalities. I do this by sharing constellations of narrative memory around writing that illustrate the various struggles and successes I experienced on my way to becoming a transnational academic writer in my home field of applied linguistics. What informs our idea of good writing (and whether it even exists) as transnational writers, as this chapter argues, is shaped by our lived experiences as teacher-scholars who oscillate between fully submitting to and subverting the expectations of academic writing along with our participation in alternative ways of constructing knowledge. Challenging the idea that fixed ideas of good writing exist, I also argue that academic work is identity work, and new discourses and rhetorical moves that diverse writers bring into academic discourses can help dispel myths about the stories we tell about good writing. The chapter illustrates examples of innovative writing practices and ends with a call for putting the self and the personal back into disciplinary writing and for reimagining scholarly discussions on creating mindful habits for reading and writing rather than chasing an ideal definition of good writing.

## Narrative Memory of Good Writing: Textual Work Is Identity Work

I did not learn academic writing, let alone "good" academic writing, but personal writing[1] has always been at the center of my life, even long before I even dreamt about being an academic in my adopted homeland of the United States. Growing up in Istanbul in the 1980s and '90s, I found that writing was a way to make sense of the world around me and to explore identities, cultural dislocations, human suffering and trauma, and conflicting affiliations. As everything around me changed, writing was my constant. It was my safe harbor that kept me in touch with my inner self and helped me engage in deep thinking and reflections. However, it was a harbor that almost no one visited. It was free of audience. My personal writing was not space-bound. Most of the writing activity I was engaged in occurred in notebooks, on napkins, on store receipts, and on random pieces of paper. I wrote while waiting for a ferry to cross the Bosphorus on my way to university. I wrote on the crowded city buses I used to ride on the weekends to teach English to economically disadvantaged kids studying at a *dershane*, a small language school in bustling Istanbul. I wrote in a small bedroom I shared with my sister after everyone went to sleep. No one was supervising my writing, but no one was reading it, either. I was writing because it was healing, and most importantly, helping me explore my identity.

Later in my undergraduate years, my father introduced me to a journalist who was at that time working for a well-known newspaper in Istanbul. After hearing about my engagement with writing, he showed interest in working with me mainly by responding to my essays and talking about Turkish literature. I was studying to be an English teacher at Istanbul University back then. The program I went through was not writing-intensive except for a few British and American literature classes

---

1   The so-called binary of *personal* and *academic* writing has always puzzled me. I usually ask myself: "Is academic writing not *personal*? How can we take the actor (the writer) out of the action of writing?" Resisting to choose a side in the academic vs personal debate, I want to acknowledge that blended scholarship exists. Still, the phrase "personal writing" that I use here relies on my earlier conception of writing that is based on the traditional personal-academic dichotomy that didn't quite recognize the continuum.

I took where we were occasionally asked to write responses to poetry and short stories. With no experience other than mimicking my favorite novelists' rhetorical moves in Turkish literature in my own writing in English and Turkish essays, I regularly shared with this journalist my handwritten essays. My favorite Turkish novelists (Ahmet Altan, Orhan Pamuk, Buket Uzuner, Elif Shafak, and Duygu Asena) distinguished themselves with their use of extensive vocabulary, metaphors, narrative techniques, storytelling, and complex and detailed descriptions of characters and plots, so these were the features I adopted in my own writing. I clearly remember the strange feeling of seeing someone else's handwriting on top of my writing when this journalist returned my essays. This was the very first time I had received genuine feedback on my writing. His initial feedback was mainly on what I was saying rather than how I was saying it. It was the first time I realized that writing can be an act of communication with others and that I did not have to write only for myself or for my college professors.

Several years after this experience I found myself sitting in my advisor's office as a first-year TESOL master's student in a new country and feeling ashamed by the B-minus mark on top of a paper with all the red-inked comments in the margins. I remember the professor talking about all the things that were wrong with my writing. He told me that I had long descriptions, strange expressions, and too many metaphors that did not have much place in a research paper. More importantly, he observed, my thesis statement didn't appear until relatively deep in the paper, and this confused the readers about where I was going with my arguments. When he explained to me what a thesis statement was and its importance in academic writing, I remember not quite understanding the urgency to tell the readers my claims on the first page. Giving away the suspense of the journey early on in my paper didn't make sense. Including a thesis statement felt tantamount to someone spoiling the end of a movie, so why would I do that to my readers? He insisted that I needed a roadmap that clearly told the reader about the main points I was about to make in this paper. But why would I need a map in a place where I was mainly exploring, getting lost, discovering, and engaging? Why were such digressions not valued?

Another area where I had to pull back my authorial self was reporting on research. In one of my research papers as a first-year master's student, I remember including detailed information about my participants and how our relationship started and evolved in the research process. I was disappointed to see that my professor had placed a big X over this section of my paper and wrote in the margin "unnecessary." In another paper that I wrote for the same professor, I remember starting my introduction with a set of questions about the topic of my research paper. I thought that posing some questions at the beginning would raise the curiosity of the readers and make my beginning more interesting to the readers. Again, I was mistaken. My professor put another big red X on this part of my writing and wrote in the margin, "I hate questions." Although I learned a great deal from this professor, I remember developing anxieties around expressing myself and being creative when I was writing papers for his class. As a new international student in the program and a novice "academic" writer, I didn't understand what readers in this setting consider important in a text.

My writing confidence took a big blow that year. What I thought good writing should look like was not working for this particular situation. I felt constrained by this professor's feedback and did not fully understand why and how I should "fix" my writing. After all, I was never trained to write in the disciplines, and I thought that perhaps what was valued in one cultural context was not valid in other cultural contexts. This was also the first time I realized that writing could be done with a particular purpose in a specific context for a particular audience and that perhaps the notion of "good" writing was dependent on and shaped by discourses and communities that were about to become more familiar to me.

Fast-forward two years. It's 2003. I'm a first-year doctoral student at Ohio State University attentively listening to a doctoral class taught by Dr. Shelley Wong, feeling fascinated by her teaching, passion, and critical look at applied linguistics. As part of this course, we were asked to write a research paper focusing on a specific issue we studied in critical language education. In Dr. Wong's course, I was deeply moved by Bonny Norton's 1997 article on social construction of identity in which Norton narrated Canadian immigrant women's estrangement from the mainstream culture and their reclaiming of the English language and identity positions to become legitimate participants of the new community they were about to enter. I was also pleasantly surprised that accomplished scholars in my field brought in stories and narrative voices in their academic writing and that academic writing in my field includes variation in textual forms and methods. Similar to the stories of the immigrant women I read about in Bonny Norton's earlier work, for Dr. Wong's final assignment I wrote a research paper blending my personal immigration story and instances where I felt marginalized at the workplace. This was the first time I dared to bring autobiographical features into my academic writing. To this day, I vividly remember reading in the margins of the paper

Dr. Wong's cursive, handwritten note in pencil: "You have a powerful voice! Your story is captivating." My eyes stopped at each word. *Powerful. Captivating. My story.* That day Shelley Wong's words validated my voice and increased my confidence as a multilingual doctoral student. Perhaps I wasn't that bad of a writer after all! Perhaps there wasn't only one correct way of writing in academic contexts. Perhaps academic writing does not have to feel hegemonic, with rigid standards and rules that have to supersede one's own identity and stories. I could still have a voice, tell my story, and do scholarship. This was the first time I realized that textual work is identity work (Kamler &Thomson, 2007).

My earlier experiences as a writer, oscillating between fully submitting to and subverting the expectations of academic writing along with participating in alternative ways of constructing knowledge, inform the questions that I ask about good writing and how to go about talking about writing with the students I work with today. These experiences usually come to my rescue as I mentor undergraduate and graduate writers and help them become the kind of writers they wish to be. Today, one of my favorite statements about writing is one by Elizabeth Wardle, who writes, "There is no such thing as writing in general. Writing is always in particular" (Wardle, 2017, p. 3). Although these are such simple statements, they tell us so much about the problems with generalized narratives of how good writing should look and what pathways one needs to take to produce good academic writing. It wasn't until much later in my graduate school years that I learned that there is no magic formula that makes someone a good writer in all situations. That is because writing, especially academic writing in the disciplines, is done with a particular purpose in a specific context for a particular audience. In this sense, writing is a social action, and writers are actors who use writing as a tool to get things done with a shared communicative purpose (Swales, 1990).

Yet due to years of standardized writing instruction, where our students are taught to treat most writing as an overextension of the five-paragraph essay structure coupled with the test-burdened education systems, many students come to university (or graduate school) thinking that academic writing can be achieved through the acquisition of discrete technical skills and a set of specific conventions. For many, a five-paragraph essay is a default writing structure for all things considered academic. Or there will be students like me, who never received much academic writing instruction and whose knowledge about writing may not always be accepted or welcomed in academic contexts. In both scenarios, learning to figure out the disciplinary expectations or making sense of the professors' assignments is a game-like practice in which novice writers are asked to learn the rules of the game, understand the roles of the participants, and learn to play the game correctly (Casanave, 2002; Freadman, 1994). Such expectations may pose various challenges especially for linguistically and culturally diverse writers and for writers who do not always have equal access to a quality writing education. One challenge for these writers is to break away from the myths that good writing is universal and that once writers learn a series of form-based categories and conventions, *good* writing can be achieved in all situations. Drawing on the game metaphor of writing, if learning how to write is tantamount to learning the rules of a board game, the idea that one's writing knowledge in one genre transfers easily to all situations is similar to saying that one can be a good chess player if they know the rules of backgammon.

This issue becomes especially complex for multilingual writers whose rich linguistic repertoires or traditions of and personal experiences with writing, whether they are speakers of World Englishes or English as a Lingua Franca, make them outsiders to Western academic discourse. The texts that multilingual writers compose, especially those who may not have received writing instruction in their home countries, may be influenced by the rhetorical choices and linguistic patterns they have seen practiced in their communities or in the literature they have read in their home languages. Additionally, there seems to be a large discrepancy between what the most recent L2 writing studies research focuses on and what ESL/EFL textbooks seem to promote in their treatment of writing. Much of the emphasis given in EFL writing courses is guided and controlled writing where learners mainly imitate language structures taught for that unit. The expectation to produce accurate language overshadows looking at the situatedness of writing. Textbooks may also present inauthentic reading materials that can be demotivating for student writers or lack coverage of genres, literacy skills, and socioculturally appropriate discussion topics for L2 writers (Ferris & Hedgcock, 2014).

Although translingual flow is an ordinary fact of multilingual life (Otsuji & Pennycook, 2010) in many communities around the world, we often fail to make space for the rich linguistic repertoires and storytelling traditions of multilingual writers within academic contexts, missing the opportunity to expand the borders of what good academic writing may look like. The linguistic multiplicity that we passionately advocate and recognize in the scholarly world is rarely reflected in the way we imagine *good* writing and writing instruction to be. Academic writing, devoid of multilingual stories, creates an artificial distance between our sensory and intellectual worlds, a distance that, as a transnational writer who is rediscovering the power of storytelling both in my teaching and scholarship, I wish to shorten (Seloni, 2019a).

## Putting *Self* Back into Writing as a Liberatory Practice

> Mini-*diálogos*: Convo with a "mentor"
> You have to place your ideas in the field!
> *Qué field?*
> The field! the field! the field!
> *La tierra? Sí! Sembramos palabras*
> *We grow the words we're going to need.*
> How is your work connecting to the field's scholarship?
> *I grow bougainvillea's y framboyanes.*
> What is your specialization?
> *I press their fallen flowers in useless oppressive books. To commune with*
> *brutalized trees.*
>
> Yanira Rodríguez, p. 8

The dialogue above between a mentor and a student comes from a powerful piece by Rodríguez (2019) about creating teaching sites that can unpack white supremacy in the university and meeting the needs of student-teacher-workers. In this piece, Rodríguez shares her antiracist classroom practices by asking the following question: "What does it mean to emphasize liberatory pedagogies in the classroom while we continue to neglect other spaces in the academy, where faculty and students with marginalized identities bump up against the oppressive workings of the institution and its actors?" (p. 9). In her composition classes, she discusses how her students make art together as a way to respond to social and political issues of interest transforming research writing courses into interdisciplinary spaces with all forms of writing styles and modalities. Reflecting on the pedagogy of refusal that extends meaning making beyond the classroom, she writes, "My classroom is always an attempt to dislodge the mechanistic way many students (due to economic and other pressures) have come to understand their education and its value" (p. 10).

Rodríguez's call to bring more liberatory pedagogies into writing spaces that extend beyond the classroom is also reflected in Casanave's (2010) advocacy for change and risk-taking in dissertation writing and pushes the boundaries of conventions in this particular genre. She writes:

> Students, recent graduates, and novice faculty do not feel free to do what they want, believing that their writing must conform closely to disciplinary norms and traditions to be acceptable to future employers and to tenure and promotion committees. Their advisors and mentors believe the same. Where, then, does change come from? Only from the top, from tenured well-known or emeritus scholars who no longer need to fear taking risks? If we take this route, change may not happen, except at the top. I do not think it automatically trickles down. (p. 2)

Rodríguez's and Casanave's calls for narrative and art-based forms of scholarship not only inspire me but also remind me that how we think about *good* writing in an academic context is not separate from institutions and institutional expectations. And institutions don't always make equitable space for adjusting and playing with the standards, as it's usually those who are in privileged positions who enjoy flexibility in writing styles and genre-bending.

As academic communities increasingly include more Black, Indigenous, and People of Color (**BIPOC**) and ethnic minority scholars whose first language is not English, new forms of academic discourse and new definitions of good writing will emerge as credible sources of knowledge-making, whether we like it or not. We can no longer expect these scholars and practitioners to act, write, speak, and behave in a way that reflects white, middle-class, Western values of academic contexts. Creative tools that many translingual writers already use in their own writing as academics, as well as the way they subvert genres and languages, can not only help all of us reimagine writing as an emancipatory practice but also put a human face to knowledge-making. Suggesting alternative practices within academic discourses, whether it's nonstandard discourses, unconventional representations of knowledge, playfulness, or genre bending, is not new to writing pedagogy, specifically writing pedagogy that recognizes and legitimizes writing done by multilingual writers (e.g., Canagarajah, 2013; Gilyard, 1991; Holdstein & Bleich; 2001; Schroeder, 2002; Tardy, 2016, 2021; Young, 2013). As many of these scholars indicate in their work, creative attempts in language use and genre bending would be more acceptable as long as the authors use them strategically. As Chris Schroeder, one of the contributors to *ALT-DIS: Alternative Discourses and the Academy*, observes, "legitimacy of stories as a form of intellectual work often depends upon who does the telling" (Schroeder, 2002, p. 183). However, it is important to note that not legitimizing local narratives and stories and instead asking the authors to conform to one way of writing or privileging certain stories over others limits academic culture, creating a tendency to assimilate and exclude underrepresented voices from the academic discourses. Young's words here about the inclusion of African American Vernacular English in academic discourses are relevant when it comes to the doublespeak we perform as academics and teachers, when on the one hand we praise students' nonstandard variations for their creative voice but on the other hand we expect them to shed their voices, whether to make them recognizable by mainstream readers or to erase linguistic and cultural differences:

> Too many teachers still on one hand praise African American students for their creative voice and renderings of black rhetoric when they write poetry but then condemn those same students when they both un-self-consciously and strategically employ those same features when speaking to non-black people, particularly white people, or to professionals of any race, or when they produce critical, academic, or journalistic writing students. . . . Often saying that they are preparing these students for the real world, one that doesn't yet value black English (read: black people), they must demand that the students switch back and forth when appropriate; be black, or as they put it, speak black, when it's safe to do, but not when your job, your grades, or your relationships with other non-black people (and sometimes other blacks who share the same prejudice) are on the line. (Young, 2013, p. 140)

Young's words remind us that demanding students conform with non-contextual ideas about what "good" writing is and who "good" writers are will keep creating exclusionary practices in classrooms. Then, as teachers of writing and teacher educators, we can ask ourselves these questions: When can we stop being gatekeepers of good writing in our classrooms? When do we finally help student writers get rid of the training wheels and let them fly as their unique selves?

## Textual Work as Identity Work: Blended Scholarship as an Alternative Way to Construct Knowledge

Teachers and scholars often forget that textual work is identity work (Kamler & Thomson, 2007). As we participate in the construction of textual work and produce academic writing as an end result, we also become the teacher-scholar we want to be by claiming certain positionalities through written language. How we choose to express ourselves, whether we are disputing ideas or exchanging information as applied linguists, is usually reflective of one version of our identities. Defining academic writing as an act of identity, Hyland (2012) observes, "writing is not just about conveying 'content' but about representation of 'self': how we portray ourselves to others in our disciplines" (p. 17). Some of the ways writers position themselves in academic writing include their use of stance and engagement markers, hedging, self-mentions, or citation practices. For instance, the inclusion of citation helps establish a persuasive framework and displays the writer's credibility as a researcher (Hyland, 2008). Just as academia is not immune to the inequalities and power imbalances around knowledge construction and dissemination, neither are academic writing practices. Several scholars have argued that practices that are considered to conform to standard written English are largely based on the norms of Inner Circle communities, and they don't represent the preferred codes and identities of minoritized communities (e.g., Canagarajah, 2013). One of these practices is academic citation practices, which are embodied in political, cultural, and historical processes in which writers engage during different stages of writing. These writing practices can allow writers to reproduce certain authorial identities while leaving out others, such as BIPOC bodies (Ahmed, 2017). While general advice for good academic writing includes an act of standing on the shoulders of oft-cited writers and scholars, sound advice would be to encourage emerging scholars to read widely and include voices that have been historically oppressed and marginalized.

Even though I know today as a transnational academic writer that there is no such thing as writing in general, as a faculty member at a U.S. institution who regularly reads and responds to graduate student work, I recognize *good enough* academic writing. I can tell if a text is organized in a way that addresses the expectations of the mainstream audience in my field by looking at things like the writer's use of previous research, their way of situating their research within the larger scholarship, and their control of disciplinary vocabulary and rhetoric. These are important rules of the academic writing game in which credentials of the writers are shared. Because I was socialized in the U.S. academic culture for most of my academic life, following these conventions was my ticket to success during my graduate school and pre-tenure years. Although I want my students to know these normalized ways of acting within a community, I also encourage them to include stories and cultural fabric of their own and embrace alternative ways of knowledge creation—the kind of knowledge creation that allows for diverse literacies and languages and new forms of discourses and writing practices. I make these expectations part of my course assignments and interactions. For instance, in undergraduate and graduate courses, I have been creating assignments where students can re-mediate an academic genre to include personal voice, creativity, and genre innovation. The inclusion of novel writing practices such as creation of content for podcasts, infographics, storybooks, or writing fictional stories has been especially empowering during the COVID-19 pandemic when students have used these writing assignments as an outlet for merging their personal traumas with academic and pedagogical interests.

Innovative and inclusive writing assignments (Ortmeier-Hooper, 2017), whether given in composition or teacher education courses, not only enhance student writers' investment in the topic and facilitate meaningful participation but also create equitable practices, especially in traumatic times, by allowing students to draw from their unique lived experiences and diverse linguistic resources. Although I still find it harder to experiment with genre departure in high-stakes writing, I try to follow a similar path in thesis and dissertation mentoring, where students are encouraged to explore alternative ways of knowledge representation, whether that means including auto-ethnographic accounts of their research or fictional story-writing. In early stages of doctoral mentoring, I now urge my students to explore why a topic is personally worthwhile to examine and research. More than anything I strive to help them make space for *self* and see how *self* can be positioned within disciplinary communities of practice—which, to me, are overlooked and undervalued aspects of good writing in our field.

Even though we have much research on genre bending, reflexivity, and alternative ways of writing in the field of second language education in the last decade or so (e.g., Belcher & Hirvela; 2005; Casanave, 2010; Seloni, 2019b; Starfield, 2013; Starfield & Ravelli, 2006; Tardy,

2009, 2016), innovative writing, whether about one's choice of methods, use of narrative voice, or modality, is still not the norm in our field. It is worthwhile to note that the use of innovation and creativity is not always a mere issue of individual choice for writers. Many emerging scholars, faculty members, and graduate writers in our field are under pressure to produce academic writing that can be published in mainstream journals. This is important because publishing in respected journals is key for future employees and for the tenure and promotion committees who evaluate the validity and quality of one's scholarship. Good writing in such contexts is traditionally believed to be the kind of writing that closely conforms to and follows disciplinary traditions and norms. Although some writers are more conditioned to write in this way and may hesitate to bring novelty into writing, such as bringing life writing into disciplinary writing, there are inspiring examples in the larger field of writing studies where scholars innovate and push boundaries of their disciplinary norms blending components of the personal and the scholarly (e.g., Robillard & Combs, 2019). Discussing the role of novelty in academic writing, Tardy (2009) writes,

> Perhaps because of the expectation in academic research for some
> new contribution, innovations that strive to offer novel ideas or
> approaches are not always stark departures from conventions. Rather,
> research that challenges previously held ideas or approaches cannot
> stand entirely apart from prior scholarship—it must instead work to
> recognize and represent a field's consensual knowledge base and then
> question it and move beyond it in some ways. (p. 81)

What Tardy observes here is important in several ways. For one, it reminds us that taking risks in academic writing does not need to completely depart from genre expectations, and innovation is not limited to a text's structure. In this view, all genre knowledge encompasses both convention and innovation, and as Tardy indicates in her 2021 piece on the potential power of play in writing, creative rhetorical and linguistic moves can reduce tensions around academic writing and "contribute to metalinguistic awareness, as well as metacognitive genre awareness" (Tardy, 2021, p. 7). It's through play that writers can feel the joy of creating. In a classroom setting, our role as writing teachers and academics in talking about good writing in our disciplines can be to show our students the complex interplay between disciplinary values, stakes, policies, and other systems that play a role in the reception of our writing and rhetorical choices that can be disputed and broadened. Writing instructors can also demonstrate that writing can be a joyful and playful activity.

# A Call for Innovative Writing in Applied Linguistics

In the last few years, the fields of composition and applied linguistics have witnessed unconventional writing in which both novice and experienced writers innovate genres and modalities in ways that challenge traditional understandings of good writing. These newly emerging genres are not limited to things like "video abstracts," which are available on some publishers' websites, and blogs, where authors re-mediate their academic writing into a shorter form of genre that can be read by a general audience. The novel writing practices also include dissertations written by emerging scholars where different forms of representation are used to construct knowledge.

The fields of communication studies and rhetoric and composition are especially rich with innovative dissertations in which writers go beyond academic conventions and use novel ways to make their arguments. For instance, A. D. Carson, who received his PhD in Rhetorics, Communication, and Information Design at Clemson University, delivered his dissertation titled *Owning My Masters: The Rhetorics of Rhymes and Revolutions* as a hip-hop album (https://phd.aydeethegreat.com/). In one of his video representations of this dissertation, Carson says, "Can the scholars not just create or speak through hip hop as opposed to having it, like, mixed with something else in order for it to be acceptable? We already know that people can have experience or talk about rap without having someone else filtering it. . . . I am just moving that filter, and being the dope" (A. D. Carson: *Owning My Masters*, introduction, 2017, 1:27). Having a space for the spoken word in the academy is not only a liberatory practice at its best, but it also allows for a range of rhetorical, linguistic, and genre- and modality-based possibilities that can create equitable academic participation practices. Similarly, Eda Ozyesilpinar's (2018) dissertation titled *Dis/orienting 'Middle East': A Cart-Rhetorical Rhizomatic Mapping* is supplemented by a story map of the Middle East using geospatial technology. The multimodal component of her dissertation includes maps, videos, images, and other artifacts that illustrate how the Middle East has been misrepresented with "unjust socio-spatial identity" (p. ii). Another interesting example of an innovative dissertation is one written by Jason Helms, now an associate professor of English and director of the Center for Digital Expression at Texas Christian University. While at Clemson he created a RhizComics dissertation that was then converted to an open-access monograph presenting comics as rhetorically complex arguments in the form of an interactive website in which he used drawings, videos, animations, and written text. As he points out in the introduction of this interactive text, although his work is unusual, "like many books, it offers a scholarly argument and attempts to persuade its reader using evidence and citing other authors where appropriate" (Helms, 2010). When I browsed through Helms's digital work, I was impressed by the richness of intertextual links made through hyperlinks and how this intertextuality shaped the way I read his work and the reading strategies I employed.

The examples of innovative writing in the context of dissertations are not limited to these. Using storytelling as resistance, Aja Martinez's 2012 dissertation titled *Critical Race Counterstory as Rhetorical Methodology: A Chican@ Academic Experience Told through Sophistic Argument, Narrative, and Allegory,* intersperses academic prose with counterstories. Additionally, video game development is used in various dissertations. For instance, Samuel Fuller at Southeast Louisiana State added a game modification to his dissertation (2018) and now teaches courses on writing and video games; and Lauren Woolbright created a feminist video game prototype with her dissertation discussing "the playful modes of identity formation and pedagogy" (Woolbright, 2016, p. ii).

I am attracted to these unconventional dissertations for various reasons. They are transformative, creative, radical, empowering, and humane because they not only include cutting-edge research but also include stories and voices of individual writers. What these examples also suggest is that knowledge creation within disciplines and what we consider to be "good" writing in the context of dissertation writing are changing. Good academic writing is no longer limited to a norm-based textual production. Writers in the discipline, if given the rhetorical space and support needed, can innovate academic writing and co-construct knowledge in a way that makes sense for other writers and readers and in a way that has an impact on the larger non-academic community (i.e., reaching a public audience such as young scholars, teachers, policymakers, and non-experts). What all these dissertation writers have in common is that they take ownership of their writing by innovating within a high-stakes genre that has been traditionally thought to bring a fixed understanding of what good writing and knowledge contribution look like. They do this by incorporating textual and visual elements such as multimodality, narrative writing, and non-standard language use. They take full ownership of what it means to create knowledge through self-expression in the mixed academic and personal discourse that includes various forms of multiliteracies, multi-modalities, and language play.

This is a prime time to start talking about and paying attention to the features of these multimodal genres and to think about ways in which we can expand our definitions of good writing in the context of emerging technologies and of the multiplicity of writing styles and rhetoric presented by diverse writers. Perhaps it is time for dissertations within the field of applied linguistics to also take a chance on pushing the boundaries of disciplinary conventions, including creativity, self-expression, play, and innovation while challenging particular language ideologies, identities, and beliefs about academic writing. And we all know that this is more possible with advisors, committee members, and departments who advocate and support this kind of work that challenges conventions and creates a rhetorical space for all writers.

## Coda: Expanding the Stories We Tell about Good Writing

In the "The Danger of a Single Story," Chimamanda Ngozi Adichie says, "The single story creates stereotypes, and the problem with stereotypes is not that they are untrue, but that they are incomplete. They make one story become the only story" (Adichie, 2009). The stories we tell our students about *good* writing are incomplete if we only stick to the guidebooks about good academic writing, with their finite rules and conventions with little emphasis on context, genre, creativity, or author personality and lived experiences. The unwillingness to subvert is a byproduct of long-held beliefs about the superiority of traditional epistemologies and academic discourse, the inferiority of creative intellectual work (Bizzell, 2002), and a rigid adherence to one type of writing. As Pattanyak (2017) states, "by perpetuating the myth of one correct way of writing, we are effectively marginalizing substantial swaths of the population linguistically and culturally" (p. 86).

My experiences as a transnational scholar have deeply shaped and continue to shape the way I read and respond to student writing. I'm increasingly finding myself more courageous to invite the graduate students I work with to innovate within high-stakes genres such as dissertations and theses, and I invite them to adopt a reflexive approach to the benefits and risks of innovation as they try to publish (Hartse & Kubota, 2014). Instead of giving prominence to style handbooks on "good" writing in college writing courses, graduate programs, or teacher training courses, perhaps it is time that we focus on practices that promote mindful habits in writing, creativity, and innovation and activities that look at writing from a cultural and historical viewpoint with all its complexities, intricacies, and backstories.

It is my hope that one big takeaway from this chapter is that definitions and frameworks around good writing become contextualized and humanized in a way that is empowering to all writers, not just selected privileged ones. Pushing the boundaries of academic writing through narrative inquiry, we can create a rhetorical and linguistic space for complexity and confusion as well as attentively listen to transnational voices without trying to categorize or assimilate them. Learning how to both play and break the rules of the game (and the tricks of the trade) should incur no penalty if we want to create an inclusive and equitable playing field for all writers.

## References


Ahmed, S. (2017). *Living a feminist life*. Duke University Press.

Adichie, C. N. (2009). The danger of a single story [Video]. *YouTube*. https://www.youtube.com/watch?v=D9Ihs241zeg

Belcher, D., & Hirvela, A. (2005). Writing the qualitative dissertation: What motivates and sustains commitment to a fuzzy genre? *Journal of English for Academic Purposes, 4*(3), 187–205.

Bizzell, P. (2002). The intellectual work of "mixed" forms of academic discourses. In C. Schroeder, H. Fox, & P. Bizzell (Eds.), *ALT DIS: Alternative discourses and the academy* (pp. 1–10). Heinemann.

Carson, A. D. (2017). *Owning my masters: The rhetorics of rhymes and revolutions* [Doctoral dissertation, Clemson University].

Canagarajah, A. S. (Ed.). (2013). *Literacy as translingual practice: Between communities and classrooms*. Routledge.

Casanave, C. P. (2002). *Writing games: Multicultural case studies of academic literacy practices in higher education*. Lawrence Erlbaum.

Casanave, C. P. (2010). Taking risks? A case study of three doctoral students writing qualitative dissertations at an American university in Japan. *Journal of Second Language Writing, 19*(1), 1–16.

Ferris, D., & Hedgcock, J. (2014). *Teaching L2 composition: Purpose, process, and practice*. Routledge.

Freadman, A. (1994). Anyone for tennis? In A. Freedman & P. Medway (Eds.), *Genre and the new rhetoric* (pp. 43–66). Taylor & Francis.

Fuller, S. J. (2018). *Modding the apocalypse: (Re)making videogames as post-structuralist free play* [Doctoral dissertation, Clemson University]. https://tigerprints.clemson.edu/all_dissertations/2219

Gilyard, K. (1991). *Voices of the self: A study of language competence.* Wayne State University Press.

Hartse, J. H., & Kubota, R. (2014). Pluralizing English? Variation in high-stakes academic texts and challenges of copyediting. *Journal of Second Language Writing, 24,* 71–82.

Helms, J. M. (2010). *Rhizcomics: The structure, sign, and play of image and text* [Doctoral dissertation, Clemson University].

Holdstein, D. H., & Bleich, D. (2001). *Personal effects: The social character of scholarly writing.* Utah State University Press.

Hyland, K. (2008). Genre and academic writing in the disciplines. *Language Teaching, 41*(4), 543–562.

Hyland, K. (2012). *Disciplinary identities: Individuality and community in academic writing.* Oxford University Press.

Kamler, B. & Thomson, P. (2007). Rethinking doctoral writing as text work and identity work. In B. Somekh & T. Schwandt (Eds.), *Knowledge production: Research work in interesting times* (pp. 166–179). Routledge.

Martinez, A. Y. (2012). *Critical race counterstory as rhetorical methodology: Chican@ academic experience told through sophistic argument, allegory, and narrative* [Doctoral dissertation, University of Arizona]. Retrieved from ProQuest. 3507744.

Norton, B. (1997). Language, identity, and the ownership of English. *TESOL Quarterly, 31*(3), 409–429.

Ortmeier-Hooper, C. (2017) *Writing across language and culture: Inclusive strategies for working with ELL writers in the ELA classroom.* NCTE.

Otsuji, E., & Pennycook, A. (2010). Metrolingualism: Fixity, fluidity, and language in flux. *International Journal of Multilingualism, 7*(3), 240–254.

Ozyesilpinar, E. (2018). *Dis/Orienting Middle East: A cart-rhetorical rhizomatic mapping* [Doctoral dissertation, Clemson University]. https://clemson.maps.arcgis.com/apps/MapSeries/index.html?appid=6f2af058c6f947bd8c69c9a1845a9e5f.

Pattanyak, A. (2017). There is one correct way of writing and speaking. In C. E. Ball & D. M. Loewe (Eds.), *Bad ideas about writing* (pp. 82–87). West Virginia University Libraries.

Robillard, A. & Comps, S. (2019). *How stories teach us: Composition, life writing, and blended scholarship.* Peter Lang Publishing.

Rodríguez, Y. (2019). Pedagogies of refusal: What it means to (un)teach a student like me. *Radical Teacher, 115,* 5–12.

Schroeder, C. (2002). From the inside out (or the outside in, depending). In C. Schroeder, H. Fox, & P. Bizzell (Eds.), *ALT DIS: Alternative discourses and the academy* (pp. 178–190). Heinemann.

Seloni, L. (2019a) Moving literacies: A need to tell transnational stories. In A. Robillard & S. Combs (Eds.), *How stories teach us: Life writing, composition, and blended scholarship.* (pp. 93–108). Peter Lang Publishing.

Seloni, L. (2019b) Enacting reflexivity in second language writing research: A personal account of cultural production of authorial self and researcher perception. In M. Grenfell & K. Pahl (Eds.), (with contributions from Cheryl McClean, Catherine Compton-Lilly and Lisya Seloni). *Bourdieu, language-based ethnographies, and reflexivity: Putting theory into practice* (pp. 107–130). Routledge.

Starfield, S. (2013). Researcher reflexivity. In C. Chapelle (Ed.), *The Encyclopedia of Applied Linguistics* (pp. 1–7). Wiley-Blackwell.

Starfield, S., & Ravelli, L. J. (2006). "The writing of this thesis was a process that I could not explore with the positivistic detachment of the classical sociologist": Self and structure in New Humanities research theses. *Journal of English for Academic Purposes, 5*(3), 222–243.

Swales, J. (1990). *Genre analysis: English in academic and research settings.* Cambridge University Press.

Tardy, C. M. (2009). *Building genre knowledge.* Parlor Press LLC.

Tardy, C. M. (2016). *Beyond convention: Genre innovation in academic writing.* University of Michigan Press.

Tardy, C. M. (2021). The potential power of play in second language academic writing. *Journal of Second Language Writing, 53,* 1–12.

Wardle, E. (2017). You can learn to write in general. In C. E. Ball & D. M. Loewe (Eds.), *Bad ideas about writing* (pp. 30–33). West Virginia University Libraries.

Woolbright, L. (2016). *Identity design: Challenging archetypes with feminist approaches to video game design* [Doctoral dissertation, Clemson University].

Young, V. A. (2013). Keep code-meshing. In A. S. Canagarajah (Ed.), *Literacy as translingual practice: Between communities and classrooms* (pp. 139–145). Routledge.

**Chapter 14**

# Reflexivity, Reflective Practice, and Good Writing: An Unfinished Journey

*Hanako Okada*

"Writing vulnerably takes as much skill, nuance, and willingness to follow through on all the ramifications of a complicated idea as does writing invulnerably and distantly." (Behar, 1996, p. 13)

## A Confession

Let me begin with a confession. Although I was honored to be asked to contribute to this volume, I could not straight away accept the offer because I was unsure if I was entitled to discuss what good writing is. I thought the discussion should be among the leaders of the field who have perfected the craft of writing—the highly proficient and confident writers who can write elegantly, sophisticatedly, eloquently, compellingly, seamlessly, and clearly, among many other features. I suppose I am expected to be a good writer, by default, especially in the eyes of those outside academia, given that I am an academic who writes for publication and teaches academic writing. I also suppose that I am not a terrible writer. But the lurking lack of confidence and discomfort made me hesitant to accept right away—the stakes seemed so high. After going back and forth, I bit the bullet, because I do have some opinions about the topic, however particular, that I wanted to share, and because I thought a chapter written by a person who feels rather uncomfortable tagging herself as a "good" writer might encourage and resonate with other academic writers who may feel the same way.

Of course, there are many overarching characteristics of good academic writing, as presented in published writers' guides (e.g., Pinker, 2014; Sword, 2012; Zinsser, 2006). But it is important to note that what is considered good writing is partisan according to the paradigm and orientation. As the chapters in this volume showcase, there is a vast array of perspectives of what "good writing" means within the field of applied linguistics and TESOL. As writing and the writer cannot be separated, in this chapter I tell a personal narrative of my trajectory as a writer. I focus on reflexivity and reflective practices as ways that helped me develop good writing in qualitative research and also develop as a writer and a writing instructor.

## Some Definitions

Before I begin my story, for brevity and clarity let me provide some concise (and hence partial) definitions, as the concept of reflexivity is complex and widely discussed within different disciplines and intellectual traditions (on the history, see Dean, 2017; Finlay, 2002; for practical guides, see Finlay & Gough, 2003; May & Perry, 2017; for discussions within applied linguistics and TESOL, see Pérez-Milans, 2016; Starfield, 2012). Reflexivity is the "process of critical self-reflection on one's biases, theoretical predispositions, preferences, and so forth . . . [that] points to the fact the inquirer is part of the setting, context, and social phenomenon, he or she seeks to understand" (Schwandt, 2015, p. 268). It is also used as evaluative criteria for establishing integrity in qualitative research (Finlay, 2006; Henwood & Pidgeon, 1992; Richardson & St. Pierre, 2018).

It is important to note that *reflexivity* and *reflection* are often confused and wrongly used interchangeably (Finlay, 2008). While *reflexivity* is "a more immediate and dynamic process that involves continuing *self*-awareness," *reflection* is "simply 'thinking about' something after the event" (p. 6, emphasis in original). *Reflective practice*, which falls between the two, is "the process of learning through and from experience towards gaining new insights of self and/or practice" (p. 1) (on reflective practice, see Schön, 1987, 2016; on writing as reflective practice, see Bolton & Delderfield, 2018; on reflective practice within TESOL, see Farrell, 2018; Mann & Walsh, 2017).

## The Beginning

When I first started reading applied linguistics literature as a graduate student, I was shocked to find that it was incredibly hard to read. This difficulty was primarily due to the APA-mandated in-text citations that cut the flow of the sentences and paragraphs and the excessive use of acronyms, both of which I was not familiar with. But I soon realized that it was also because many pieces were written in a detached manner with no appearance of the author/researcher. I recall thinking how strange that was when the focus was on languages and their users—that is, real, living people. Although I was discouraged, I told myself that this was the field's style, and I needed to get used to it. And I did. Soon the in-text citations no longer bothered me, and I learned the acronyms very quickly. But I never got used to the detached, non-personal style.

As I proceeded with my studies and read more widely, it was clear to me that I was drawn to qualitative research, and one small yet important reason was that I preferred reading qualitative over quantitative studies. (Let me note that I do by no means discard the importance of quantitative studies. I am focusing here on my interests and what I found pleasurable to read.) In particular, I thoroughly enjoy reading in-depth ethnographic studies of language learners' lives. To give an example, I recall how much I enjoyed reading Yasuko Kanno's *Negotiating Bilingual and Bicultural Identities: Japanese Returnees Betwixt Two Worlds* (2003), because it was written eloquently and clearly and read like a novel, including rich descriptions about both the participants and Kanno herself. Although I had not met the author at that time, I felt as if I had gotten to know Kanno personally—both as a researcher and as a friend—and to see the participants and their community through her eyes.

I believe my preference roots in my background. From a young age, I was fascinated by people's stories—both written and oral. I found great interest in why and how people think in a certain way and act and speak according to their thinking. Put together with my habit of critical reading that I acquired through studying philosophy and religious studies as an undergraduate, it was no surprise that I particularly appreciated situated qualitative research—the kind of qualitative research that has reflexivity built into it (Atkinson, 2005; cf. Haraway, 1988). I wanted a more critical outlook. I wanted more context. I wanted in-depth details—not only about the participants but also about the authors/researchers themselves. I wanted to know who they were, where they were coming from, and why they perceived the world in a certain way.

## Reflexivity and Reflective Practice in My Writing: Finding and Nurturing My Voice

It is no surprise that most of my research was the situated kind, employing narrative inquiry as a method. Due to my research interests and, I must also admit that because of the accessibility of research sites, I was often an insider in the community I was researching (Okada, 2009, 2017; cf. Kuwayama, 2004; Narayan, 1997). In some cases, I was also an "intimate insider" (Taylor, 2011) with preexisting friendships with the participants (Okada, 2009, 2011). Such positions brought not only advantages but also tensions associated with power imbalances affecting interpretation, representation, bias, and disclosure of sensitive issues. These methodological and ethical dilemmas forced me to consider my positionality in relation to my participants carefully, which led me to use reflexive writing strategies that considered myself as part of my own inquiry (Pelias, 2011)

Even though reflexivity is widely used, it is by no means free from criticisms and risks. First, it is criticized as narcissistic and self-indulgent (Finlay, 2002; Maton, 2003; Swan, 2008). Other criticisms include too much focus on the research process (Fortune & Mair, 2011) and an undue legitimization of the research processes (Sharma, 2021). Publicly displaying oneself honestly and vulnerably also involves risks, particularly for novice writers (Behar, 1996; Kleinsasser, 2000; Okada, 2008). Although I was concerned about criticisms and risks, I did not regret situating myself in my own work. First, as Chiseri-Strater (1996) noted, "to be reflexive demands both an other and some self-conscious awareness of the process of self-scrutiny" (p. 130). Therefore, reflexivity, in its true sense and when employed correctly, is not mere "navel-gazing." Second, acknowledging our partial "view from somewhere" (Haraway, 1988, p. 590) is essential in qualitative studies. Drawing from poststructuralism, Richardson (in Richardson & St. Pierre, 2018) articulates the idea:

> Specifically, poststructuralism suggests two important ideas to qualitative writers. First, it directs us to understand ourselves reflexively as persons writing from particular positions at specific times. Second, it frees us from trying to write a single text in which everything is said at once to everyone. *Nurturing our own voices* releases the censorious hold of "scientific writing" on our consciousness as well as the arrogance it fosters in our psyche: writing is validated as a method of knowing. (p. 821, emphasis added)

I remember the excitement I felt when I first read this passage in the earlier edition of *The Sage Handbook of Qualitative Research* (Richardson, 2000, p. 929). It is no exaggeration to call it a turning point for me as a graduate student. I felt that the writing that situated me was justified and legitimized, and I was encouraged to continue "nurturing my own voice."

However, I did not know what my "own voice" as a writer was. I was too preoccupied with completing heavy coursework and then my dissertation and did not have the luxury of considering voice or writing styles. Now that more than a decade has passed since I earned my doctorate, I feel that I am in the process of nurturing and developing my own voice. I can now characterize my writing as detail-oriented, and the stories that I tell are more personal, honest, and (I hope) evocative and compelling than in my previous writing. I believe this is the result of years of considering reflexivity and employing reflective practices.

One important reflective practice that I have been employing is journal writing. Ever since I was encouraged to do so in one of my earlier doctoral courses, I maintained the habit of keeping a research journal. This was not hard to do given that I was already an avid diary writer. Although I still kept my diary, the boundaries between it and the research journal soon became slim, as I included substantial introspective, retrospective, and reflexive accounts along with research memos and analytic memos (Maxwell, 2012). In my journal, I asked questions, explored concepts and ideas, and documented concerns, tensions, uncertainties, anxieties, and other feelings. I also included diary-like details such as my physical well-being. Because of this, my research journals were often quite extensive. To give an example, the journal that I kept during the data-collection period for my dissertation amounted to 170 typed double-spaced pages.

Here are some partial snippets from an entry written immediately after one of the interviews for my dissertation research (Okada, 2009):

October 24, 2007 Ayako's third interview

The alarm goes off, and I'm feeling terrible. I'm exhausted, groggy, and awfully sleepy. I kept waking up from pain last night. I struggle to get up, but I open the curtains and realize it's a gorgeous fall day. I take a shower, get dressed in my usual white long-sleeved T-shirt and black maxi-length skirt attire. I don't have an appetite, but I don't want to get hungry and feel faint during the interview, so I have a banana and a cup of yogurt and finish by popping two Advils.

. . .

Ayako starts by telling me when she was born. Soon the story becomes darker with her parents' failed marriage, and her mother getting very sick and her older sister having to take care of her. I tell her that she doesn't have to tell me things that she doesn't want to tell. I notice that her eyes are beginning to fill up. Big drops of tears start rolling down her face, and her eyeliner begins to smudge. I give her the box of tissue paper, console her, and tell her she can stop. But she says, "It's okay," and continues telling her story while sobbing. . . . A part of me is glad that she's opened up so much, and another part of me feels bad making her go back to her difficult times, and my heart begins to ache.

. . .

I wonder if she would mind if I write about all this. At one point, she tells me a "big secret." While I'm glad she's now feeling comfortable enough to confide in me, I worry about the outcome of this interview. Would she mind if I write that her mother left the kids behind to be with another man? Would she mind if I write that her father is stingy? Does she realize what she's doing? And how am I going to represent her and her dramatic life? . . .

Although some of the accounts in the example may appear trivial and irrelevant, the entries in the research journal played an essential role in both the process and the product (cf. Borg, 2001) of the dissertation. They evoked vivid memories enabling me to revisit the events virtually. They helped me recall and then write about the events in ways that recordings and transcripts could not capture. They functioned as a data source and helped me weave my perception and interpretation into each participant's stories. They helped me be more critical in my observations and analysis and be more sensitive in interacting with my participants. They helped me organize my thoughts and make my thinking transparent. Writing and rereading the entries helped me learn from my experiences and functioned as a springboard to gain new insights. The list of the benefits I found in keeping a research journal goes on (see Bolton & Delderfield, 2018; Borg, 2001, 2003; Casanave, 2011; Janesick, 1999;

Vicary, Young, & Hicks, 2017). Above all, I also believe that extensive journal writing was instrumental in nurturing my voice as a writer.

Whether it was for personal or research purposes, the journal was a private and risk-free space with no judgment or criticisms from readers. My poor health, busy-ness from work, and lack of confidence as a writer did not affect this space—it was my very own private and "sacred" world where I wrote down whatever came into my mind. Even when I was experiencing writer's block, I was still able to write in my journal, as it was a place for me to vent and let go of anxieties and frustrations. It did not matter how I wrote, what I wrote, how much I wrote, or how often I wrote. When I wrote longer entries, I indulged in details and engaged (and often wrestled) with my thoughts and ideas. I frequently reread my research journal and wrote questions, comments, and responses to earlier questions in the margin and separate entries; at times, I wrote newly constructed narratives based on the rereading. As a reflective practice, journal writing did not end once I finished writing an entry. It was an ongoing, layered practice that involved multiple rounds of revisiting and renewing. In tandem with the influences from the body of literature in situated qualitative research and narrative inquiry, this reflective practice helped my writing become more detail-oriented, personal, honest, and sometimes confessional (cf. Pillow, 2003; Van Maanen, 1988). I am aware that this type of writing style is particular and not to everyone's taste, but finding my distinct voice seemed like a milestone to me as a struggling writer.

## Reflexivity and Reflective Practice in the Classroom: My Development as a Writing Instructor

My own experiences with reflexivity and reflective practice in writing also found a place in the classroom. As a first-year writing instructor, I taught students from multiple linguistic and cultural backgrounds. As part of the course curriculum, I had to teach rules and structure in academic writing, including style guidelines and sometimes also grammar and mechanics. I also had to guide the students to write essays without the first-person pronoun "I," with the exception of the personal narrative essay. In my early days of teaching, I noticed that students were often preoccupied with rules and structure—to them, a "perfect paper" meant an error-free paper. At times, I came across these "perfect" error-free papers, but sadly, most of them were terribly boring as there was hardly any commitment to the content.

Contrary to the essays without much substance, the learning journal entries that students submitted every other week were rich and engaging (cf. Bolton & Delderfield, 2018; Casanave, 2011). In these entries, students were asked to reflect on what they were learning in class (note that I purposely refrained from using the word *reflexivity*, as I thought the concept was too challenging for many of my first-year students). They were intended to help the students "personalize" their learning through reviewing and reflecting and address any questions or concerns. Students did not have to use academic English that they were learning in class, and the only requirement other than to reflect was to write in prose form with a minimum word length of 300 words. Alongside timed freewriting that was done as an opening ritual in every class meeting (thank you, Peter Elbow, 1973), the journals permitted them to go beyond the rules and structures. Once the entries were written, students read each other's entries in groups of three or four and commented on each one, focusing on the content and not on the errors. Students' comments included those showing solidarity, responses to questions through direct answers and examples, questions, and praise and encouragement. I then collected all the entries and commented on each one. These entries were interesting and pleasurable to read, and they were also useful to me as an instructor. First, they showed critical thinking and depth of engagement; second, they were often creative and original in style; third, they provided an opportunity for authentic and personal communication among all the persons involved; and fourth, they enabled me to know what the students were interested in and finding difficulty with, which led to modifications of the lessons, tasks, and writing assignments.

Students appreciated the journals too. In the course feedback, students commented on how the process of reflecting through writing helped them think, learn, review, and find purpose and meaning in their learning and track their development. They also said they appreciated the written communication with me and their peers. I did not think they were trying to please me—most wrote extensively, exceeding the minimum length requirement by far, and some students even wrote extra entries on their own. At times I was asked to read them, and of course, I gladly did.

The success with the learning journals encouraged me to use more reflective practices in the classroom. For example, aside from verbally encouraging students to select essay topics that were meaningful to them as well as their peers, I assigned a short writing task asking them to critically reflect on the topic of their choice and explain why they found it to be important, interesting, and meaningful and how it might interest their primary audience, i.e., their peers. Topic selection was particularly important as they had to commit to that topic over a series of short writing tasks and two essays. In the journal entry that followed this task, many students reported that selecting a topic of their interest was more challenging than they expected, especially because topics were often given to them, and when they had a choice, they tended to select topics quickly and randomly without giving them much thought. Even after they completed the tasks and essays, students continued to examine their topics in their journals critically. At times, the carefully selected and thought-out topics turned out to be more challenging to research and write about, but students became more committed to their writing, and the finished products were far more interesting, showing more originality and engagement than the abovementioned "perfect" essays. Although they did not use the first-person pronoun "I," their essays were personal in the sense that they had personal relevance and commitment. Students often reported their satisfaction in completing the assignments and expressed their wish to pursue their topics further. I believe an increasing number of students no longer wrote for the mere purpose of just completing the assignments and/or following rules and structures in writing. They began to notice that writing is not only a communication tool but also a "method of inquiry" (Richardson & St. Pierre, 2018).

Some colleagues have commented that we do not need to include reflection in the curriculum, as students should be writing objectively—they are already too focused on themselves, and they are already used to writing about their thoughts. Though I understand where this line of thinking comes from, I do not think reflection is a mere indulging of the self. I agree wholeheartedly with Clarà (2015) that "reflection consists of giving coherence to a situation that is initially incoherent and unclear" (p. 262; cf. Dewey, 1986; Schön, 1987, 2016) and is essential, not only in writing but in learning. I also believe that it is imperative for students to consider reflexivity and reflective practices in this "post-truth" era, where critical thinking and information literacy are crucial. Circling back to the Richardson quote above, these abilities also aid not only students, but all of us, to "understand ourselves reflexively as persons writing from a particular position at specific times" (Richardson & St. Pierre, 2018, p. 821) and to engage in meaningful, detailed writing—my own included.

## Conclusion

Although it may read like one, my narrative is certainly not a success story or a model of writer-development. Rather, it is a documentation of a trajectory—an unfinished journey. I believe the journey is an endless one, but I do not say this with despair. I hope that I will continue to steadily develop as an academic writer, however small each step may be. This is a message that I convey to my students, too—although we are all at different developmental stages as academic writers, we are in this together, and every step we take matters. I do not know how I will evolve as a writer, but I am certain that I will not cease from valuing reflexivity and reflective practice in my pursuit of good writing, both as an academic and a writing instructor. I hope that my story acknowledging my vulnerability and tensions will help me move forward and encourage other fellow writers struggling amid their unfinished journeys.

## References

Atkinson, D. (2005). Situated qualitative research and second language writing. In P. K. Matsuda & T. Silva (Eds.), *Second language writing research: Perspectives on the process of knowledge construction* (pp. 49–64). Lawrence Erlbaum.

Behar, R. (1996). *The vulnerable observer: Anthropology that breaks your heart*. Beacon.

Bolton, G., & Delderfield, R. (2018). *Reflective practice: Writing and professional development* (5th ed.). Sage.

Borg, S. (2001). The research journal: A tool for promoting and understanding researcher development. *Language Teaching Research, 5*(2), 156–177. doi:10.1177/136216880100500204

Borg, S. (2003). Pulp fiction? The research journal and professional development. In T. Murphey (Ed.), *Extending professional contributions* (pp. 39–46). TESOL.

Casanave, C. P. (2011). *Journal writing in second language education*. University of Michigan Press.

Chiseri-Strater, E. (1996). Turning in upon ourselves: Positionality, subjectivity, and reflexivity in case study and ethnographic research. In P. Mortensen & G. E. Kirsch (Eds.), *Ethics and representation in qualitative studies of literacy* (pp. 115–133). NCTE.

Clarà, M. (2015). What is reflection? Looking for clarity in an ambiguous notion. *Journal of Teacher Education, 66*(3), 261–271. doi:10.1177/0022487114552028

Dean, J. (2017). *Doing reflexivity: An introduction*. Policy Press.

Dewey, J. (1986). How we think: A restatement of the relation of reflective thinking to the educative process. In J. A. Boydston (Ed.), *John Dewey: The later works, 1925–1953, volume 8: 1933* (pp. 105–352). Southern Illinois University Press.

Elbow, P. (1973). *Writing without teachers.* Oxford University Press.

Farrell, T. S. (2018). *Research on reflective practice in TESOL.* Routledge.

Finlay, L. (2002). Negotiating the swamp: The opportunity and challenge of reflexivity in research practice. *Qualitative Research, 2*(2), 209–230. doi:10.1177/146879410200200205

Finlay, L. (2006). 'Rigour,' 'ethical integrity,' or 'artistry'? Reflexively reviewing criteria for evaluating qualitative research. *The British Journal of Occupational Therapy, 69*(7), 319–326. doi:10.1177/030802260606900704

Finlay, L. (2008). Reflecting on 'reflective practice.' *Practice-based Professional Learning Paper 52.* The Open University.

Finlay, L., & Gough, B. (2003). *Reflexivity: A practical guide for researchers in health and social sciences.* Blackwell.

Fortune, D., & Mair, H. (2011). Notes from the sports club: Confessional tales of two researchers. *Journal of Contemporary Ethnography, 40*(4), 457–484. doi:10.1177/0891241610377093

Haraway, D. (1988). Situated knowledges: The science in question in feminism and the privilege of partial perspective. *Feminist Studies, 14,* 575–599.

Henwood, K. L., & Pidgeon, N. F. (1992). Qualitative research and psychological theorizing. *British Journal of Psychology, 83*(1), 97–110.

Janesick, V. J. (1999). A journal about journal writing as a qualitative research technique: History, issues, and reflections. *Qualitative Inquiry, 5*(4), 505–524. doi:10.1177/107780049900500404

Kanno, Y. (2003). *Negotiating bilingual and bicultural identities: Japanese returnees betwixt two worlds.* Lawrence Erlbaum.

Kleinsasser, A. M. (2000). Researchers, reflexivity, and good data: Writing to unlearn. *Theory into Practice, 39*(3), 155–162. doi:10.1207/s15430421tip3903_6

Kuwayama, T. (2004). *Native anthropology: The Japanese challenge to Western academic hegemony.* Trans Pacific Press.

Mann, S., & Walsh, S. (2017). *Reflective practice in English language teaching: Research-based principles and practices.* Routledge.

Maton, K. (2003). Reflexivity, relationism, & research: Pierre Bourdieu and the epistemic conditions of social scientific knowledge. *Space and Culture, 6*(1), 52–65. doi:10.1177/1206331202238962

Maxwell, J. A. (2012). *Qualitative research design: An interactive approach* (3rd ed.). Sage.

May, T., & Perry, B. (2017). *Reflexivity: The essential guide.* Sage.

Narayan, K. (1997). How native is a "native" anthropologist? In L. Lamphere, H. Ragone, & P. Zavella (Eds.), *Situated lives: Gender and culture in everyday life* (pp. 23–41). Routledge.

Okada, H. (2008). Learning to do graduate school: Learning to do life. In C. P. Casanave & X. Li (Eds.), *Learning the literacy practices of graduate school: Multicultural perspectives on writing, academic enculturation, and identity* (pp. 247–262). University of Michigan Press.

Okada, H. (2009). Somewhere "in between": Languages and identities of three Japanese international school students [Doctoral dissertation, Temple University].

Okada, H. (2011). Negotiating the invisible: Two women making sense of chronic illness through narrative. In P. McPherron & V. Ramanathan (Eds.), *Language, body, and health* (pp. 145–169). De Gruyter.

Okada, H. (2017). Researching people with illnesses and disabilities: Ethical dimensions. In J. McKinley & H. Rose (Eds.), *Doing research in applied linguistics: Realities, dilemmas, solutions* (pp. 124–133). Routledge.

Pelias, R. J. (2011). Writing into position: Strategies for composition and evaluation. In N. K. Denzin & Y. S. Lincoln (Eds.), *The Sage handbook of qualitative research* (4th ed.), (pp. 659–668). Sage.

Pérez-Milans, M. (2016). Reflexivity and social change in applied linguistics. *AILA Review, 29*(1), 1–14. doi: https://doi.org/10.1075/aila.29.01per

Pillow, W. (2003). Confession, catharsis, or cure? Rethinking the uses of reflexivity as methodological power in qualitative research. *International Journal of Qualitative Studies in Education, 16*(2), 175–196. doi:10.1080/0951839032000060635

Pinker, S. (2014). *The sense of style: The thinking person's guide to writing in the 21st century.* Penguin Books.

Richardson, L. (2000). Writing: A method of inquiry. In N. K. Denzin & Y. S. Lincoln (Eds.), *The Sage handbook of qualitative research* (2nd ed.), (pp. 923–948). Sage.

Richardson, L., & St. Pierre, E. A. (2018). Writing: A method of inquiry. In N. K. Denzin & Y. S. Lincoln (Eds.), *The Sage handbook of qualitative research* (5th ed.), (pp. 818–838). Sage.

Schön, D. A. (1987). *Educating the reflective practitioner.* Jossey-Bass.

Schön, D. A. (2016). *The reflective practitioner: How professionals think in action.* Routledge.

Schwandt, T. A. (2015). *The Sage dictionary of qualitative inquiry* (4th ed.). Sage.

Sharma, B. K. (2021). Reflexivity in applied linguistics research in the tourism workplace. *Applied Linguistics, 42*(2), 230–251. https://doi.org/10.1093/applin/amz067

Starfield, S. (2012). Researcher reflexivity. In C. A. Chapelle (Ed.), *The encyclopedia of applied linguistics* (Vol. 8, pp. 4931–4937). Wiley-Blackwell.

Swan, E. (2008). Let's not get too personal: Critical reflection, reflexivity, and the confessional turn. *Journal of European Industrial Training, 32*(5), 385–399. doi:10.1108/03090590810877102

Sword, H. (2012). *Stylish academic writing.* Harvard University Press.

Taylor, J. (2011). The intimate insider: Negotiating the ethics of friendship when doing insider research. *Qualitative Research, 11*(1), 3–21. doi:10.1177/1468794110384447

Van Maanen, J. (1988). *Tales of the field: On writing ethnography.* University of Chicago Press.

Vicary, S., Young, A., & Hicks, S. (2017). A reflective journal as learning process and contribution to quality and validity in interpretative phenomenological analysis. *Qualitative Social Work, 16*(4), 550–565. doi:10.1177/1473325016635244

Zinsser, W. (2006). *On writing well: The classic guide to writing nonfiction* (30th anniversary ed.). Harper Collins.

**Chapter 15**

# My Experience with Second Language Writing as a Non-Native Speaker of English: Struggles, Successes, Setbacks, and Lessons Learnt about "Good" Writing

*Icy Lee*

In this chapter, I share my firsthand experience with English writing as a non-native speaker born and educated in Hong Kong, a British colony until 1997 when its sovereignty was handed back to China. I began my journey as a diffident second language writer obsessed with the display of advanced grammar and vocabulary in my writing. I had been an inexpert secondary English teacher who paid inordinate attention to standard (British) English in writing and moved on to become a second language teacher educator-researcher with broadened perspectives on teaching, learning, and assessment of writing through my research and professional practice. My own struggles, successes, and setbacks in my journey as a writer and researcher have taught me valuable lessons about writing: what it is and what to focus on when I research, teach, and evaluate writing. They are also life-changing experiences that have enabled me to discover who I am as a writer, and more important, what good writing entails. In this chapter, I reflect on how my understanding of good writing has informed my practice as a teacher educator and researcher of second language writing, a journal editor and manuscript reviewer, and a doctoral supervisor, with implications for academic/research writing, teaching, and learning.

## As a Secondary Student: "Flowery Language! Write in Simple English!"

Born in Hong Kong in the 1960s, I began to learn English at the age of four. Hong Kong was then a British colony. I studied at a Chinese-medium primary school, and English happened to be my best subject. I did very well academically and took pride in being able to attend one of the best girls' secondary schools run by the colonial government, which had adopted English as the medium of instruction. With a strong foundation in English grammar, I always did well in English writing. In those days, marks were deducted for each grammatical mistake in writing. I knew very well how to avoid mistakes, so I always got good scores in my English compositions. To me, written accuracy was the be-all and end-all of good English writing. My obsession with displaying advanced grammar and vocabulary in writing intensified until Secondary 4 (i.e., 10th grade). I remember I kept a vocabulary book in which I entered a wide range of newly learnt vocabulary items; each time I wrote a composition I tried my best to use some new words I had learnt by searching my vocabulary book. When I received my English teacher's feedback on my first composition in Secondary 4, however, I was flabbergasted. I failed! It was my very first failure in English writing, and the teacher's overall remark was: *Flowery language! Write in simple English!*

That fiasco was followed by another one. Still with pretty high self-esteem about my own English writing ability, I was determined to publish my writing in a local English newspaper. I shared my draft essay with my English teacher, who read it and told me it was not up to scratch. "You have to learn to write in simple English!" she repeated. I was perplexed. What is "simple English"? Shouldn't I embellish my written language to make it less bland and commonplace?

Gradually I lost interest in choosing "exotic" words or expressions to display my knowledge of vocabulary in writing. My failures were a humbling experience; they taught me a precious lesson and made me more cautious of my language choice when I wrote. I realized that rarely are two words exactly identical in meaning; in writing I have to mean what I say and say what I mean without going over the top. Looking back, my initial failures are significant episodes that give me a constant reminder that good writing is natural and simple, rather than artificial and turgid. As a teacher educator, I always find myself telling my pre- and in-service teachers that good writing is easy to read and understand and that it is important to use vocabulary for the right context, the right purpose, and the right audience. Such principles were true when I was a school student decades ago, and they are still true in the twenty-first century. According to Pinker, good writing in the twenty-first century is characterized by clarity and simplicity (*The Current*, 2014).

## As a Secondary Teacher: Primacy of Language in English Writing

When I grew up, I became an English teacher at a secondary school. With just a bachelor's degree in English literature and linguistics, I had no idea how English should be taught. Quite naturally I brought with me my ingrained belief about the primacy of language in writing, which I had acquired from my previous English teachers. I loved teaching English grammar and vocabulary and perhaps inadvertently sent my students the message that writing was primarily a vehicle for language reinforcement. In line with the policy of the school, I deducted marks for each grammatical mistake and filled all of my students' papers with red ink. I prided myself on my detailed written corrective feedback and thought that my strong grammar knowledge helped me perform my job well. Without the benefit of teacher training, I did what my previous English teachers did—i.e., apprenticeship of observation (Lortie, 1975)—by putting predominant emphasis on the language form in my responses to student writing. Like many other ESL teachers around the world, I approached "good writing" in the way criticized by Zamel (1987):

> It seems that ESL writing teachers view themselves primarily as language teachers, that they attend to surface-level features of writing, and that they seem to read and react to a text as a series of separate pieces at the sentence level or even clause level, rather than as a whole unit of discourse. In fact they are so distracted by language-related problems that they often correct these without realizing that there is a much larger, meaning-related problem that they have failed to address. (Zamel, 1987, p. 700)

Upon reflection, when I was a secondary teacher, I did ignore the meaning conveyed by my students and focused primarily on language in my written feedback. What's worse, I insisted that my students adhere to British English; it was a time when Hong Kong was a British colony, and I happened to be a big fan of British English. I still remember prohibiting the use of American spelling like "center" and "color" in my students' writing.

In retrospect, my preoccupation with and pedantic insistence on correct grammar and mechanics as well as one single variety of English demonstrated my narrow-mindedness and lack of understanding of "good" writing. Today I believe that it is not necessary to impose a native speaker standard (be it British or American) in academic writing and that there is more to good writing than written accuracy.

## My PhD Research: Realization of the Importance of Macro Issues in Writing

My professional development began in earnest as I moved from secondary to tertiary teaching, prompting me to upgrade myself professionally by undertaking further studies. My PhD research marked an important turning point in my understanding and pursuit of good writing.

Perhaps subconsciously it was because of my earlier fixation on micro issues in writing that drove me to focus on macro concerns in my PhD research. Somehow I was intrigued by the notion of coherence in writing and decided to investigate what coherence is, how it can be taught in writing classrooms, and whether and how it can improve students' writing performance. As I read up on the literature, I became fascinated with all the ideas that helped me understand how to organize a text to achieve overall coherence, for example through a focus on purpose, audience, and context as well as the information structure, rhetorical organization, and genre of texts. I still remember my PhD supervisor's comment on my writing after reading my first draft: "You write well!" I heaved a sigh of relief.

Through my PhD study, I realized that good academic writing is coherent in the sense that it communicates ideas clearly, taking into consideration the needs of the readers. There must be something meaningful in the message communicated; hence, writing is thinking, and good writing is good thinking (Nauman, Stirling, & Borthwick, 2011). Grammar, vocabulary, and mechanics are still important but they are subsidiary to purpose, communication, and clarity as well as to overall coherence.

# Critical Incident: I Almost Failed My PhD!

As I continued to work on my PhD research, my supervisor gave me encouraging feedback, boosting my confidence in my academic writing. I developed a set of pedagogical materials about the teaching of coherence, submitted them to TESOL for the Excellence in Materials Development Award, and won the award. Such thrilling news reinforced my belief in the significance of my topic on coherence in writing. At the same time, I started to publish papers from the preliminary study of my PhD research, with some success. When I submitted my dissertation for examination, I thought that I would get a good pass.

Much to my shock, my external examiner, whom my supervisor and the dissertation committee members did not know personally and who had probably not examined any PhD dissertations at Hong Kong universities, appeared to have a low opinion of my dissertation. I was told that she read only the first two chapters and stopped reading as she did not like the way I presented the literature review—mainly how I conceptualized "coherence" in my dissertation. Without examining the entire piece of work, she could not complete the external examiner's assessment form. So it was neither a pass nor a fail. The dissertation committee, now in a state of limbo, spent over an hour discussing my case after the oral examination, which the external examiner did not attend. The committee's joint decision was to give me several months to revise my dissertation and to appoint a new external examiner to assess my work, without another oral examination. In the end, I passed.

Ironically, when I believed that my understanding of writing had broadened significantly and that I had become better at academic writing through my PhD research on coherence in writing, my first external examiner was flatly unimpressed by my writing, particularly the literature review chapter. My thinking about "coherence" was considered by the external examiner to be inadequate, though I later learnt that all of my internal examiners would have passed my first submission. My setback had driven home the message that writing is thinking and that good academic writing is quality thinking—to be judged by the readers and especially the gatekeepers (in the case of my PhD research, the key gatekeeper was my external examiner). However, judgment of quality thinking in academic writing can be a subjective matter. As long as a single significant gatekeeper does not appreciate the thinking in my work, I have to improve it to strongly defend my original choices. I later learnt from my scholarly publishing experience that this is also how the publishing game is played.

# My Academic Publishing Experience: I Can Write and Publish!

After getting over the emotional shock of my PhD oral examination, I completely lost interest in research on coherence in writing. This lacuna was soon filled by my growing interest in error feedback (now more commonly known as "written corrective feedback"), which was triggered by Truscott's (1996) landmark article in *Language Learning*, where he vehemently argued for the abandonment of grammar correction in writing. Since the early 2000s, I have been researching written corrective feedback and have gradually broadened my research focus to include feedback in writing, classroom writing assessment, and writing teacher education and development (e.g., teacher beliefs and identity), producing an ongoing stream of publications in international journals. While I kept plugging away at scholarly publishing without consciously addressing the fundamental question of what good academic writing is, my continuous success in getting my work published in international journals, especially the *Journal of Second Language Writing* (JSLW), turned out to be a significant milestone in my academic career, also culminating in my understanding of what good academic writing entails.

I used to think that research conducted in Hong Kong, an underrepresented context, could not be of much interest to researchers in the United States, where second language writing research is the most vibrant. That was why when I learnt that I won the JSLW Best Article Award for my 2008 article "Understanding Teachers' Written Feedback Practices in Hong Kong Secondary Classrooms," I simply could not believe it. Through the JSLW award, however, I came to the realization that if my work is original and provides new insights that push the field forward, it is considered "good" academic writing. I later learnt from fellow researchers in the field that they appreciated this award-winning paper because it approached the topic of feedback from a new vantage point, not only unraveling the reasons why teachers' feedback practices departed from recommended principles but also bringing sociocultural perspectives into the picture to account for the gulf between research and practice. One of my PhD students, who is now a very well-established researcher in second language writing, told me that he had resolved to come to Hong Kong to pursue his PhD under my supervision after he had read that 2008 paper. In his informal communication with me, he explained:

> I could see something new about feedback in L2 writing in this article. It has provided new insights into our understanding of teacher

feedback in EFL contexts by explaining why Hong Kong secondary English teachers gave feedback in the ways they did. The paper is very easy to follow . . . and I enjoyed reading it very much!

My PhD student's additional remark that my writing was easy to follow has, in fact, been echoed by others. Throughout the years, the informal comments I have received from my readers are that my writing is clear, concise and simple, easy to follow, and always to the point. One reader told me in his informal communication:

You write in a unique style—simple language but intricate and delicate thoughts and ideas. Your writing is crystal clear as your ideas are very logically organized, which are easy for the readers to follow . . . I mean your language is not flourished. . . . No unnecessary information.

Back in my secondary school days, I was unable to write in simple English; through my professional learning and practice as an academic, I think I have a built a reputation for my ability to communicate ideas in simple English. If good writing is precise and easy to follow (Leki, 1995), I hope my writing can provide an example, among many others, for novice second language writers.

## We Write What We Are: My Voice as a Unique Individual and as a Writing Teacher Educator-Researcher

It is gratifying to know that I have finally overcome my major weakness in writing—inability to write in a simple manner. As I matured as a person, I also grew in my thinking and writing. I have probably learnt to digest complicated information and present it in a simple fashion. Through developing my expertise in my specialist areas, I have refined my thinking, developed insight, and found my own voice in my writing. I am reminded by Elbow's (2007) words: "Everyone has a real voice and can write with power. Writing with a strong voice is good writing. Sincere writing is good writing. My voice is my true self and my rhetorical power" (p. 168). Through projecting my voice, my readers can see me in my writing, and they know who I am through my work. My sincere writing speaks to my guilelessness as a person, and my concise writing parallels the clean language I use in my daily life communication. My writing allows me to express my voice not only as a person but also as a second language writing teacher educator and researcher, who no longer treats writing as a vehicle for language reinforcement but instead as both a means and an end to achieve a higher purpose. I write for the sake of knowledge contribution and knowledge mobilization, and I hope that through my writing my readers will become inspired. As a PhD student who knows my work very well commented, "I can see where you are coming from—your concerns, passion, and intentions as a writer, researcher, and teacher educator." I am glad that my readers appreciate my voice as a writer and understand that as a second language writing teacher educator-researcher I want to help teachers enhance their instructional and assessment practices through my writing.

Although there is a perception that good academic writing has to be scientific and objective and hence should not express a personal voice, good academic writing indicates the stance of authors who "show the kind of engagement or involvement with their topics that comes with taking a particular point of view" (Leki, 1995, p. 33). Gemmell (2008) refutes the conventional thinking about the inappropriateness of personal voice in academic writing: Putting students' ideas and opinions at the center of our classroom has freed students' voices. They know that I care about what they have to say, and in turn, they care more about what they write. They produce better writing—writing that sounds like them, writing that I enjoy reading (Gemmell, 2008, p. 67). Indeed, good academic writing has a strong personal voice, giving the writer a unique sense of identity.

## As a Journal Editor and Manuscript Reviewer: What I Look for in Good Academic Writing

In my multiple roles as a journal editor and manuscript reviewer, my conceptions of good writing as explicated in the above have been guiding my practice.

The very first thing I look for is whether the author has something important and meaningful to say. As McKinley and Rose (2019) hold, "communication of meaning is key" (p. 116). Manuscripts cannot be accepted for publication just because they are well-written or neatly organized; they have to produce new knowledge or perspectives that move the field forward in a significant way.

In terms of language use, to present ideas in an unambiguous manner is the goal of academic writing, rather than to sound like a native speaker of English (McKinley & Rose, 2018). In my review of manuscripts, I never use nativeness as a yardstick but consider clarity of ideas as an important criterion of good writing. As a non-native speaker of English myself, I actually cannot claim to possess full understanding of the notion of nativeness in writing and, indeed, it is a nebulous concept to me; in fact, "expertise" is much more pertinent to discussion of good academic writing than "nativeness" (Römer, 2009). Citing McKinley and Rose (2018) again, I believe that good academic writing "can easily be understood by a broad, heterogeneous, global, and multilingual audience" (p. 1). To elaborate, meaning has to be clearly expressed to a global community comprising L1 and L2 users/writers: There is "a need for linguistic clarity in journal publications so that research can be understood with unambiguity; and a need to be inclusive of a global academic community, many of whom are L2 writers" (McKinley & Rose, 2018, p. 9).

As for textual organization, although the standard expectation for a research article is introduction-literature review-methodology-findings-discussion-conclusion, i.e., a predictable organization, I do not look for these elements in all journal papers in a decontextualized manner. Instead, good organization is content-driven (Leki, 1995); that is, the textual organization may vary according to the content of the paper. Using book reviews as an example, I do not expect a rigid organizational format for a book review published in a journal—e.g., a chapter-by-chapter summary of the book followed by an overall evaluation of the book. The JSLW guide for authors on "how to write a book review" alludes to a flexible structure that is driven by the content:

> The journal seeks reviews that include a concise descriptive and evaluative summary of the contents (about one-third of the review) and a discussion of the significance of the work in the context of current L2 writing theory, research and/or practice, with references to other related work as appropriate (about two-thirds of the review).

Recently, Lewis's (2020) hints on how to write a book review for academic journals conclude by pointing to the importance of an individual style characterized by a flexibility that allows book reviewers to connect with the readers: There is not one perfect format for a book review, as reviewers have their own styles, perspectives, and priorities, and it is important that these come through in a book review, as it will allow the readers to "connect" with the ideas and perspectives (Lewis, 2020, p. 3).

The individual style is the voice that comes through, and that is what characterizes good writing.

Echoing my earlier idea about conciseness and reader-friendliness as crucial to good academic writing, I have specifically learnt from my journal editing experience that any manuscript could be truncated to meet the word limit requirement of the journal. In general, the longer a paper gets, the more likely it is to get convoluted and hence hard to follow and understand. Somehow, even for qualitative papers with abundant details, quotes, and excerpts, oftentimes the final product becomes more readable after it has been shortened to meet the journal's word require-ment. The magic of conciseness cannot be overstated; good writing is always to the point (Leki, 1995).

All in all, good academic writing allows the authors to achieve their communicative purpose through a language and structure that accom-modate a global academic community, express their individuality in a unique way, and connect their ideas with the readers in a concise manner.

## Bringing "Good Writing" to My Own Research Writing and Teaching

My own understanding of "good" academic writing has informed my research writing and teaching in different ways. To begin with, as an author I write with a clear purpose to communicate ideas on a topic that is of significance to the academic community. I always start with a takeaway from my readers' perspective, asking myself what my readers can get from my writing. Good writing is quality thinking: "All academic papers, whether the first draft in a composition class or the final version to appear in a top-ranked journal, are judged first on the originality and quality of the ideas within" (Stapleton, 2002, p. 187).

Good academic writing communicates new knowledge in a clear, concise, and transparent manner so that the readers can easily connect with the authors; it is not confusing and difficult to understand. As Pinker (2014) humorously suggests, good writing does not "stink." To create writing that is clear and easy to understand, I find Grice's (1975) maxims of conversation helpful, though they were originally intended to assist in effective oral communication:

> The maxim of quantity—Be as informative as possible; give as much information as is needed (just the right amount).

The maxim of quality—Be truthful and ethical. No fabricated information.

The maxim of relation—Give information that is relevant to the study.

The maxim of manner—Be clear, to the point, and provide information in an orderly manner.

For example, the maxim of quantity is particularly relevant to the methods section, where authors are expected to provide sufficient details of the research design, research context, participants, data collection, and data analysis procedure. The ethics of research is addressed in the maxim of quality—be truthful and ethical. The maxim of relation is pertinent to the literature review, where only relevant literature should be reviewed. The maxim of manner points to the need to present ideas in a clear and organized fashion. As a writer, I benefit from these maxims.

Although there are style or formatting guidelines that I need to conform to, as required by target journals or publishers (such as the APA reference style, line spacing, and font size), the organization of my writing is guided and driven by its content (Leki, 1995), which allows me to express my individuality and voice as a writer. My writing is not dictated by a single variety of English, such as British or American English, but I write in a language that is intelligible to an international academic community. The voice expressed in good academic writing is that of authors who project "an identity invested with individual authority, displaying confidence in their evaluations and commitment to their ideas" (Hyland, 2002, p. 1091).

As a non-native speaker of English, my prior learning experiences have tended to develop a bias in me toward seeing writing as a vehicle for language practice. I still remember being encouraged to memorize a range of connectives so that I could use a different connective or a phrase to connect paragraphs (e.g., "on the other hand," "apart from that," and "in addition"). Now I realize that connectives, or other metadiscoursal devices, are useful only when they are really needed to express the meaning I truly want to convey. For instance, whether I should use a hedge or a certainty marker depends on what I want to say, as well as my stance. Indeed, language is a tool for meaning making; it is important to move beyond mere obsession with correct grammar and vocabulary and zero in on the meaning and overall communicative purpose of academic writing. As a researcher, I seek to communicate with my readers to connect with them and to make a difference through the message conveyed in my writing. That is the essence of knowledge contribution as well as the research impact I wish to achieve through my writing.

Translating my beliefs about good academic writing into instructional practice at the graduate level (I mainly teach graduate students), I see the teaching of writing as the teaching of thinking—quality thinking, with an emphasis on writing as a communicative tool to make an impact through disseminating the ideas that we are passionate about. As suggested by Elbow (2007), the goals of teaching writing are to develop the self and a personal voice in students' writing. These goals cannot be achieved if the primary focus is on the language form. As a doctoral supervisor, my feedback on students' drafts focuses primarily on ideas and meaning rather than language use—i.e., what students have to say in their writing. My PhD students often tell me that back in the country where they are from, their previous master's supervisors used to point out the various grammatical errors they make in writing. I tell them, contrary to their prior learning experiences, that I comment on language only when communication is impeded and meaning unclear. In my doctoral supervision, I provide instruction through asking higher-order questions that help my students enhance the quality of their thinking. I also share with them the concerns of the audience and sensitize them to the clarity of the meaning and message they want to convey through their research. My focus on lucidity often makes them reexamine the formulation of ideas from the readers' perspective; my query about the meaning expressed drives home the importance of language as a communicative tool and conciseness as a rule of the thumb. Verbosity is something they have to learn to avoid. I state very explicitly that no readers like to read a dissertation that is overly long; unnecessary information has to be taken out and the entire dissertation has to be presented in a reader-friendly manner, which is what good writing is about.

## Closing Thoughts

The way we write is deeply influenced by the norms and expectations of the specific cultural and professional communities with which we are familiar or affiliated (Abdollahzadeh, (2011). As someone brought up in an environment that privileged the British culture, I find myself easily empathizing with Anglophone academic conventions like authorial identity and personal voice. However, second/foreign language writers from other cultures may have a different view of good academic writing. They may find promoting an individual self in writing an alien idea (Hyland, 2002), or they may find it hard to apply text conventions or discourse patterns that differ from those of their own culture (Scott, 2015). In conceptualizing "good" academic writing, there are bound to be cross-cultural differences. It is important that teachers acknowledge and show understanding of such differences and provide support and instruction that help multilingual student writers cope with the challenges in what a particular culture considers to be good academic writing.

Even though my personal and research experience has prompted me not to give excessive attention to linguistic accuracy in writing, I do not mean to downplay the importance of language use in academic writing. If an author can convey significant and meaningful ideas in writing that uses a range of appropriate vocabulary, as well as varied and sophisticated sentence structures to express meaning with clarity and perhaps an element of idiomaticity (see Reichelt, 2003), readers can readily recognize it as good writing.

In closing, although I have shared my understanding of "good writing" in rather explicit terms based on my personal experience, I am cognizant of the fact that behind explicit standards always lie subjective interpretations of terms that are typically associated with good writing, such as "clarity" (e.g., clarity of meaning) and "appropriateness" (e.g., appropriate vocabulary) (see Leki, 1995; Reichelt, 2003). Despite its apparent status as a simple notion, "good writing" is in fact a complex concept that is hard to pin down, especially with universally agreed definitions. I hope that my reflections on "good writing" can make a tiny contribution to this neglected yet significant conversation in L2 writing scholarship.

## References


Abdollahzadeh, E. (2011). Poring over the findings: Interpersonal authorial engagement in applied linguistics papers. *Journal of Pragmatics, 43*(1), 288–297.

Elbow, P. (2007). Reconsiderations: Voice in writing again: Embracing contraries. *College English, 70*(2), 168–188.

Gemmell, R. (2008). Encouraging student voice in academic writing. *The English Journal, 98*(2), 64–68.

Grice, H. P. (1975). Logic and conversation. In P. Cole & J. J. Morgan (Eds.), *Syntax and semantics 3: Speech Acts* (pp. 41–58). Academic Press.

Hyland, K. (2002). Authority and invisibility: Authorial identity in academic writing. *Journal of Pragmatics, 34*(8), 1091–1112.

Leki, I. (1995). Good writing: I know it when I see it. In D. Belcher & G. Braine (Eds.), *Academic writing in a second language: Essays on research and pedagogy* (pp. 23–46). Ablex Publishing Corporation.

Lewis, M. N. (2020). Here's a good book: Hints on writing a book review for academic journals. *RELC Journal, 53*(1), 253–260.

Lortie, D. (1975). *Schoolteacher.* University of Chicago Press.

McKinley, J., & Rose, H. (2018). Conceptualizations of language errors, standards, norms and nativeness in English for research publication purposes: An analysis of journal submission guidelines. *Journal of Second Language Writing, 42*, 1–11.

McKinley, J., & Rose, H. (2019). Standards of English in academic writing: The authors respond. *Journal of Second Language Writing, 44*, 114–116.

Nauman, A. D., Stirling, T., & Borthwick, A. (2011). What makes writing good? An essential question for teachers. *The Reading Teacher, 64*(5), 318–328.

Pinker, S. (2014). Why academics stink at writing. *The Chronicle of Higher Education,* September 26. https://stevenpinker.com/files/pinker/files/why_academics_stink_at_writing.pdf

Reichelt, M. (2003). Defining "good writing": A cross-cultural perspective. *Composition Studies, 31*(1), 99–126.

Römer, U. (2009). English in academia: Does nativeness matter? *Anglistik: International Journal of English Studies, 20*(2), 89–100.

Scott, N. (2015). Academic writing and culture: A study of Austrian tertiary-level EFL learners. *AAA: Arbeiten aus Anglistik und Amerikanistik, 40*(1/2), 75–97.

Stapleton, P. (2002). Critiquing voice as a viable pedagogical tool in L2 writing: Returning the spotlight to ideas. *Journal of Second Language Writing, 11*(3), 177–190.

*The Current.* (2014). Steven Pinker says good writing in the 21st century needs clarity and simplicity. CBC Radio. October 1. https://www.cbc.ca/radio/thecurrent/oct-1-2014-1.2907475/steven-pinker-says-good-writing-in-the-21st-century-needs-clarity-and-simplicity-1.2907478

Truscott, J. (1996). The case against grammar correction in L2 writing classes. *Language Learning, 46*(2), 327–369.

Zamel, V. (1987). Recent research on writing pedagogy. *TESOL Quarterly, 21*(4), 697–715.

Chapter 16

# What "Not-So-Good" Writing Looks Like

*Lía D. Kamhi-Stein*

I have to begin this chapter by acknowledging that, in spite of having been in academia for thirty years, defining "good" writing is still a challenge for me. In search of a description of features of "good" writing, I will in this chapter chart how my own writing has evolved since my days as an English as a foreign language (EFL) learner. In looking back at my own texts and my reflections on them, I attempt to provide an explanation of how my writing did not meet my teachers' (or my own) expectations of what "good" writing looked like at the time I produced the texts. I then discuss what "not-so-good writing" looks like and end the chapter with a call for looking at "good" writing in translingual literacies.

## From "Composiciones" to Monographs

I am a Spanish-English bilingual and biliterate TESOL professional. I was born and raised in a middle-class immigrant Sephardic Jewish family in Buenos Aires, Argentina. Like all immigrant families in Argentina, my parents placed a lot of value on my education since it was perceived as the ticket to a better life. In fact, my mother saw English as a language of power and prestige, and as such, she believed that, as adults, it would provide my brother and me "symbolic and material resources" (Peirce, 1995, p. 17) that she saw herself lacking. Therefore, my mother enrolled me in my EFL neighborhood institute, where classes were offered twice a week for a total of two hours. My teacher, Omar Mariani, was an energetic young man who over the years has taught thousands of EFL learners.

While my mother had what in the field of TESOL is known as instrumental motivation (Gardner & Lambert, 1972), my motivation was significantly more ambitious. As a child, I saw *The Sound of Music,* the Julie Andrews movie about a singing governess. After the movie was over, I remember walking out of the movie theater singing in what I thought was English, just as Julie Andrews did in the movie. However, unlike the movie's heroine, I did not know a word of English.

In the late 1960s and early 1970s, when I was in elementary school, my EFL neighborhood institute emphasized the Audiolingual Method combined with a strong emphasis on grammatical correctness. Writing did not have much of a place in my EFL classroom until I entered high school, when EFL writing instruction was limited to the production of "composiciones" (compositions), one-page, single-spaced handwritten personal narratives focusing on topics assigned by the teacher. These compositions were a mere excuse to get EFL learners to use vocabulary or grammatical structures that had been explicitly taught in the classroom. For example, in a composition titled "Visiting a Friend in Hospital," I was required to include the following information: (1) friend ill; (2) journey to hospital; (3) find room; (4) reception desk; (5) nurse; (6) doctor; (7) flowers; (8) fruit; (9) friend's room; (10) conversation with friend; (11) reflections.

In reviewing my "Visiting a Friend in Hospital" composition written in 1972, I can see that my teacher's implicit definition of "good" writing in English was writing that was devoid of grammatical errors. In this view, "good" writing in English was simply perceived as writing that showed mastery in the use of verb tenses and prepositions as well as vocabulary and spelling (Hirvela, 2004). Unfortunately, my composition, which had errors in the use of prepositions, did not meet my teacher's expectations. In fact, she put an "!X" next to every single error I made— only five!—and at the bottom of my composition wrote "Be very careful please!" followed by another big "!X."

My teacher's view of "good" writing as free of errors was not unique to her and indeed reflected the view of many EFL teachers in Buenos Aires, whose attention was focused on the manipulation of linguistic forms for the purpose of producing grammatically accurate texts that were not necessarily motivating to read or write. Raimes's (1991) argument, that writing in the 1970s went beyond the notion of "sentence combining and controlled composition" (p. 409) and instead switched attention to issues of process and multiple drafts, is far from the reality of the EFL classroom in Buenos Aires in the 1970s. "Good" writing was expected to conform to standards of grammatical form and was done in a decontextualized manner in that it did not consider issues of purpose and audience. To put it simply: Writing was the conduit for grammatical accuracy.

My writing experience in my public high school, where all instruction was done in Spanish, the official language of the country and my home language, was not much different from what was happening in my EFL classes. Although my peers and I were assigned to read authors from the Spanish Golden Century, only on very few occasions were we asked to do any writing and, when we did, our objective was to analyze the work of famous authors. One more time, writing played a limited role in my education.

In contrast to what was happening in my formal schooling, the situation could not have been more different on my home front. My mom, who wanted me to have access to all the cultural capital she saw herself as lacking, created an environment that contributed to making me an avid reader and writer of narratives and poetry. In fact, I enjoyed reading great Latin American and European authors—in Spanish or translated into Spanish—like Ernesto Sábato, Julio Cortázar, Gabriel García Márquez, Herman Hesse, Antonin Artaud, and others. I saw these authors as representing "good" writing because of their creativity and their ability to create magical worlds or challenge readers' views through the use of extensive vocabulary and complex prose.

When I went to college (first to obtain a degree as Certified Public Translator and then to graduate with an EFL teaching degree), all of the coursework was in English. During my first year of college, I was introduced to a wide range of authors such as Jane Austen, D. H. Lawrence, T. S. Eliot, and James Baldwin. Much of the written work I did focused on the literary analysis of the books we read. However, my first recollection of being asked to write for academic purposes was when a U.S. instructor, who was teaching in an Argentine university for the first time, assigned her U.S. Culture class, in which I was enrolled, to write a 20-page monograph focusing on a topic of our choice (in my case, twentieth-century artists in the United States). I still remember our collective reaction. *Twenty pages? And based on research? And all of this done without having had the opportunity to read or understand how to write a monograph?* Even though I was able to complete the assignment successfully, what was not, and still is not, clear to me is how my instructor defined "good" writing.

During my college studies, I was not asked to write a 20-page paper ever again; however, I was required to write shorter papers that were graded in terms of grammatical accuracy. Much like the case of my EFL teachers in elementary and high school, "good" writing was not associated with issues of syntax, text coherence, and style (Pinker, 2014a). One more time, "good" writing was limited to grammatical accuracy in English.

What *did* change in college is that, in contrast to the reading that I did in elementary school and high school, I became an avid English reader. Besides doing the required reading of British and U.S. authors mandated in my college courses, I read magazines like *Time*, *Glamour*, and *Good Housekeeping* (among others) and the highly respected Argentine newspaper *The Buenos Aires Herald* (whose director, Robert Cox, was a leader in the defense of human rights during Argentina's military dictatorship). These materials exposed me to different genres and registers and provided me with valuable information on current topics outside those that were of interest in mainstream Argentine society.

## Writing in Graduate School

After I spent several years working as an EFL teacher in various EFL institutes in Buenos Aires and teaching EFL and serving as a program administrator at the Buenos Aires Binational Center—a nonprofit EFL institute that promotes the mutual understanding between the United States and Argentina—in 1990 I immigrated to the United States when I married my Texan husband. That same year I set out to enroll in a master's program in TESOL at California State University, Los Angeles, where I currently teach. My initial experience as a novice graduate student was similar to that of many other non-native English-speaking professionals, whose self-perceptions are often affected by the change in setting (from experienced EFL professional to graduate student in an Inner Circle setting) (for a discussion on this topic, see Kamhi-Stein, 2013). However, in spite of my initial negative self-perceptions, what was *not* lost in me was my sense of agency and determination to grow as a professional.

As a novice graduate student, my definition of "good" academic writing was quite simplistic: I believed that the authors who were published in *TESOL Quarterly* had to be good writers. After all, they were published in the leading journal in the TESOL field. To me, these authors had to have an in-depth understanding of the topic on which they were writing; they wrote with fluidity and with a specific audience in mind; they had extensive vocabularies; they were coherent in their arguments; and they knew how to structure their papers to get published. In addition, I saw these "good" writers as showing linearity in their discourse structure and argumentation. This was a particularly important issue to me given that, as a native speaker of Spanish, a Romance language, I perceived my writing and speech in Spanish *and* English to take digressions that, from the point of view of an English-speaking reader, were irrelevant to the discussion at hand. At that point, I was deeply influenced by Kaplan's (1966) idea of contrastive rhetoric and was under the impression that to be a "good" writer by Inner Circle standards, I had to demonstrate strict linearity in my discourse. Although my digressions did not create problems with my Spanish-speaking interlocutors and were indeed welcome, I perceived them as creating confusion among my English-speaking interlocutors. Therefore, as shown in an excerpt of the very first paper I wrote in graduate school in 1990 (Excerpt 1), in search for what I perceived as "good" writing, I emphasized the notion of linearity as the driving force in my text:

Excerpt 1

. . . Below are the four major points in my philosophy which will be described in detail in the main portion of this paper:

1. Social interaction and its role in second language acquisition;
2. Comprehensible input and its role in second language acquisition;

. . .

## 1. Social Interaction and Its Role in Second Language Acquisition

Vygotsky (1978) recognizes two developmental levels in the human being: the actual developmental level (Krashen's—1982—"i") and a potential developmental level ("+1"). Between the two levels is the zone of proximal development. Through interaction, the individual goes from the actual developmental level to the potential level.

What are the implications of these ideas for the ESL classroom? If we apply Vygotsky's ideas to what Freire (1970) called a "libertarian" education, teachers and students will engage in a dynamic educational process. The question to ask is, "What kind of activities will make students go from the actual to the potential level?"

As the excerpt above shows, the paper did not depict any features of what I thought was "good" writing. First, the text's direct rhetorical structure did not contribute to my idea of "good" writing because it resulted in writing that was unmotivating to read. In fact, I now question the extent to which readers, at that point my own professors, would be interested in engaging with my own texts—for any purposes other than giving me a grade. There was a second reason why the paper can't be considered "good" writing: Even though it is clear that I knew that "good" academic writing had to reflect "traces of other texts" (to use Hyland's 2004 terms, p. 80) by weaving paraphrases and quotations into my own text, the paper I produced too heavily relied on the work of authors that I considered authorities. Therefore, I was practically speaking through the authors' mouths, resulting in what is known as "ventriloquism" (to use Ruddick's 2001 term, cited in Blanton, 2003, p. 182). To make matters worse, my text suffered from a feature that is considered to be typical of novice writers for academic purposes: the use of the topic-comment pattern (Dobson & Feak, 2001), which involved summarizing an author's idea and then making a comment in response to a question.

My subsequent papers showed significant improvement due to the fact that I engaged in a practice that is common to many novice authors: I carefully read and analyzed *TESOL Quarterly* articles (Casanave, 2003) and engaged in a process of modeling my writing after the "good" *TESOL Quarterly* authors. In reading what I thought were "good" writers, I paid attention to their vocabulary, their hedging, paraphrasing, and quoting strategies as well as the conventions they used to provide cohesion within and across paragraphs. It was by doing this kind of work that my writing moved along the writing continuum from "poor" to "more developed."

In fact, a year and a half after producing my first paper in graduate school, I wrote a paper that allowed me to see myself as, not necessarily producing "good" writing, but producing "more competent" writing. What follows is an excerpt (Excerpt 2) from the paper, titled "In Search of a Balance Between the Process Approach and the English for Academic Purposes Approach":

Excerpt 2

. . . In the process approach, students frequently select their topics, or respond to a piece of expository writing or a work of literature (Raimes, 1991). Instead, in the English for academic purposes approach, students are taught how to deconstruct (Johns, 1986) prompts and respond to the writing assignments of different academic disciplines.

While the process approach is critical, in the sense that it introduces students to the idea of multiple drafts and revisions, in my view, it fails to consider an important point. Advanced ESL students at the university level usually do not have experience writing for academic purposes in the U.S. university system. Thus, university students often lack an understanding of the conventions of U.S. academic prose and may not know what professors require to successfully fulfill academic writing assignments.

Should not writing courses in university programs attend to the immediate needs of at-risk advanced students of ESL?

. . .

Writing classes, in my view, should be organized around a curriculum that helps students develop a schema for academic writing in English. With this purpose in mind, students would be given models of appropriate academic prose in English. Moreover, having students analyze such models would help at risk ESL students further develop a schema for the different rhetorical models of academic writing in English. After this modeling state, students could be introduced to the idea of writing multiple drafts and revisions.

As can be seen in the excerpt, the text shows features of manifest intertextuality (Fairclough, 1992) through the use of paraphrases and parenthetical citations. However, I am no longer a ventriloquist speaking through the ideas of other authors. On the contrary, the paper presents my authorial voice (or the beginning stages in the development of an authorial voice) in the sense that, in contrast to the first paper, I engaged here in a process of knowledge transforming (Bereiter & Scardamalia, 1987) that allowed readers to see my voice or, as Hirvela and Belcher (2001) put it, allowed readers to see the "person behind the written words" (p. 85). On the other hand, the excerpt shows only one question as a cohesion-making device (just as the first paper did). However, in my defense, I should note that in contrast to the first paper, where questions were used in practically every paragraph, in the latter paper there was only one question in the whole text.

Looking back on the text, I can see that what made me more competent as a writer is that as I began to see my professional identity in academia as more legitimate, I began to feel comfortable using strong language (e.g., "in my view," "fail") that showed my position on the topic discussed. I also think that the focus of the paper, dealing with issues of classroom instruction and English for academic purposes, was another factor contributing to my self-portrayal as a more competent writer. Even today, after my many years in academia, it is when I write on issues of classroom instruction and novice teachers' practices that my academic voice is strong and clear.

## So What About Spanish?

In his groundbreaking volume focusing on bilingual education in the twenty-first century, García (2009) argues that "the languages of an individual are rarely socially equal, having different power and prestige, and they are used for different purposes, in different contexts, with different interlocutors" (p. 45). In my case, although I have done some academic publishing in Spanish, most of my academic writing has been done in English, the dominant global language of academe. In contrast, in my personal life, both English *and* Spanish are the languages that I use to communicate with my daughter, friends, and some colleagues, both orally and in writing. In fact, in my writing for personal purposes, I engage in translanguaging, involving the use of "multiple discursive practices in which bilinguals engage in order to make sense of their bilingual worlds" (García, 2009, p. 45). After analyzing my writing depicting instances of translanguaging, I can see that while I straddle between languages (as well as registers and dialects), I subconsciously use English to write about concrete facts and events, in particular those connected with my professional life. On the other hand, my Spanish, both orally and in writing, is used to express deep emotionality and feelings (a point shown in research by Pavlenko, 2008, and later confirmed by Williams et al., 2020). However, central to my personal writing is the fact that it is highly creative, that it draws on emotion, and that I am not afraid to bend the languages and the structure of the texts in order to convey meaning. Instead, I believe that my writing for academic purposes in English is more timid because it is concerned with issues of conformity to audience expectations and acceptability.

# On What Is "Not" Good Writing

In this chapter, I charted my bilingual writing development and attempted to explain why my teachers or I did not consider my writing to be "good." Drawing on the ideas already discussed, in this section I summarize three of the features that I believe do *not* contribute to "good" writing. Although the list is not meant to be comprehensive, it deals with issues that I see as having implications for writing instruction of English language learners (ELLs) in a variety of settings.

First, "good" writing is not context-free. As explained by Leki (1995) in her seminal article on writing in higher education, when we write for academic purposes, what counts as "good" writing in one discipline may be different from what counts as "good" writing in a different field. For example, years ago, when I was collaborating with a biology professor in an undergraduate adjunct class, my biology colleague made me aware that, contrary to what we do in the TESOL field, her disciplinary expectations were to read the results of an experiment in the introduction of a scientific paper. In a more recent example, graduate students from a variety of disciplines enrolled in a writing class that I taught were asked to identify reporting verbs in several of their discipline journals. My students found that the hard sciences make more frequent use of objective than evaluative reporting verbs (a fact that they later confirmed in a follow-up exercise in *Academic Writing for Graduate Students: Essential Tasks and Skills* (Swales & Feak, 2012). Taken together, these examples, as well as the body of research in the TESOL field, support Leki's (1994) assertion that different discourse communities have different expectations. Therefore, engaging students in writing tasks that are devoid of context (as I was asked to do as a child) or that are not associated with a particular audience or discourse community is a futile exercise given that it is the latter that ultimately determines whether the writing is acceptable.

Second, "good" writing is more than just grammatically accurate writing. In fact, a perfectly grammatically accurate sentence does not necessarily contribute to meaningful or motivating writing. For example, in my "Visiting a Friend in Hospital" composition, the local error I made in the preposition following the verb "arrive," (as in "When I arrived *to* the third floor, a nurse asked me if I wanted to speak with my friend's doctor") does not prevent the reader from understanding the meaning of the sentence. Different would have been the case had the error been a global one and the reader's comprehension of the text had been impeded. In fact, other than affecting my self-esteem when I saw five red marks on my paper, my teacher's feedback strategy did not have a meaningful impact on me: I continued producing the same error until years later, when I became a more strategic reader and writer. This recollection shows that an overemphasis on grammatical accuracy at the expense of issues of syntactic, rhetorical, and vocabulary choices results in writing that is boring or dry and is solely produced for the purpose of mastering the language. English language learners like me would benefit more from participating in activities that connect reading and writing in which authentic (or modified) texts provide ELLs with rich language input and, at the same time, serve as a springboard for creating linguistic awareness that can ultimately translate into ELLs' enhanced writing fluency.

Finally, "good" writing is not writing that is "impossible to understand" (Pinker, 2014b, para. 3). Much like Casanave (2003), I have to admit that I sometimes find the publications in the TESOL field challenging. As a novice reader and writer in academia, I used to doubt my English language proficiency, my English vocabulary, and my content knowledge. Eventually, I realized that the problem was none of the above. I would argue that in search of recognition as a valid field of study, the TESOL field has produced highly valuable work that, at the same time, sometimes misses providing clear or humanistic descriptions of the people or events that are the focus of our research. I should note that it could be the case that my own bias in favor of qualitative and narrative work, which are rich in holistic descriptions, leads me to see this type of academic writing as communicating ideas in a manner that is clear and engages readers in a conversation with the author.

## Coda

Elsewhere in this chapter I have referred to myself as a bilingual and biliterate Spanish-English TESOL professional. In his work, Canagarajah (2013) makes a strong case for no longer using terms like "multilingual" and "plurilingual," and by extension "bilingual" and "biliterate," because they give the impression that the languages are compartmentalized and function as separate entities. To address this problem, he proposes replacing the terms with "translingual" (to use Canagarajah's, 2013, term, p. 1), given that the latter depicts "the ability to merge different language resources in situated interactions" (p. 1). As a resident of Los Angeles, I am immersed in contexts (both at home and at work) where I am exposed to and engage in translingual practices, both in oral and written discourse.

However, with the exception of the work by Canagarajah (2013) and García (2009) and her colleagues (García, Johnson, & Seltzer, 2017), the fields of TESOL and applied linguistics have given limited attention to issues of literacy as translingual practice. Given this limitation, it remains to be seen how "good" writing can be defined in such a complex and diverse milieu.

## References


Bereiter, C., & Scardamalia, M. (1987). *The psychology of written composition*. Lawrence Erlbaum.

Blanton, L. L. (2003). Narrating one's self: Public-personal dichotomies and a (public) writing life. In C. P. Casanave & S. Vandrick (Eds.), *Writing for scholarly publication: Behind the scenes in language education* (pp. 175–188). Lawrence Erlbaum.

Canagarajah, A. S. (2013). *Literacy as translingual practice: Between communities and classrooms*. Routledge.

Casanave, C. P. (2003). Narrative braiding: Constructing a multistrand portrayal of self as writer. In C. P. Casanave & S. Vandrick (Eds.), *Writing for scholarly publication: Behind the scenes in language education* (pp. 157–174). Lawrence Erlbaum.

Dobson, B., & Feak, C. (2001). A cognitive modeling approach to teaching critique writing to nonnative speakers. In D. Belcher & A. Hirvela (Eds.), *Linking literacies: Perspectives on L2 reading-writing connections* (pp. 186–199). University of Michigan Press.

Fairclough, N. (1992). *Discourse and social change*. Polity.

Freire, P. (1970). Pedagogía del oprimido [Pedagogy of the oppressed]. Tierra Nueva.

García, O., Johnson, S. I., & Seltzer, K. (2017). *The translanguaging classroom: Leveraging student bilingualism for learning*. Caslon.

García, O. (2009). *Bilingual education in the 21st century: A global perspective*. Wiley-Blackwell.

Gardner, R. C., & Lambert, W. E. (1972). *Attitudes and motivation in second-language learning*. Newbury House.

Hirvela, A. (2004). *Connecting reading & writing in second language writing instruction*. University of Michigan Press.

Hirvela, A., & Belcher, D. (2001). Coming back to voice: The multiple voices and identities of mature multilingual writers. *Journal of Second Language Writing, 10*(1–2), 83–106.

Hyland, K. (2004). *Genre and second language writing*. University of Michigan Press.

Kamhi-Stein, L. D. (2013). From "The Sound of Music" to "the Sound of Silence" and back: Language learning, teaching, and identity. In L. D. Kamhi-Stein (Ed.), *Narrating their lives: Examining English language teachers' professional identities within the classroom* (pp. 18–26). University of Michigan Press.

Kaplan, R. B. (1966). Cultural thought patterns in inter-cultural education. *Language Learning 16*, 1–20.

Leki, I. (1995). Good writing: I know it when I see it. In D. Belcher & G. Braine (Eds.), *Academic writing in a second language: Essays on research and pedagogy* (pp. 23–46). Ablex.

Pavlenko, A. (2008). Emotion and emotion-laden words in the bilingual lexicon. *Bilingualism: Language and Cognition, 11*(2), 147–164.

Peirce, B. N. (1995). Social identity, investment, and language learning. *TESOL Quarterly, 29*(1), 9–31.

Pinker, S. (2014a). *The sense of style: The thinking person's guide to writing in the 21st century!* Penguin Random House.

Pinker, S. (2014b). Why academics stink at writing. *The Chronicle of Higher Education.* September 26. Retrieved from https://www.chronicle.com/article/why-academics-stink-at-writing/

Raimes, A. (1991). Out of the woods: Emerging traditions in the teaching of writing. *TESOL Quarterly, 25*(3), 407–430.

Swales, J. M., & Feak, C. M. (2012). *Academic writing for graduate students: Essential tasks and skills* (3rd ed.). University of Michigan Press.

Vygotsky, L. S. (1978). *Mind in Society: The development of higher psychological processes.* Harvard University Press.

Williams, A., Srinvasan, M., Liu, C., Lee, P., & Zhou, G. (2020). Why do bilinguals code-switch when emotional? Insights from immigrant parent-child interactions. *Emotion, 20*(5), 830–841.

# Chapter 17

# Good Writing: Learning to See How Others See It

*Guillaume Gentil*

It is difficult to write a text about good writing without becoming self-conscious. Wouldn't it be paradoxical to produce bad writing about good writing? How can I write about good writing without sounding patronizing? How can I, a middle-aged white man, make pronouncements about what good writing is or should be without reproducing the cultural legacy of colonialism and imperialism? Not to mention the added linguistic insecurity of doing so in a language, English, that I acquired late. In grappling with these questions as I wrote several drafts of this text, I concluded that the best, and perhaps the only, way I could explore good writing is through a reflexive and dialogical approach by reflecting on personal encounters with texts and writers in context and hopefully engaging you, readers, in their interpretation. Let me call this a critical hermeneutic approach to good writing, a label that I hope will become clearer as you read on.

An important source of inspiration for this approach has been Leki's (1995) rather sobering and yet still relevant piece, "Good Writing: I Know It When I See It." In it, she reported the results of a study where she asked ESL students, writing teachers, and content area teachers to rank four essays written by ESL students and then interviewed them about the reasons for their rankings. Rankings and criteria differed widely both within and among each group of readers, even though some respondents appeared quite confident in their assessments. Leki came to two conclusions that still haunt me: First is the idea that there are no universally agreed-upon standards of good writing that hold across rhetorical situations and disciplinary contexts, but rather that good writing is "writing that meets particular requirements set for a particular readership at a particular time and place" (p. 41). In other words, good writing is situated, context-bound, and potentially eminently subjective. Second is the observation that even with the best intention of making evaluation criteria as explicit as possible, there is no guarantee that they will be interpreted and applied in the same ways to specific pieces of writing. What counts as good writing will remain largely tacit or implicit and therefore elusive for our students to understand.

Taking Leki's conclusions as premises, I propose first to examine whether, to what extent, and under what conditions this intuitive sense of "knowing good writing when we see it" can be made explicit verbally. Next, I venture to offer tentative formulations about good writing by considering texts and contexts, as Leki suggests, but also by trying to abstract from the particulars of writing situations some characterizations of good writing that I hope will make some sense to you, readers, in your respective contexts. While doing so, I am less concerned about whether you will agree with how I have come to characterize good writing but rather wish to illustrate a way of generating insight into good writing through a reflexive, dialogical, and contextualized approach. In keeping with the scope of this book, my exploration will be limited to good academic writing, specifically good nonfiction writing in university and college contexts, the context I know best. I will let readers judge whether the approach described here could be extended to other forms of writing such as literary and creative writing.

## Making Good Writing Explicit

Can good writing be defined and explained in words? This question harks back to the long-standing debate on the role of explicit writing instruction. In her landmark "show and tell" think piece, Freedman (1993) cast serious doubts about the possibility of teaching the genre knowledge that writers require to respond to writing situations, given the largely tacit nature of genre knowledge and genre learning. The possible role of explicit instruction in facilitating language learning has also been at the core of much research in second language acquisition (e.g., Norris & Ortega, 2000). However, whether instruction can have a desired effect on oral or written language development is a question that can be investigated empirically. Good writing, on the other hand, is a matter of evaluative interpretation. In fact, the empirical assessment of the effect of explicit writing instruction presupposes an evaluative frame within which writing quality can be assessed. Can these evaluative frames be articulated in language?

Questions about whether one can explain in language the type of understanding that is expressed though a skillful practice like good writing have preoccupied philosophers too. From a philosophical hermeneutics perspective (Kögler, 1996; Taylor, 1991), human understanding is mediated by language in that we make sense of ourselves, others, and the world through language. For example, cats cannot understand themselves as Canadian or American, gay or straight, because they do not have a vocabulary to interpret themselves in terms of national belonging or sexual orientation. When these vocabularies exist, it is next to impossible not to interpret oneself through the distinctions they not only afford but also impose. Given current vocabularies, we cannot but interpret ourselves in terms of nationality, gender, race, or sexual orientation. At the same time, the paradox is that although human experience is transformed by language, it cannot be reduced to it or fully expressed by it. Although national, racialized, or gendered vocabularies are an inescapable part of my interpretive horizon, they remain for the most part in the background, coming to consciousness, partially, only in certain circumstances. Our understanding of ourselves relative to others and the world is largely holistic, tacit, embodied, and expressed in how well we respond to a situation at a given place and time.

I believe the same applies to good writing. Writing as an activity and as a concept is enabled by language, but it cannot be fully explained by language. I find it paradoxical to see some of my students struggle with the very writing issues they read and write about when they review writing research. For example, I have witnessed students write about cohesion and coherence and yet struggle to achieve good textual flow. Clearly, the articulation of writing knowledge is not a sufficient condition of skillful practice. It may not even be a necessary condition, judging from the observation that other students manage textual flow well and yet cannot describe why. That said, it is also my experience that reading, talking, and writing about writing has made me a more reflective writer. Developing a language about writing has helped me attend to aspects of my practice, arguably in a very partial and limited way, and yet has allowed me to better direct the gaze to a dimension that may require more explicit attention and control.

Writing knowledge may well be ineffable. A piece of writing looks good when somehow it works for us. It may be impossible to articulate exactly why we feel it works, but displaying good writing at work can help to highlight, through show and tell, aspects of what makes a piece of writing respond well to the writing situation. Michael Halliday (1985) made a similar argument about grammatical knowledge:

> Even those [grammatical systems] of which we have some conscious understanding . . . cannot be fully defined—that is, glossed in exactly equivalent wordings. They have evolved in order to say something that cannot be said in any other way; they are strictly ineffable. The best one can do is to display them at work, in paradigmatic contexts, so as to highlight the semantic distinctions they are enshrining.
> (p. xxvi)

In her experiment, Leki (1995) elicited views of good writing around specific exemplars of writing. However, for the purpose of her study, she took essays written for ESL writing classes out of their native context; the essays were deemed good in that context but then subjected to evaluation in a new context constructed for the study: the research interviews with students, L1 and ESL writing faculty, and instructors in other disciplines. This experiment was successful in underscoring the absence of universally agreed-upon writing standards. However, if the goal is to raise awareness of what makes a piece of writing work for specific readers in its intended context at a given time, displaying good writing at work *in situ* would be best. That is why contextualized feedback on writing is so effective. That said, discussion of good writing around exemplars taken into the writing classroom from other contexts could remain fruitful as long as contextual considerations remain centre stage: How well and in what ways does the text respond to the exigence of the target writing situation? What changes may be necessary to make it work in a new context? And what may be predisposing us to respond to the text the way we do? These could also be productive questions.

## Good Writing Reduces Distance

To illustrate how good (and not-so-good) writing can be displayed at work in context, here are two emails that I received within an hour of each other. The first one was sent by the Labour Relations Office to graduate program administrators and program directors. The second was sent by the teaching assistants' union to students. Both describe a special TA application procedure of relevance to international students. Here is email 1, from Labour Relations:

> New Application Form for International TAs with Priority (Spring/ Summer Term)
>
> Hello everyone,
>
> It has come to our attention that International TAs with future Priority Status are unable to apply for Outside Priority TA Appointments in the Spring/Summer Term through [System Name].
>
> To remedy this, we have created a specific form (See attached) for these individuals to submit when applying to individual departments. If you receive this form, please treat it as a regular application/ indication of interest pursuant to Article [number].
>
> If you could please advise all those responsible for Teaching Assistant allocations as soon as possible it would be greatly appreciated.
>
> Regards,

It is likely that this internal email does not make much sense to you or anyone outside my university. This does not mean that it is not well written, because outsiders were not the intended audience. It did, however, create some confusion both for me and my administrative assistant who were both intended recipients as persons "responsible for Teaching Assistant allocations." Luckily, when an international student sent her TA application shortly after, she copied the email she had received from the union. Here is email 2, from the teaching assistants' union:

> Info for International TAs: Application Process for Spring/Summer TA Work
>
> Hello International TA Members,
>
> If you are an international student with any future priority TA terms of work (ie. Fall 2020, Winter 2021), and you would like to work as a TA in the Spring/Summer 2020 terms, please complete this form and deliver a copy to each Department you are interested in working for.
>
> The form can be submitted to Departments by email.

> International students with priority in future Fall and Winter terms
> can apply for work in the Spring/Summer terms. [. . .] Unfortunately,
> there is an error in the TA Management System that prevents
> international students with future priority from applying for work
> in the Spring/Summer terms. Your union and [University Name]
> management have agreed to the use of this form as interim measure.
> We hope to have the online system fixed in the months ahead.
>
> [. . .]
>
> If you are an international student and encounter any difficulties with
> the application form or process, please contact us at email.
>
> In solidarity,

The union's email is longer but arguably clearer. The student who forwarded it to me knew exactly what to do and emailed me her application form. The email also clarified for me important details such as why international students were unable to apply online ("there is an error in the TA Management System") and how they should submit the form ("to Departments by email"), However, I suspect this second email remains somewhat difficult for you to follow, because it still assumes too much background knowledge. I could unpack it further for you and explain why only some TAs have "priority" in the fall/winter and/or summer terms, but I don't think you need to be bothered with the intricacies of TA allocation at my university. The point I rather wish to bring home with these examples is that good writing reduces the distance between oneself and another, between oneself as a writer and the imagined and actual others who will read the text, so that the text makes (at least some) sense not only for oneself but also for another. The more cultural and cognitive distance there is, the more work there is to do to reduce it. Good writing thus requires of a writer a decentering of perspective from her point of view to a reader's point of view, with concerns over readers' needs and wants driving decisions about the selection and management of information, text organization, word choice, and all other aspects of the text production. Linda Flower (1981) described such decentering as the shift from writer-based to reader-based prose.

Putting oneself in the reader's shoes is one of the greatest difficulties I have seen student writers and other university writers struggle with. I struggle with it too. What information is it necessary to provide to establish a shared context of understanding? How much is too much? With the two email examples, I have tried to give you a sense of how read-ers may respond to a text when they do not quite have enough context. I wonder if a source of confusion for students about academic writing is that the texts they are given to read, especially in the upper under-graduate years and at the beginning of graduate studies, are research articles that are not intended for them but for disciplinary specialists who have more background knowledge than they have. I recently taught a master-level course meant to introduce research methodology. When we examined sample research studies, students complained about the dense, shorthand writing they encountered. Why don't authors explain what they mean by "quasi-experimental study," "post hoc pairwise compari-sons," or "ANOVA"? In a way, they found themselves in the position of an outsider reading an email about TA application rules in a university context they do not know. The text must be contextualized and unpacked for them lest they might be socialized into thinking that academic writing is meant to mystify.

## Oh My. . . . There Is Meaning to Be Had!

My first teaching experience taught me something else about good writing and what may impede students from producing it. It was a course in effective communication for first-year engineering students twenty-odd years ago. This memory is obviously reconstructed, but I remember to this day a teaching moment that may have been more epiphanic for me than for my student. One assignment asked students to popularize a technical or scientific text for a lay audience. One stu-dent wrote a piece that hardly made sense to me, so I asked for the text he had been trying to popularize. That source text was somewhat challenging to read too, for despite my STEM background as a former biologist and agricultural engineer, it was about a topic and a branch of engineering I was not familiar with. However, it did make more sense to me than the student's text. In a one-on-one conference with the student, I began to map out on a blank sheet of paper the con-nections and causalities I saw among the ideas and concepts, writing down keywords and drawing arrows and circles with a pencil. The stu-dent appeared surprised and remarked that writing was "like logic," as though he had just then come to the realization that there was mean-ing to be had in dense technical prose. I was surprised that one could so easily give up on meaning.

Good writing is good thinking, and with clarity of thought come ease and clarity of expression. This idea is not new. French poet and literary theorist Nicolas Boileau, contemporary of Molière, put it in alexandrine verses: "Ce que l'on conçoit bien s'énonce clairement / Et les mots pour le dire arrivent aisément." More prosaically: *What is clearly thought out is clearly expressed / And the words to say it flow with ease.* With hindsight, what I was trying to do with this first-year student was to demonstrate the thinking and meaning-making process at the heart of reading and writing. As with examining good writing as text that works well in a specific context, demonstrating good writing as process is best done in context. One possible misunderstanding to dispel is that clarity of thought should be obtained before clarity of expression can be achieved, as if writing simply puts down in words ideas previously thought out, when it is through the act of expression that thinking develops and takes shape.

When I argued earlier that good writing "feels good," I did not mean to say that it cannot be challenging to read. There are different types of fulfilment that good writing can provide, one of which is the intellectual satisfaction of expanding one's understanding when successfully engaging with an exacting yet rewarding text. Mapping the articulation of ideas is an activity that I find helps students deconstruct more cognitively demanding academic texts. Some like idea maps to visualize the text organization; others prefer to make the text organization explicit through a more traditional outline with headings, subheadings, and keywords or by writing in the margin of each paragraph a short phrase that encapsulates the main idea. All these activities provide practice with seeing how ideas can be organized and supported in others' texts, preparing them to lay out their own ideas in their texts for others.

Writing to express, not to impress, is a common exhortation in professional communication courses and can serve well as a principle to good academic writing too. Why would student university writers want to impress in the first place? I pointed out one possible reason earlier: the mistaken belief that academic writing is meant to mystify. Another possible reason is that, like all language use, academic writing is at the same time ideational, interpersonal, and textual, to borrow Halliday's (1985) three language metafunctions: As writers arrange and express ideas in their texts, they also project and negotiate identities with presumed and actual readers. Trying out ways to sound like an academic writer is part of the process of becoming an academic writer. Sometimes, however, this voice imitation game runs counter to the imperative of clarifying for oneself and for others what one wants to say, as it can make simplistic ideas sound more complicated than they are.

Complex thinking naturally leads to complex phrasing that must then be simplified through distillation. Blaise Pascal, another contemporary of Molière and Boileau, apologized for the longer letter he did not have the leisure to shorten ("Je n'ai fait celle-ci plus longue que parce que je n'ai pas eu le loisir de la faire plus courte," *Les Provinciales*, lettre 16). Simplicity in writing takes more time because it follows a detour through an expansive and messier stage. The ideas must decant. Another image that comes to mind is that of a wine reduction: the mixture must boil and bubble out before it can thicken to a rich and flavourful sauce. The text that you are reading now is a shorter version of a longer draft.

## An Armchair Is Not a Chair . . . in French: Good Writing in the Age of Linguistic and Cultural Relativism

In the preceding sections, I have backgrounded the cultural and power dimension of good writing, perhaps giving the impression that good writing as a form of effective transaction simply rests on universal principles of good thinking and good communication. My views on good writing inevitably betray my cultural biases and experiences as a privileged white middle-aged man educated in French and in France for the first half of my life before settling in Canada for the second half. Is there a way to come to an understanding of good academic writing that can transcend or cut across linguistic, cultural, and national traditions? What conditions could help begin the conversation?

It would be ideal to engage in the sort of deliberative democracy described by Jürgen Habermas whereby all stakeholders debate on the same footing, but in a postcolonial age when questions about white privilege, cultural imperialism, and unequal encounters loom large, such an approach seems untenable. Starting from the guiding principle that good writing is writing that works well in its ecological context, the conversation need not limit itself to assessing how well and in what ways a piece of writing meets it communication purpose, addresses readers' expectations, and responds to the rhetorical exigence of the writing situation. The conversation should also acknowledge the positionalities and perspectives of all the participants in the conversation. In what contexts have they learned and experienced writing? What literacy practices and linguistic, cultural, and national traditions of writing (and knowing) have they been exposed to, in and out of school? How much writing experience do they have producing what written genres and in what contexts? What are their social roles and statuses within the institutional context, the selves they feel that they have inherited, aspire to be, and are boxed into? How much authority might be vested in them as judges of a specific piece of writing at hand, in its presumed and imagined contexts, and on what grounds could this authority be contested? These might be productive questions for problematizing conversations about good writing.

One challenge in assessing writing quality in an age of postcolonialism and globalization, with the hopes of arriving at some areas of agreement by anchoring conversations in specific texts and contexts, is to negotiate the fine line between the developmental and sociocultural and political dimensions of writing. On the one hand, New Literacy Studies has made a compelling case that what may count as good writing is a sociocultural and ideological construct. On the other hand, textual, cognitive, and ethnographic studies of writing development, particularly longitudinal case studies of multilingual writers, underscore that becoming skillful at "writing games" (Casanave, 2002) can take years of guided practice even in the more enabling contexts. As a sociocultural practice, writing can be seen as an art, which like painting or sculpting is learned through apprenticeship in communities of practice. This is why, when engaging in cross-cultural conversations on writing quality, I believe it is important to acknowledge not only the traditions and communities we come from but also the degree of expertise and social recognition we may have gained within them. To return to a culinary analogy I have used to describe the conditions of the cross-cultural validation of genre knowledge (Gentil, 2011), developing student writers who suddenly encounter a new cultural context of writing through study abroad or resettlement are more in the position of an apprentice cook than a French chef being thrown from a French restaurant to a Chinese restaurant. They must learn new language and writing games before they have had a chance to master the previous ones.

One dimension of writing knowledge that takes time to develop is the level of linguistic precision that appears to be a common expectation of good academic writing. Achieving linguistic precision can be challenging, especially in a language in which one did not have the benefit of years of exposure from a young age in a variety of formal and informal contexts. I was in my mid-twenties when I first immersed myself in English for over a year. This sojourn in the American Midwest was instrumental to my English language development. At the same time, I realized later that many of the words and phrases that I had picked up in context did not quite mean what I had guessed them to mean, which also made me realize that other English users probably had not quite construed my intended meanings. When using English as a common language, writers and readers with different linguistic experiences inflect it with accents, voices, uses, and understandings that reflect these experiences, contributing to the heteroglossia of English. I subscribe to calls for pluralizing English norms and approaching "difference in language . . . as a resource for producing meaning in writing" (Horner et al., 2011, p. 303). It is impossible to know how other speakers will construe our words and utterances; no one can enter another person's mind. We can only hope from the readers' response that the meaning they construed is close enough to the meaning we intended for the conversation to continue. It is not unreasonable to expect of all English language users, whether considered first language or additional language users, to make an effort to interpret the meanings others are trying to express. At the same time, I am not convinced that language systems are as fluid or unstable as they are sometimes depicted to be or that such fluidity and instability are inherently more desirable than some degree of stabilized-for-now fixity. The meanings recorded in dictionaries and grammars attest to the possibility of intersubjectively shared meanings while contributing to fixing (for some time) language through codification. My impression of the writing produced by students who do not quite grasp the stabilized-for-now meanings that are commonly agreed upon in the language they compose in is that their writing is fuzzy, as if their expression was not in sharp focus.

As a bilingual writer, there are times when I would like to reproduce in my academic writing the kind of code-meshing that goes on in my mind, simply using whatever resources available in my linguistic repertoire most spontaneously express my developing thought. However, I know that few readers would be able to makes sense of the resulting text. I also have come to realize that thinking in two languages and yet writing in one can be generative of new insight and both sharpen and deepen my understanding of what it is I am trying to express. Despite considerable crossovers resulting from a thousand years of contact, English and French today each bring a distinctive "potential" (Halliday, 1985) for meaning making, predisposing to certain ways of breaking up and attending to the world within and around us. To take a concrete example, in English an armchair may be seen as a type of chair, whereas in French the lexical difference between "fauteuil" (an armchair) and "chaise" (a chair) does not make such categorization as obvious. Interestingly, while the common (Old French) origin of "chair" and "chaise" remains noticeable today, the

Germanic origin of "fauteuil" (*faldestoel*, literally "folding stool") is now lost on most French speakers. Nor would contemporary French speakers associate a *fauteuil* with the image of a folding chair in the Paris Métro.

The innumerable cognates resulting from centuries of contact between English and French can be a great help for speakers of one language in acquiring the other but also a source of difficulty, because many cognates today overlap only for some uses but not for others. To give just one example, the French verb *demander* is closer in meaning to the English *ask* or *request* than it is to *demand*. Having to disentangle such webs of English and French meanings has forced me to attend to the nuances and layers of meaning each word can carry in given linguistic contexts, trying to bear in mind the various resonances they could have for speakers with various linguistic experiences with each language. I believe this constant effort at cross-linguistic disentanglement has sharpened my written expression in both English and French and made me more sensitive to my readers' language needs. After my English immersion in the American Midwest, my second most formative experience as an English writer happened when I moved to the bilingual city of Montréal for graduate studies, because it forced me to shuttle back and forth between English and French. Having to translate into French those English words I had learned through exposure and guessing helped me to clarify their meanings.

Challenges in finding translation equivalents has also confronted me with the apparent limitations of each language as a meaning potential. The concept of "agency," for example, is central to educational scholarship in English. It was the main theme of the 2019 Symposium on Second Language Writing. And yet this concept is virtually nonexistent in Francophone scholarship. It is not that one could not come up with a French word for it: *agentivité* has been proposed. However, its use appears to be much more limited and specialized, not to say pedantic, in French, than *agency* in English, which begs the question: Are Francophone scholars missing out on a major tool for thought or is the level of attention generated around the concept in English an artifactual effect of the language? An unjustified obsession? What other ways of talking and writing about agency are available in French, and what complementary insight could they bring? Similar questions arose with *literacy* and *gender* in the 1990s and more recently *translanguaging* (Gentil, 2019), or when scholars construct arguments around distinctions between pairs of related terms (e.g., awareness vs. consciousness, evaluation vs. assessment) that may appear somewhat suspicious when there is only one term in French. And of course, similar questions arise when rethinking in English theoretical perspectives developed in French (e.g., Moore & Gajo, 2009).

In short, cross-linguistic and cross-cultural contact complicates the development and assessment of good academic writing, but it also has the potential to improve thinking through writing and enrich the conversation about good writing. The very concepts of "writing" and "good writing" do not translate easily into French, because there is no single equivalent of the -ing form. Depending on the contexts, "writing" may be rendered by the nouns "écriture" or "rédaction," a nominalized participle "l'écrit" (literally, "the written"), or the infinitive form "écrire" ("to write"). This forces us to unpack the various dimensions of writing as an activity, a practice, a process, a product, a mode, or a field of study. Similarly, "good writing" requires some spelling out in French: whether it refers to an art ("l'art du bien écrire": "[the art of] good writing"), writing quality ("rendre la qualité de l'écriture explicite": "making good writing explicit"; "expliquer le bien écrire": "explicating good writing"), or a well-written text ("un bon texte: je le reconnais quand je le vois": "good writing: I know it when I see it").

## Learning to Meet the Eyes of the Other

By sharing examples and observations arising from my encounters with texts and writers, I have tried to illustrate both a view that good writing engages the writer and reader in dialogue and a proposal for understanding good writing dialogically as well, through an exchange of perspectives on texts in context. There is no guarantee that the contextualized, text-based conversations on good writing I have been advocating will lead to consensus. In fact, disagreements may be productive in revealing expectations and underlying assumptions and impositions. They may also bring about common understandings. Writing specialists have a facilitative role to play by providing vocabularies and theoretical lenses that help writers and readers articulate their perception of a text and its quality given its intended and conceivable contexts. Writers can bring insider perspectives on the texts and contexts they know and outsider perspectives on the texts and contexts they have not yet encountered, while writing specialists can help formulate possible explanations about the workings of texts and the conditions of their social validation given the underlying power dynamics among readers and writers. This kind of dialogue can be seen as a form of critical hermeneutics (Kögler, 1996). Critical hermeneutics is premised on the hope that by learning to interpret the world dialogically through another's perspective, we can become more reflexive and aware of (some of) the linguistic, social, and cultural presuppositions that frame our interpretations and evaluations. The critical hermeneutic approach to good writing I have tried to propose here is premised on such a hope, which Kögler calls "the power of dialogue."

Writing this chapter made me more reflexive about my views of good writing. In writing this chapter, I had images of you, readers, but of course I could only engage in an imaginary dialogue in my mind. I will let you decide to what extent and in what ways some of the characterizations of good writing I have offered here resonate with your own experiences and contexts. I remain optimistic, however, that areas of agreement on writing quality can be found amidst the diversity of views, values, and interests that cross-cultural encounters and postcolonial legacies bring to the fore. For example, I was first struck by the apparent contradiction between Flower's (1981) observation long ago that good writing is reader-based and Hinds's (1987) claim of cultural differences in writer vs. reader responsibility. According to Hinds, whereas responsibility for effective communication is primarily borne by the writer in writer-responsible languages such as English, it is borne by the reader in reader-responsible languages such as Japanese. Thus, a writer trying to follow Flower's advice of restructuring a text from a reader's point of view may end up insulting a reader's intelligence by trying to make the logic of the ideas too clear and explicit. Of course, Hinds's reader vs. writer responsible typology can be seen as an instance of the stereotyping tendencies that intercultural rhetoric has been criticized for (Belcher, 2014). In his defence, Hinds himself cautioned that there may be exceptions to cultural tendencies. Nonetheless, Hinds's argument may also uncover some of the cultural biases implicit in Flower's (1981) advice for reader-based prose. Because of my French schooling, perhaps, I am surprised by American composition textbooks' insistent advice to state the thesis early when I was taught to save it till the end, as the term of a dialectical development of a problem space ("problématique") opened at the beginning. That said, the principle of reader-based prose does not have to translate into a text that chews up all the ideas for the readers like a mother who cuts food into small pieces for her child. It rather invites writers to adopt a reader's perspective. Reader-centered prose can turn out to be reader-responsible if a writer perceives this to be desirable from a reader's perspective. Moreover, a writer's intent may not necessarily be to please readers but to provoke an effect. While there may be different ways for writers to see a text a from reader's perspective, and for readers to reciprocate, this movement toward meeting the eyes of the other may well be a key to good writing that transcends the local and the cultural.

While starting from my experiences with texts and writing, I made certain characterizations of good academic writing as reducing the distance with the reader, thinking clearly through precise expression, and being reader-based. I am uneasy about making such generalizations and yet claiming that good writing can only be assessed locally, examining a given text in specific writing situation. My views reflect my experiences with writing, and there is no escaping it, but I remain confident that we can arrive at some common understandings by interpreting our responses to texts dialogically.

Leki (1995) underscored the disagreements among different assessors on the same pieces of writing. In contrast, I have been surprised more than once by how different assessors can independently arrive at very similar observations, for example during thesis defences or when co-supervising a student with a colleague. This seems to happen when, unlike in Leki's study, the assessors share not only a common understanding of the writing situation but also shared disciplinary expectations. Our agreement likely emerges as the byproduct of a shared *habitus* or disposition toward academic writing that we have developed through our socialization into overlapping discourses and practices. Greater differences in disciplinary socialization likely also explain the greater disagreement that Leki (1995) observed between writing teachers and content area teachers than within each group. When we help students increasingly approximate the type of writing that is expected of them, we are socializing them into our disciplinary ways of seeing and doing. We are helping them to see and perform writing as other, more experienced members of their disciplines do. The challenge is finding ways to do this while acknowledging the power imbalance in the relationship and mitigating the risk of cultural imposition. There is an opportunity for professors, too, to question and expand their habitual ways of seeing good writing by learning to see how others see it through critical dialogues around texts in context.


## References

Belcher, D. (2014). What we need and don't need intercultural rhetoric for: A retrospective and prospective look at an evolving research area. *Journal of Second Language Writing, 25,* 59–67. https://doi.org/10.1016/j.jslw.2014.06.003

Casanave, C. P. (2002). *Writing games: Multicultural case studies of academic literacy practices in higher education*. Lawrence Erlbaum Associates. http://www.loc.gov/catdir/toc/fy031/2001055592.html

Flower, L. (1981). *Problem-solving strategies for writing*. Harcourt Brace Jovanovich.

Freedman, A. (1993). Show and tell? The role of explicit teaching in the learning of new genres. *Research in the Teaching of English*, *27*(3), 222–251.

Gentil, G. (2011). A biliteracy agenda for genre research. *Journal of Second Language Writing*, *20*(1), 6–23. https://doi.org/10.1016/j.jslw.2010.12.006

Gentil, G. (2019). Translanguaging and multilingual academic literacies: How do we translate that into French? Should we? Pour en faire quoi? (et pourquoi s'en faire?). *Cahiers de l'ILOB/OLBI Working Papers*, 3–41. https://uottawa.scholarsportal.info/ottawa/index.php/ILOB-OLBI/article/view/3831

Halliday, M. A. K. (1985). *An introduction to functional grammar*. Arnold.

Hinds, J. (1987). Reader vs. writer responsibility: A new typology. In U. Connor & R. Kaplan (Eds.), *Writing across languages* (pp. 141–152). Addison-Wesley.

Horner, B., Lu, M.-Z., Royster, J. J., & Trimbur, J. (2011). Language difference in writing: Toward a translingual approach. *College English*, *73*(3), 303–321.

Kögler, H. H. (1996). *The power of dialogue: Critical hermeneutics after Gadamer and Foucault* (P. Hendrickson, Trans.). MIT Press.

Leki, I. (1995). Good writing: I know it when I see it. In D. Belcher & G. Braine (Eds.), *Academic writing in a second language: Essays on research and pedagogy* (pp. 23–46). Ablex Publishing.

Moore, D., & Gajo, L. (2009). French voices on plurilingualism and pluriculturalism: Theory, significance, and perspectives [Special Issue]. *International Journal of Multilingualism*, *6*(2), 137–227. https://doi.org/10.1080/14790710902846707

Norris, J. M., & Ortega, L. (2000). Effectiveness of L2 instruction: A research synthesis and quantitative meta-analysis. *Language Learning*, *50*(3), 417–528. https://doi.org/https://doi.org/10.1111/0023-8333.00136

Taylor, C. (1991). The dialogical self. In D. Hiley, J. Bohman, & R. Shusterman (Eds.), *The interpretive turn: Philosophy, science, culture* (pp. 304–314). Cornell University Press.

# Part IV
# Readers, Reading, and Writing

# Chapter 18

# Reader-Orientedness Is a Central Tenet of Good Qualitative Research Reports: Why So, How So, and What Now?

*An Cheng*

## *Why So?* This Chapter as an Opportunity to Reflect on My Belief in Reader-Orientedness as Central to Good Writing

I have always believed strongly that good academic writing is "readerly," "reader-oriented," "reader-based," or "reader-focused," to use the terms that I have repeated to my students. As I drafted this chapter, I started to question why I was so sure that I even know anything about what good writing is, especially when others have written eloquently on the topic. For example, Billig (2013) highlights the problems in academic writing in the social sciences. These include abusing nominalization and passivization to "avoid describing people and their actions" (p. 7), to "conceal aspects of what occurred in . . . experiments" (p. 8), and to exaggerate to promote one's work. Pinker (2014) believes that good academic writing "starts strong" (p. 13), uses parallel constructions strategically, contains "a touch of the poetic" (p. 14), "flip[s] the way the world is perceived" (p. 14), "is understood with the mind's eyes" (p. 16), juxtaposes "different senses of a single word" (pp. 20–21), and uses "surprising transitions" (p. 21), among other attributes. Thomson and Kamler (2013) flesh out how good academic writing textualizes one's scholarly self, while Belcher (2019) argues that a good journal article is driven by a "single significant idea" (p. 67). How does my belief in good academic writing as fundamentally reader-oriented stack up against these cogently argued ideas?

In addition, why am I so committed to reader-orientedness as a central aspect of good writing? After all, readers, often used interchangeably with audiences, have become a threshold concept in the study of rhetorical situations and the teaching of writing (Bitzer, 1968; Lunsford, 2015). As early as 1984, for example, Ede and Lunsford (1984) argued that viewing one's audience as merely "audience addressed" and a writer's task as mainly to meet the needs of the audience neglects the agency of the writer. They also believed that perceiving the audience as "audience invoked" and a writer's task as mainly to invent and to write to an imaginary audience downplays the importance of analyzing and meeting the needs of one's real audience.

Meanwhile, the importance of readers may not be as apparent to others or to myself as I thought. Thomson and Kamler (2013), for example, notice that novice writers often don't know or haven't thought of the reader as important, and the question of who the reader is for one's journal article "startles so many people" (p. 28). Why not take the writing of this chapter as the opportunity to reflect on my belief in good writing as readerly writing? I started to comb through the peer-review comments I have written and received, notes from the graduate seminars I have taught, and my feedback on graduate students' qualitative research reports, including their seminar papers, qualifying papers, theses/dissertations, and journal article manuscripts, hoping that these documents would clarify to me what it means to say that good writing is reader-oriented.

Qualitative research reports become the focus of my reflections because of the challenges in writing them (Casanave, 2020). In addition, I teach my department's "Introduction to Graduate Studies" course regularly to first-year PhD students and students in the master's research track in applied linguistics and in writing studies. The course concentrates on research approaches and pays close attention to qualitative research. I also see myself as a qualitative researcher who has published qualitative research reports. Through my teaching and research, I have recognized not only the importance of learning the technical aspects of doing qualitative research but also the significance of learning to think and write as a qualitative researcher. How to reach one's readers effectively when composing qualitative research reports is part of thinking and writing as a qualitative researcher and has thus become the focus of my reflections on readerly writing.

Given my interest in genre theory, the concept of discourse community also guides my reflections on reader-centeredness. Genre is "a class of communicative events . . . [that] share some set of communicative purposes" (Swales, 1990, p. 58). The experienced members of a discourse community often possess some threshold knowledge of expertise to enable them to recognize the communicative purposes in a genre in question. These members thus understand the communicative purposes of genres much better than the apprentice members do (Swales, 1990). Although other scholars have subsequently added further dimensions to the concept of discourse community (e.g., Casanave & Li, 2008), writing researchers and teachers tend to agree that writers who match maximally the assumptions of the established discourse community members holding the greatest genre-specific expertise will likely achieve the highest level of reader-orientedness.

In fact, "who is the reader," to some (e.g., Thomson & Kamler, 2013), means "what is the discourse community into which this article is to go" (p. 36). The "specific practices, histories, conventions, and expectations" (p. 31) of the discourse community one's writing targets are often recognized and mediated by journal editors, reviewers, dissertation committee chair and members, and other gatekeeping members of the discourse community who also often are the readers of one's research reports.

In sum, my interest in qualitative research in applied linguistics and in the concepts of genre and discourse community prompts me to conceptualize readers as the established members in the discourse community of qualitative researchers in applied linguistics. Often with "the greatest genre-specific expertise" (Swales, 1990, p. 54), these members have certain assumptions and expectations about how qualitative research is conducted and how high-stakes qualitative research reports such as qualifying papers, dissertations, and journal articles are written. Writers aware of these assumptions and able to meet these expectations would have a better chance of producing reader-oriented, or good, qualitative research reports. In this sense, good writing is, to me, reader-oriented writing above most other things.

## *How So?* Textual Clues that Have Triggered My Thinking about Reader-Orientedness in Qualitative Research Reports

To illustrate what readerly writing means in the sense described in the last paragraph, I expand here on five textual clues that have set me thinking about reader-orientedness in qualitative research reports.

*Textual Clue 1: Asking Research Questions.* Some student writers or journal authors of qualitative research reports would ask *why* or *how* questions without asking *yes* or *no* questions first. For example, they would ask, "What did the students learn from the genre samples, and how did they learn from the genre samples?" without first asking "Did the students learn anything from the genre samples" and "If not, why not?" To me, asking *why* or *how* questions without asking *yes* or *no* questions raises the question of whether the authors have truly committed to the constructivist worldview underpinning any qualitative research project. Such a worldview values how research participants possess or develop varied meanings related to the objects of study. Varied meanings include the possibility that the participants may not possess or develop any meanings at all. Asking *yes* or *no* questions alongside *why* or *how* questions respects such a possibility and is thus expected as part of the ethos of a qualitative researcher/writer. Not asking the *yes* or *no* question suggests that the qualitative research report writers may be prioritizing their *a priori* thoughts or claims either developed by the researchers themselves or gleaned from the literature instead of emphasizing the meanings their research participants may *or may not* bring to the investigated phenomena. Such a priority, or the perception of it, clashes with the assumptions of the experienced members of the discourse community. The conflict thus raises questions about whether the writing at issue is reader-oriented or readerly enough to a reader like me who reads the research questions section.

Qualitative research report writers cannot superficially compensate for the neglect of the *yes* or *no* questions through appending a *yes* or *no* question at the last minute. Regardless of whether I see the *yes* or *no* question or not, I look closely at whether the qualitative research report writers have paid any special attention to displaying the participants' diverse meanings toward the investigated phenomena through quotations, themes, and subthemes. I would study whether the authors have described any surprising codes in relation to the expected codes. I would examine whether these surprising codes show any sign of being artificially manufactured instead of organically coming out of the authors' analysis of their participants' situated meaning-making processes. Therefore, minding the presence and absence of *yes* or *no* questions and the way they are asked may be part of the assumptions or expectations of the seasoned members of the discourse community regarding whether a writer has *become* a qualitative researcher and, through the process of *becoming*, has emerged as a readerly writer.

*Textual Clue 2: Naming the Section That Describes the Study.* How do qualitative research report authors name the section that describes how the qualitative study had been conducted? Is that section called "research design," "research methods," "research methodology," "research approach," a combination of these or other terms? Whichever term is used, have the authors demonstrated their understanding of the links between the chosen term and other related terms? For example, if "research methods" is chosen, are its connections to "research approach" or "research design" apparent and convincing in the qualitative research report?

The naming of that section is another textual clue that sets me thinking about whether the writers have become readerly in the sense that they are aware of some of the assumptions and expectations of the experienced members of the discourse community. In this case, the writers have the opportunity to show that they have systematically studied the components involved in qualitative research. These components, as Creswell and Creswell (2018) clearly describe, include the philosophical—the epistemological and ontological—worldviews (constructivism or social constructivism for qualitative research). The philosophical worldviews influence the chosen research design (case study, narrative inquiry, or a broad theme-based grounded theory design, for example). The research design leads to specific research methods that encompass data collection, analysis, and interpretation. A qualitative research report writer could, indeed, use one term, such as "research methods" to describe the qualitative project to be reported in the research genre, but the use of that chosen term needs to invoke the other related terms explicitly or implicitly (the philosophical worldview and the overall research design, for example, in this case). Mere rhetorical work is not enough. For example, merely stating that "in this study, I adopted the social constructivist worldview as a researcher" is inadequate. An experienced reader may pay quiet but close attention to whether the chosen term and its connections to the related terms have permeated the way the research project has been conducted. For example, naming social constructivism means that one has used it to carefully guide data collection, analysis, and reporting. Any indication of the mismatch of related terms raises questions about the authors' reader-orientedness. For example, invoking social constructivism as a worldview but asking research questions in an *a priori* manner (see Textual Clue 1) or, worse, describing research methods that involve the testing of hypotheses would raise a red flag about reader-orientedness.

*Textual Clue 3: Presenting Findings or Results?* Calling the findings in a qualitative research project "results" can seem a negligible matter. As has happened many times, however, such a textual clue would prompt me to study how the "results" have been obtained and reported when no variable-controlling, result-yielding experiments should normally have been a part of a qualitative research project. Have the researcher/authors carefully teased out the perspectives of the participants to reveal the subtleties and complexities in the way participants, as social beings, experience the world and a particular research phenomenon? Have the researchers/authors reported these subtle and complex perspectives as "findings" instead of "results"? Or have the qualitative researchers reported the "findings," instead of "results," in a way that prompts the experienced readers' suspicion of the writers' lack of adherence to the constructivist worldview that rightfully underpins a qualitative research project?

*Textual Clue 4: Conducting a "Mixed-methods" Study?* Calling a study with one part involving numbers or statistics and another part involving verbal data a "mixed-methods study" is a textual clue that prompts me to ponder the authors' reader-orientedness. Have the authors explained how the two parts interact with each other? Is this a convergent mixed-methods study, an exploratory mixed-methods study, or an explanatory mixed-methods study? Even if the authors have named the nature of the "mixed-methods study" correctly, have the authors clarified the inherent merits, if any, in having these two parts in a study? Has the relationship, if any, between these two parts helped the researchers arrive at a deeper understanding of the research phenomenon? Or do the researchers/authors believe that it is fancier to have a study that looked at both numbers and words? Most importantly, have the authors explained how they have reconciled the inherently incommensurable positivist worldview underpinning the quantitative approach to research and the constructivist worldview driving the qualitative approach to research in a mixed-methods study? Are the attempts to bridge the divide between the two worldviews successful as seen in the way the data were analyzed and reported?

*Textual Clue 5: Comparing Findings.* In "Week 2: Advancing Your Argument," Wendy Laura Belcher (2019) discusses how an author can develop a single argument to drive a journal article. The chapter is an outstanding, and very rare, example of an experienced writer and discourse community member unpacking a complicated assumption about academic writing to benefit novice writers. Belcher points out that a journal article "organized around *one important new idea* that is demonstrably related to the scholarship previously published" and centered on "*a single persuasive idea*" takes "a giant leap closer to publication" (p. 66; emphasis added). To her, if the ideas in an article "are multiple but not organized around one new idea," the article "won't be published" (p. 62). Belcher's claim speaks directly to what I have noticed in many discussion sections of qualitative research reports that I perceive as not reader-oriented or not readerly oriented enough. The authors of these discussion sections may be aware of the rhetorical moves they are supposed to perform through which they compare their Finding 1 with Finding A of Previous Author One, their Finding 2 with Finding B of Previous Author Two, and so on. However, how such a comparison has amounted to a coherent argument in the form of critiquing a previous claim or addressing a burning issue is not obvious. Consequently, the comparison does not lead to "a single significant idea . . . emerging from or linked to some scholarly conversation . . . supported with evidence" (Belcher, 2019, p. 67). Instead, the discussion sections look like the authors are just showering the readers with multiple ideas in a piecemeal, patchwork manner and mindlessly latching on to multiple previous findings. The comparison of the findings has not been whipped into one coherent argument that answers the "so-what" question or serves as the "take-home" argument for the article.

Belcher (2019) points out that "editors and reviewers may not mention the lack of an argument as a reason for rejection." They may state that the article is "not original or significant" or "disorganized" or that it "reads like a student paper" (p. 66). Belcher (2019) is not alone in emphasizing the importance of maintaining one single argument in a research report. Creswell (2016), the well-known author of guidebooks on qualitative research, points out that "the difficulty with much qualitative writing is that the reader is left with multiple big ideas, each one distracting from the overall message that you would like to deliver" (pp. 209–210). The similarity between the "overall message" in Creswell (2016, p. 210) and the "a single significant idea" of Belcher (2019, p. 67) is apparent.

Admittedly, a longer and more complex qualitative research report, such as a dissertation, can be driven by multiple arguments. Even such a longer report can be well served by a limited number of carefully developed umbrella thoughts—the core ideas to get across in the study—with each umbrella idea reinforced, clarified, or elaborated by several big thoughts, as suggested long ago by Tarshis (1982). Each of these umbrella thoughts in the dissertation, with its underlying supporting big thoughts, could serve as one single significant argument that is the basis for a journal article.

I did not read Belcher's (2019) chapter until after I had published quite a few journal articles and taught research approaches and research writing for a while. Upon reflection, however, I noticed that, no matter how imperfect they may be, my own journal articles have been driven by this quest for a central idea or argument, a quest I now consider a central tenet of readerly, or good, academic writing. For example, in Cheng (2008), I present seventeen excerpts to document a student's analysis of genre samples and her writing. I then use my analysis of these excerpts to advance my "journal article's single significant idea" (Belcher, 2019, p. 66). The central argument is: We need to extend our understanding of what being "needs-based" means in genre-focused learning to "include [how] students' immediate and long-term learning needs . . . have been mediated by their histories and trajectories of learning" (Cheng, 2008, p. 409). Such an argument is stated clearly early in the abstract (Cheng, 2008, p. 387) and is the only argument advanced in the discussion section of the journal article. I strived to steer clear of the problematic "showering ideas" trap that some journal manuscript authors noticeably fall into when they compare findings without a coherent single significant idea that ties the comparison and, by extension, the whole article together.

## *What Now?* Two Suggestions to Foster Reader-Orientedness in Qualitative Research Reports

This chapter advances this main argument: Good writing is fundamentally reader-oriented at least in qualitative research reports, as discussed here. Good writing reveals the writer's keen awareness of the often subtle and sophisticated expectations and assumptions that expert members of the discourse community possess. Good writing means more than showing one's awareness of these expectations through merely deploying the expected rhetorical structures and lexico-grammatical features in a qualitative research report. It means that the researchers and writers in their research reports show that they have carefully thought through qualitative research. Good writing means that, through their qualitative research reports, the authors have indicated clearly to the readers, who are often the mediating gatekeepers and expert members of the discourse community such as journal editors and reviewers, their maximal efforts to approximate such assumptions and expectations.

I have presented five textual clues that often make me question whether some novice writers have met the threshold level of reader-orientedness in their writing. These textual clues serve only as examples to illustrate the importance of understanding some of the deeply held, often taken-for-granted but frequently unstated assumptions and expectations that expert members of the discourse community hold. Admittedly, other textual clues may be more relevant to other researchers. For example, Creswell (2016) points out that many novice researchers and writers may know the "scientific way" of writing a qualitative report that uses "the standard headings of introduction, literature, methods, results or findings, and conclusions or discussions" (p. 244). However, they may not know the "literary" way of writing a qualitative report that uses headings and topics to report on the study as a narrative story. Such a "literary" approach is preferred or even expected by experienced members of the discourse community when reading studies adopting certain research designs (p. 244). Therefore, not adopting this preferred writing style when reporting on studies guided by these designs would be a textual clue that gives away the novice writers' lack of reader-orientedness.

My hope for reader-orientedness in writing leads to two suggestions. First, novice writers would benefit from studying the worldviews, designs, and methods associated with qualitative research thoughtfully and carefully, either through graduate course work or through diligent self-study. This suggestion may seem obvious, but it is not. Some qualitative research reports I have reviewed have given me the impression that the writers may be learning to write by mimicking how research has been reported on in published research genres such as journal articles. The writing does not inspire confidence in the kind of rigorous research training that should have undergirded the study. The research reports include textual clues to indicate that the writers may not have met some deeper assumptions about conducting qualitative research or writing qualitative reports that the readers—the gatekeeping or experienced members of the discourse community—have. The writing is thus not reader-oriented, and the novice writers may not know why their writing does not connect meaningfully with their readers who are the experienced members of the discourse community. The problem can be ameliorated after the researchers/writers have systematically and thoughtfully concentrated on the different layers of details related to qualitative research. These layers of details cover the epistemological and ontological worldviews underpinning different approaches, the different research designs falling under the umbrella of different approaches, and the research methods that are associated with different research designs. Only then would their writing have a better chance of being readerly or reader-oriented, as discussed in this chapter.

Meanwhile, research training provided to novice writers in applied linguistics could attend to these layers of details in qualitative research more carefully and meaningfully. Some of the research guidebooks in applied linguistics often focus on research methods—how data are collected and analyzed. These guidebooks' reference to the research designs guiding the chosen research methods or the worldviews driving the work of a qualitative researcher could be more explicit than they are now (e.g., Groom & Littlemore, 2011; Richards, Ross, & Seedhouse, 2012; see also Mackey & Gass, 2016). Some guidebooks outside of the field, such as Creswell and Creswell (2018), make stronger and more explicit connections among the different layers of qualitative research and could be useful to those in applied linguistics who provide research training to novice researchers/writers. Integrating worldviews, designs, and methods consciously in research training will convey to novice researchers and writers the importance of not only learning to *do* qualitative research at the level of designs and methods but also learning to *be* a qualitative researcher through adopting a certain worldview that guides one's designs and methods. Learning to *be* a qualitative researcher will be more conducive to educating novice qualitative researchers/writers in applied linguistics about the highly sophisticated assumptions and expectations possessed by the expert members of the discourse community. It will be more conducive to producing the kind of readerly qualitative research reports argued for in this chapter.

The second suggestion is to connect the teaching of research approaches with the teaching of the types of writing specific to these approaches. When discussing writing, if they do at all, many guidebooks on research in applied linguistics often limit themselves to describing the basic rhetorical moves in the research reports specific to the research approach in question (e.g., Groom & Littlemore, 2011; Mackey & Gass, 2016; Paltridge & Phakiti, 2015). Mackey and Gass (2016), for example, describe what to include in the "final stages in reporting qualitative research" and offer a checklist of what to include in a qualitative research report (p. 353). The discussion of writing in these guidebooks is also mainly through *telling*—describing what to include—and not so much through *showing* with, ideally, textual samples to show why specific sections in qualitative research reports have been written the way they have. In fact, this lack of attention to teaching writing in conjunction with teaching research approaches as well as the tendency in "most methods texts" to "simply ignore" the close attention to writing have been noticed as a problem plaguing guidebooks on research in general, rather than just guidebooks on research in applied linguistics (Creswell, 2016, p. 208).

Books focusing on teaching research writing to novice applied linguists, which are few and far between to begin with, also often focus on the rhetorical organizational structures and lexico-grammatical features (e.g., Bitchener, 2010). The careful attention to the impact of some of the assumptions underpinning the way qualitative research reports are written is often lacking. Consequently, apprentice writers are left to their own devices to bridge the two.

Future authors of guidebooks on research and on writing in TESOL/applied linguistics may need to connect the teaching of research approaches and the teaching of the types of writing associated with specific research approaches more consciously. Meanwhile, guidebooks on research outside of TESOL/applied linguistics that have closely integrated the discussion of research approaches and writing within specific approaches may be useful to those who work with novice qualitative researchers/writers. Examples of these include Creswell (2016), who discusses how to write in a qualitative way, how to write reflexively, how to conclude a qualitative report, and how to form good writing habits as someone who often writes qualitative research reports. Creswell's book not only includes a substantial number of examples illustrating how to write, but it also unpacks some of the assumptions underpinning qualitative research and qualitative research reports. Those interested in how to write qualitative research reports using specific research designs, such as ethnography or case studies, can also benefit from such classic texts as Richardson (1990) or van Maanen (2011), where the assumptions underpinning the research design in question and the impact of such assumptions on writing have been discussed extensively.

Using these resources, experienced members of the discourse community of applied linguistics could emphasize to novice writers the importance of thoughtfully connecting research approaches (worldviews, designs, and methods) with research writing. For example, they could explain to novice researchers that dissertations need explicit references to how the three levels of a qualitative research project—worldviews, designs, and methods—have been carefully attended to. By contrast, in a journal article, only one level may need to be brought up, with the other two levels explicitly invoked or implicitly referenced. They could, to take another example, guide novice writers to examine how a qualitative research report on a study that adopted a specific qualitative research design, such as narrative inquiry, may be written differently from a report on a study adopting a different design, such as a qualitative phenomenology study. Doing so either explicitly through formal, classroom-based training or through informal mentoring of novice researchers/writers will help make deep-seated assumptions visible and make novice writers' reports reader-oriented, as is hoped for in this chapter. Notably, a new journal called *Research Methods in Applied Linguistics* published its first issue in 2022. The scope of the journal "encompasses . . . reporting practices" and could be among the venues where expert discourse community members can show how they have thoughtful connecting research approaches and writing to achieve the maximal level of reader-orientedness.

I would like to wrap up this chapter by reflecting on the research design class I mentioned earlier that I just finished teaching in the spring semester of 2022. Among the various assignments that I adopted to guide students to learn about many aspects of research, the most rewarding one to me was the one in which I asked my students to find some research writing samples. I asked them to use their burgeoning knowledge of research to reflect specifically on the way the authors of these samples write. To a larger extent, the assignment expected them to reflect on the reader-orientedness or the lack thereof, that they might have noticed in the chosen samples they analyzed. My students told me at the end of the semester that they really enjoyed this assignment and felt that they had benefited from it. I would argue that it benefited me equally, if not more so. Every other week, I would eagerly read my students' reflection journals, wondering how they might have reacted, as readers, to the writing they chose to analyze and which concepts related to research methods might have prompted their reflection on which specific points in the writing. I would read the research articles they chose to analyze myself and to try to react to them as a reader first before responding to my students' reflections. My responses to my students' reflection journals often became a sort of written conversation with them. We would each bring our perspectives as readers to our analysis of the writing at issue. We often made comments on our shared Google Docs such as:

> Well. You know what. I didn't realize the authors were making
> that assumption in the second sentence in that paragraph until
> you brought it up. I am not sure the readers necessarily share that
> assumption. Do you share that assumption with the authors? Should
> the authors have said more there?

or:

> I am not sure I agree with you that the authors should have provided
> an explanation in the last paragraph. Is it possible that we didn't know
> enough about [a specific aspect of research] and that is why that place
> seems puzzling to us? Is it possible that it may not be puzzling or may
> even be an overkill if the authors had added an explanation there?

Upon further reflection on my teaching after the semester ended, I realized why this assignment was especially rewarding to me. Yes. Good writing is reader-oriented. Good writing should reveal the writer's keen awareness of the often subtle and sophisticated expectations and assumptions that expert members of the discourse community possess. We should not, however, rest with that understanding. The devil is in the details. It would be helpful if we, instead, engage in figuring out why a piece of writing or a place in a piece of writing is reader-oriented or not. In other words, making one's writing reader-oriented in the sense discussed in this chapter requires active learning about the underlying sophisticated assumptions about writing qualitative research reports and sustained practice. More important, it requires, among many other things, that one continue to reflect on how the writers have engaged either successfully or not so successfully with the readers. The assignment was rewarding to me because it allowed me the opportunity to reflect on reader-writer engagement together with my students.

I know that, in this chapter, I have projected myself, quite uncomfortably and self-consciously, as a seasoned member of the discourse community who attempts to posit what reader-oriented research writing is about. I realized that I am more comfortable in my role as a lifelong learner of writing who constantly reflects on how the authors have interacted with the readers, among many other aspects of "good writing," as the chapters in this book have attempted to explore. Though it may be a strenuous one, the journey to constantly reflect on reader-orientedness to make one's writing increasingly readerly can be a satisfying and, ultimately, a rewarding one. I would like to invite others to embark on or to continue this journey.

## References

Belcher, W. L. (2019). *Writing your journal article in twelve weeks: A guide to academic publishing success* (2nd ed.). University of Chicago Press.

Billig, M. (2013). *Learn to write badly: How to succeed in the social sciences*. Cambridge University Press.

Bitchener, J. (2010). *Writing an applied linguistics thesis or dissertation: A guide to presenting empirical research*. Palgrave Macmillan.

Bitzer, L. (1968). The rhetorical situation. *Philosophy and Rhetoric, 1*, 1–14.

Casanave, C. P. (2020). *During the dissertation: A textual mentor for doctoral students in the process of writing*. University of Michigan Press.

Casanave, C. P., & Li, X. (Eds.). (2008). *Learning the literacy practices of graduate school: Insiders' reflections on academic enculturation*. University of Michigan Press.

Cheng, A. (2008). Individualized engagement with genre in academic literacy tasks. *English for Specific Purposes, 27*, 387–411. https://doi.org/10.1016/j.esp.2008.05.001

Creswell, J. (2016). *30 essential skills for the qualitative researcher*. Sage Publications.

Creswell, J. W., & Creswell, J. D. (2018). *Research design: Qualitative, quantitative, and mixed methods approaches* (5th ed.). Sage Publications.

Ede, L., & Lunsford, A. (1984). Audience addressed/audience invoked: The role of audience in composition theory and pedagogy. *College Composition and Communication, 35*, 155–171.

Groom, N., & Littlemore, J. (2011). *Doing applied linguistics: A guide for students*. Routledge.

Lunsford, A. A. (2015). Writing addresses, invokes, and/or creates audiences. In L. Adler-Kassner, & E. Wardle (Eds.). *Naming what we know: Threshold concepts of writing studies* (pp. 20–21). Utah State University Press.

Mackey, A., & Gass, S. M. (2016). *Second language research: Methodology and design*. Routledge.

Paltridge, B., & Phakiti, A. (Eds.). (2015). *Research methods in applied linguistics: A practical resource*. Bloomsbury.

Pinker, S. (2014). *The sense of style: The thinking person's guide to writing in the 21st century*. Viking.

Richards, K., Ross, S., & Seedhouse, P. (2012). *Research methods for applied language studies: An advanced resource book for students*. Routledge.

Richardson, L. (1990). *Writing strategies: Reaching a diverse audience*. Sage Publications.

Swales, J. M. (1990). *Genre analysis: English in academic and research settings*. Cambridge University Press.

Tarshis, B. (1982). *How to write like a pro*. Button Adult.

Thomson, P., & Kamler, B. (2013). *Writing for peer reviewed journals: Strategies for getting published*. Routledge.

van Maanen, J. (2011). *Tales of the field: On writing ethnography*. University of Chicago Press.

**Chapter 19**

# To Write Well, Read Everything, Especially Fiction

*Stephanie Vandrick*

*"Read, read, read. Read everything. . . . You'll absorb it. Then write."* William Faulkner

~~~~~~~~~~~~~~~~

*"Writing comes from reading, and reading is the finest teacher of how to write."* Annie Proulx

As applied linguists and TESOL scholars, we teach our students that reading and writing are inseparably intertwined: One cannot write well without reading extensively. Many of us who have made our careers in academe could perhaps broaden our reading and reflect more on connections between our reading and our scholarly writing. I believe that it is beneficial to read not only in our own disciplines but in related and even far-flung fields. For example, those of us who write about social and critical topics often read in sociology, gender studies, diversity studies, critical theory, and critical pedagogy. I advocate for this kind of extended reading; it broadens our conceptual frameworks, helps us make illuminating connections, and enriches our writing.

In this chapter, I focus mainly on a kind of reading that is not obviously connected to academic writing (except when authors write about literature itself): reading *fiction*. My own lifelong love of fiction and my desire to bring scholarship and the virtues and pleasures of fiction together were intensified some years ago when I had an epiphany: I read

<div align="right">**271**</div>
~~~~~~~~~~~~~~~~

Ilona Leki's book, *Undergraduates in a Second Language* (2007). I already admired this influential second language writing scholar and her work, but the book particularly struck me because its case study approach was executed in an almost novelistic fashion. It was compelling and vivid in its portraits of the students being studied. The approach was and is highly effective as well as fascinating. Since then, Leki's book has been a sort of lodestar for me as a model of writing that is both scholarly and literary.

Reading novels and short stories can influence the content, depth, and style of our writing (Prose, 2006). Literary reading enriches our general knowledge, providing context for our scholarship. It stimulates our intellects, increases our understanding, and positively affects our empathy and our sense of aesthetics, thus enhancing and elevating our writing. It reminds us that writing is a craft and an art. Academic writing is less formulaic now than formerly, and it occasionally includes elements of memoir, poetry, creative nonfiction, and theater (Willard-Traub, 2006). Note, for example, the "narrative turn" in the social sciences (Czarniawska, 2004) and the increased use since the 1990s of personal narrative in various disciplines (e.g., Behar, 1993; Ellis, 1997). Even when academic writing is not explicitly experimental, "hybrid," or "creative," reading fiction positively affects that writing. After all, whose English-language writing cannot benefit from exposure to the glorious fiction of, for instance, Jane Austen, Willa Cather, Henry James, Penelope Lively, Toni Morrison, Colm Tóibín, and Virginia Woolf?

I acknowledge that I have a personal stake in asserting the importance of reading fiction. Such reading has been an important part of my life since childhood; I was a classic bookish child. Perhaps nerdily, when I was ten years old, I started a list of all the books I read, and I have maintained that list ever since in a (pre-digital) series of now slightly battered notebooks. Early appearances on the list included *Charlotte's Web*, *Anne of Green Gables*, and *Little Women*. Mysteries and boarding school stories were favorites, including various series (Nancy Drew, Trixie Belden, Cherry Ames). By age 13 I was reading Dostoevsky's *Crime and Punishment*, although admittedly understanding only a small part of its meaning. Ever since, I have continued to read fiction extensively, several dozens of books a year. I was an English literature major in college (of course I was!). In 2010, I started a blog (StephanieVandrickReads) about books, reading, libraries, and bookstores. I know that many scholars in our field are also avid readers of fiction.

I confess that at one point I (like so many English major types!) wished that I could not only read but *write* fiction. I soon realized that I did not have that talent. But over the years, I also realized that I could incorporate aspects of literature, especially essayistic, memoiristic, and narrative aspects, into my academic writing. This was a liberating discovery, and it greatly influenced several of my publications on such topics as identity, social class, and gender (Vandrick, 2009, 2010, 2016). At about the same time, I discovered a major topic of my research and writing, that of missionary work and its part in the colonial enterprise, including the role of the spread of the English language. As a "missionary kid" myself, who had spent her childhood in India, I could draw on my own experiences and those of other "missionary kids." This confluence of feeling freer to write in a less traditional academic way, on the one hand, and finding a topic that was so personally and viscerally important to me, on the other hand, was immensely freeing and inspiring. It provided an opportunity for me to blend several aspects of my personal life, my reading life, and my academic research. This strand of my work began with a chapter in which I engaged and struggled with the connections between my missionary kid background and my career in TESOL/applied linguistics (Vandrick, 1999). I further addressed the topic in other publications (2009, 2013) and conference papers. I then carried out an analysis of forty-two missionary kid memoirs, identifying themes and supporting examples that connected those memoirs to the colonial project. This research culminated in my 2019 book, *Growing up with God and Empire: A Postcolonial Analysis of "Missionary Kid" Memoirs*. An integral part of my analyzing the memoirs as data was referring to fiction by authors such as Chinua Achebe, Pearl Buck, E. M. Forster, Ruth Prawer Jhabvala, Somerset Maugham, James Michener, and Paul Scott, all of whom addressed colonialism and sometimes specifically missionary work. It was my gradually increasing thinking about my uses of literature and my focus on the topic of "good writing" in my scholarly work that led me to write the chapter you are now reading.

## Literature about Good Writing

There are numerous books on good writing in general; Kidder and Todd's *Good Prose* (2013) is just one example. A smallish subset of these are books specifically on academic writing. Some, such as Billig (2013), are very critical of how many scholars use excessive technical vocabulary ("jargon") and employ other practices that obfuscate rather than clarify their ideas. Willard-Traub (2006) writes that "increasingly . . . approaches to writing that incorporate autobiography and personal narrative are being used by scholars . . . as methods of scholarly analysis and argumentation" (p. 424). Laurel Richardson, a sociologist whose own publications are known for their creativity and literary qualities, writes about the importance of narrative in social science writing, eloquently stating, "Narrative displays the goals and intentions of human actors; makes individuals, cultures, societies, and historical epochs comprehensible as wholes; humanizes time; allows us to contemplate the effects of our actions and to alter the directions of our lives" (1990, p. 20).

The emphasis of scholars and others on the uses of *narrative* in scholarly writing is one of the biggest influences that fiction has on that writing. Ethnography and autoethnography, especially, clearly depend heavily on narrative writing. Further, as Christine Pearson Casanave and I put it (Casanave & Vandrick, 2003, p. 2):

> Narratives allow for understanding and connection in ways that straight exposition does not. Truth in academic writing, particularly in the more scientific fields, has been characterized as objective, as written in the third person, as distanced from personal feelings and experiences. . . . Yet we contend . . . that there is another kind of truth to be obtained from narratives, stories, and first-person viewpoints, which people use to construct their realities and interpret their experiences.

There is an increasing amount of writing by applied linguistics/TESOL scholars that employs not only narrative in the more traditional places, such as case studies, but also *personal* narratives, stories that illuminate research topics. Many of these are found in edited collections, including those of Curtis and Romney (2006) on race and English language teaching, Kamhi-Stein (2013) on language teachers' identities as manifested in classrooms, and Yazan, Canagarajah, and Jain (2020) on language teachers' transnational identities. Instances of personal narratives in articles or non-edited books are Lin et al. (2004) on racism and sexism in language studies; Sharkey (2004), addressing sexual identities of language educators; Simon-Maeda on being a North American language teacher in Japan (2011); and Sister Scholars (2021), about women of color addressing obstacles in professional lives in academe.

An important issue for scholars is the tension between following the traditional "rules" and practices of academic writing, on the one hand,

and being free to be creative and occasionally "break" those rules, on the other. Students and novice scholars need to have the tools to fit in with their disciplinary conventions, and often not knowing these conventions can be especially detrimental to those with marginalized identities. Those who don't know the conventions well are often penalized for not following them, but also do not know them well enough to challenge them. Further, often only majority (generally White, male, well-established) scholars are permitted to be flexible and creative about trying less restricted types of writing styles, such as using personal narrative. The broader issue is the role of privilege in writing: Which academics with which privileged identities (regarding race, gender, class, sexual identity, academic address, etc.) are given the further privilege of deciding when to follow the rules and when to break those rules?

When I narrow the focus to the main topic of this chapter, it is less easy to find publications specifically about how reading *fiction* influences academic writers doing scholarly writing. Regarding academic writing, Kara (2013) writes of "using fiction to enhance academic research and writing" and "as a way of studying 'messier' aspects of the process, such as emotion" (p. 70). Antoniou and Moriarty's (2008) perspective on the contributions of creative writing (mainly fiction) is that scholarly writers are whole persons, a combination of personal and professional selves, and should not suppress "the voice of our non-academic or personal selves," nor accept the "false divide" between the academic and the creative (p. 159).

## Ways That Reading Fiction Can Heighten Good Academic Writing

Reading fiction can positively influence our scholarly writing in several ways. When we read, we unconsciously store up examples of good writing in fiction (to emulate) and examples of poor writing (to avoid). I personally would be sad not to have read George Eliot, E. M. Forster, Alice Munro, Barbara Pym, Richard Russo, and so many more literary giants past and present. Reading great novels for so many years means I have taken these works, individually and cumulatively, into my mind and spirit. Although I can't draw a direct line from my having read their work to their influences on my writing, I know in my bones that they influence me indirectly, whether the influences are detectable or undetectable, obvious or subtle, known or not to the reader or even to me as the writer.

Wide reading of fiction helps us understand the effectiveness and power of *story*, which humans crave, and then perhaps use it in our own writing, such as in the examples we choose, and in ethnographies and other reports on qualitative research. Regular reading of fiction, in which the plotting, character development, and themes are often complex, helps us "go deeper" in our own writing and not settle for mediocre or merely adequate insights and language. As writers we develop an awareness of the reader and thus a sense of connection between the writer and the reader is enhanced. We develop our sense of empathy, which makes us consciously very aware of both the subjects we write about and our readers.

More specifically, reading fiction influences our writing in both *content* and *style*. In describing these elements, I briefly mention ways in which some specific authors illustrate these characteristics, and ways in which the authors have inspired me.

First, the *content* of our writing is affected by our reading. Sometimes we directly draw on what we read, often as examples. In my book (2019) on "missionary kid" memoirs, I began by discussing the way Barbara Kingsolver's novel *The Poisonwood Bible* (1998) had negatively influenced so many people's perception of missionaries. I wrote that many people, when hearing of my topic, asked me, "Oh, have you read *The Poisonwood Bible?*" Other novelists whose work I have drawn on and been profoundly influenced by in my academic writing include Jane Austen, Tsitsi Dangarembga, Joan Didion, Isak Dinesen, Amitav Ghosh, Rumer Godden, Nadine Gordimer, Doris Lessing, and Jane Gardam. Regarding content, I often feel connected to novels by authors such as these through their drawing attention—directly or indirectly—to social justice and identity issues. Nadine Gordimer and Tsitsi Dangarembga, among others, address racial issues. Doris Lessing and Sylvia Plath, also among others, confront sexism. Joan Didion explores what it means to be American. Jane Austen's novels, each of which I have read numerous times, at first appealed to me for the stories and the witty portrayals of the characters and the mores of the time. I soon noted that Austen was also illustrating the constricted choices of women and addressing other social issues such as slavery in England's colonies. The connection to the content of my own writing is that my publications have also very often addressed issues of identity and of (in)equality regarding gender, race, sexual identity, the colonizers and the colonized, and related identities.

Shifting from *content* to ways in which reading fiction influences our writing *style*, and therefore good writing, I believe it does so regarding the overlapping qualities of *clarity, voice, control, vividness,* and an intangible quality of *engagingness.*

Everyone gives lip service to *clarity,* but many scholars do not in reality practice being as clear and readable as possible in their writing. On some level, many academics seem to believe that if one's scholarly writing is "too" clear, it risks seeming too accessible, too obvious, and not academic enough. As Booth, Colomb, and Williams (2003) put it, too often scholars "take as a model those writers whose prose is terminally dense, because they think that a complex style bespeaks academic success" (p. 265). I do not ask that scholars oversimplify the genuine complexities of their research, but we need to be aware of readers and make every effort to write in a way that is understandable and even welcoming. I know that I have sometimes felt inadequate because of not completely understanding certain heavily theoretical works, yet when I finally had them explained in a clearer way by someone who could more adeptly cut through the thickets of jargon, I felt illuminated and was able to use those concepts as contextual lenses for my own thinking and writing. Despite evidence to the contrary in too many cases of academic writing, good writers can in fact write about complex topics in clear ways. I believe that fiction writers, who if they are not clear, will lose their readers, have something to teach academic writers. Austen, again, is a perfect example of a writer whose complexity and subtlety have many layers of meaning but who never hides in tangled, turgid prose. I am inspired by her, as well as by the way Joan Didion cuts through obfuscation and the way Rumer Godden gently leads readers to realizations.

Another aspect of style is *voice.* Voice is hard to define, but it involves a combination of such factors as point of view, tone, emotion, and word choice. The case of voice may be one that really is an instance of "I know it when I see it!" Who among us does not recognize certain prose as that of scholars whose other publications we have read? Even if readers don't recognize a certain author's work, they can get a sense of an actual person, with specific characteristics and viewpoints, behind the written product. Voice does not have to announce itself, but is always, subtly at least, present in good writing. The topic of voice has at times been controversial in applied linguistics and TESOL (see, e.g., Atkinson, 2003). But to me the phenomenon of voice in writing is so common, so evident, that I cannot deny its existence and importance. I am inspired by novelists such as Barbara Pym, who wrote in an understated way and who was for too long underestimated. Her gently witty voice is punctuated by moments of absolutely piercing observations. Academic writers could well aspire to the same combination.

*Control,* too, is an important factor found in good academic writing. Readers need to know that someone is firmly in charge. There should be no feeling that the piece of writing is just following a template, or—on the other hand—that the writer is ineffectually casting about to pull everything in the article or essay together. There needs to be an awareness of focus, of intentionality that provides a sense of unity in the writing. Who is more firmly in control of her work than George Eliot, especially in her masterpiece, *Middlemarch?* Or, for a contemporary example, the great short story writer, Alice Munro? I have a tendency in my writing to overexplain; reading Munro reminds me to be more controlled in my writing. Another part of control is that the reader can sense that the writer has taken care with the composition of the written work, with consciousness of aesthetics and art, and with creativity.

Even the most quantitative work, but especially qualitative publications, can be greatly enhanced by the quality of being *vivid,* reaching out to draw the reader's attention. This may be through artful sequencing, through striking images and language (think of Sylvia Plath's work, fiction and poetry, which practically epitomizes "striking images and language"), and most of all through telling details. "Telling details" may be the most critical quality of vividness of both fiction and academic writing. Important elements of vividness include an aliveness, a sense of a highly purposeful, thoughtful, and reader-aware writer behind the work. Toni Morrison's work exemplifies these elements. In my own writing, I am constantly fighting the temptation to settle for the easy words, phrases, or images, and although I am sometimes discouraged by how hard it is to write vividly, I at least keep that goal in front of me.

An overarching characteristic of a writing style that benefits from the writer's experiences reading fiction, one that draws on all of the qualities discussed above, is the intangible one of *engagingness.* (I had to look up whether this is in fact a word, which fortunately the internet assures me it is.) When the reader feels that the writer is thinking of her/him and is drawn into the academic article or book and reads it with pleasure, the work can be described as engaging. The writer does not pander but trusts and truly wants to communicate with the reader. This is another "I know it when I see it" quality, such a welcome one when we encounter it. I will always trust putting myself in the hands of contemporary novelists such as Ann Patchett and Anne Tyler. Both display absolute control, without the mechanisms of control being distractingly visible, and thus completely engage the reader.

# My Colleagues' Ideas

As I was thinking about this chapter, I wanted to draw on the knowledge and experiences of some of my colleagues in our discipline(s) whom I consider excellent academic writers. I wrote to several of them, spread over several continents, asking for their informal answers to my broad questions on whether and how reading widely, and particularly reading fiction, influences their and other scholars' writing. Several of these scholars/writers were kind enough to take time from their busy lives to reply, which I deeply appreciate and for which I thank them very much. Many of them addressed some of the same themes as I have discussed in this chapter. I only wish I had had the space to include more of the thoughtful comments they provided. I promised anonymity, so I will quote from them without names.

Here are the relevant parts of my introduction to my letter to my colleagues, followed by the four broad questions I asked them, and a selection of their replies:

> My thesis is basically that good (clear, engaging, non-jargony) writing is enhanced by reading a lot of non-academic material, and especially fiction (but could be biography, memoir, history, politics, science, and other nonfiction as well) . . . . Please answer some or all of the questions, as briefly or in as much detail as you want.

## 1. Please comment on my thesis that extensive non-academic reading enhances the quality of scholars' academic writing.

Selected comments:

> *"Reading good writing means witnessing how it has been crafted. When you judge whether or not you like it, even though you might not realise this, it is on the basis of how convincing it is. Being convincing, just as in academic writing, is about reference to evidence. . . . A crucial part of this is being curious about how good writers do what they do—about how the writing is crafted—about . . . how authorial voice is employed, how message and argument are constructed. . . ."*

> *"I feel most satisfied with my academic writing when it 'sounds' good, when a sentence has an evocative cadence."*

> *"Yes, I totally agree. I'd extend your point to reading all multimodal forms of meaning making, which can expand our aesthetic attention to what we write.*

> *I've been playing and writing music all my life. . . . I've come to appreciate*
> *commonalities in crafting 'texts,' whose meaning and impact are inseparable from*
> *their creative production."*

Note that these comments speak of writers' absorbing lessons about the *craft* of writing. They also emphasize the important point that all writing, including academic writing, needs to use evidence in order to be convincing. The "data" of academic writing are similar to the "evidence" in fiction, such as striking details and examples. Even though I have made this point to writing students for decades, I am also struck by my colleagues' reinforcement of the idea that the process and product in writing (and music and other arts) are inseparable.

## 2. Please comment on the idea that reading *fiction* is especially effective in enhancing one's academic writing.

Selected comments:

> *"The features of fiction that might enhance academic writing are narrative,*
> *sentences of varying length . . ., a larger vocabulary, dialogue, and descriptive*
> *passages and titles. The use of narrative is particularly enhancing because it*
> *prevents the author from hiding behind a façade of objectivity, including passive*
> *voice, and forces a reckoning with the subjectivity and creativity of interpreting one's*
> *data. I enjoy the inclusion of stories, fragments, bits of dialogue (including different*
> *varieties of English), vivid descriptions of the social context, and creative titles*
> *in academic writing. They . . . encourage lingering over an article or book chapter*
> *rather than simply gleaning information."*

> *"[Other] features of fiction that might enhance academic writing are uncertainty*
> *and speculation. This can be seen when academic writers hedge, using modals*
> *such as might, could, may be, etc. Taking this speculative posture, rather than*
> *one of certainty, demonstrates that research is a tentative and ongoing process,*
> *not an endpoint or the final and incontrovertible word. When we adopt hedging*
> *in our academic writing, we're showing humility about our research process and*
> *conclusions."*

> *"Yes, definitely! I think the enhancement especially relates to its effects on*
> *readers. . . . Fiction has a rhetorical or illocutionary effect that acts on us and*
> *mobilizes our emotions (and agency) in ways unrealized in abstract academic*
> *writing. . . . [I]n terms of social welfare policy and labour laws to mitigate the*
> *hardships of industrial capitalism, Dickens was far more effective and influential*
> *than Marx and Engels on British parliamentarians."*

> *"Fiction tells a story, and there is nothing more compelling. Fiction teaches us to consider a truth from inside another's heart and mind, how to pay attention to detail and to use detail to make our writing come alive. It reminds us that we are living in a body, using our senses, and that is part of everyone's life, even an academic's!"*

I was excited to read these eloquent comments, with their very specific points about ways in which reading fiction may well influence academic writing. These respondents referred to narrative, structure, language, speculation, voice, characterization, emotions, and the senses as factors in fiction that at least indirectly influence and elevate one's academic writing. I agree that these are all characteristics of excellent academic writing, although aiming for these attributes in scholarly writing is seldom discussed.

## 3. Do you feel that what you personally read (in addition to academic writing) influences/shapes your own writing style?

Selected comments:

> *"I read lots of contemporary fiction, especially writers of color who deal with issues of oppression, racism, sexism, and immigration. So, speaking thematically, there's definitely an overlap between my reading of fiction and my academic writing. I guess this means that I don't perceive fiction and academic writing as diametrically opposed. Just different ways of presenting a topic."*

> *"I seem to be especially attracted to what are for me new lexical and grammatical arrangements for saying things I often say but in tired, formulaic ways. I think my music background affects how I hear what I'm reading, in terms of prosody, rhythm, intonation. I'm a brutally slow and error-prone writer on a keyboard, so I find myself voicing out a text before and during entering it into script. I think this adds to my compositional awareness of its audibility or how it 'sounds' to a reader."*

> *"In some book chapters more recently I've tried to adopt a more 'personal' voice and challenge some conventions as to presentation/style. . . . I do feel more 'resistant' to the power of academic genres as I get older but I guess that's a privilege in some ways."*

> *"Absolutely. I seek out writing that influences and shapes my own writing. . . . When I'm stuck . . . I re-read stories, poems, memoirs, passages from novels that*

> *have helped me in the past. Recently, for example, I have re-read the short memoir* Still Life *by Mary Gordon, parts of Ian McEwan's* Saturday, *some of Amy Bloom's short stories, Eva Hoffman's* Lost in Translation.*"*

Some of these replies address topics and themes; some address structures, voice, and even musicality; some address using specific readings intentionally to shape one's writing. It makes me very happy to think of academic writers concerning themselves with "musicality" and carefully "shaping" their writing, and even specifically seeking out good fiction in order to inspire and enhance their writing!

## 4. What genres of publications (besides academic ones) do you personally like to read? Examples of specific books (etc.) are very welcome!

Selected comments:

> *"I love to read contemporary fiction. . . . A novel I recently read,* Girl, Woman, Other, *uses a genre-bending style called verse fiction, a hybrid of prose and poetry, that I found very appealing. There's no sentence punctuation so the reader has to rely on line breaks which work really well in this novel for highlighting topics, moods, and characters. I found it very evocative and would like to experiment with this hybrid genre in future writing . . . My favorite non-fiction book,* The Warmth of Other Suns *by Isabel Wilkerson, blurs the line between history and narrative, between efferent and aesthetic. It's history, sociology, and narrative, brought together in a compelling and heartbreaking way."*

One respondent listed novels that he has used in his academic writing as follows:

> *"*Half of a Yellow Sun *and* Americanah, *by C. N. Adichie;* Only in London, *by H. Al Sheykh;* We Need New Names, *by N. Bulawayo;* The Pleasure Seekers, *by T. Doshi;* The Moor's Account, *by L. Lalami; and* Istanbul: Memories and the City, *by O. Pamuk."*

> *"I prefer to read fiction that includes a lot of character development and psychological interiority," such as Yaa Gyasi's* Transcendent Kingdom *and Emily Ruskovich's* Idaho.*"*

Another respondent lists her non-academic reading material as follows:

> *"Novels (my latest are* The Revisioners, The Other Half, Redhead by the Side of the Road, Heartberries, On Earth We're Briefly Gorgeous*); non-academic books about social issues, such as race;* The New York Times, *usually just on Sundays; mindfulness/meditation books; parenting books; books about organizing schedules;* Real Simple Magazine; *and* Sunset Magazine.*"*

I couldn't resist asking this last question, because it offers the kind of detail that fiction itself does, and—candidly—because I always love to know what people, especially my colleagues and friends, are reading! And I was not disappointed, as I was rewarded with both the variety and the specificity of the answers to this question, as well as, in some cases, the reasons why the respondents read what they do.

As I read the thoughtful replies to the four questions I asked, it is clear to me (although I am not surprised!) that many applied linguistics/TESOL scholars are widely read in many areas besides their own discipline(s), and that this wide reading is an integral and essential part of their knowledge base and of the factors that influence their thinking and their academic writing. Even though the sample size of my respondents is small, I am thrilled to have my beliefs about the effects of wide reading, especially fiction, confirmed.

## Keep Reading Everything, Especially Fiction!

The intriguing and creative comments of my colleagues inspire me by allowing me to see "behind the curtain" of the beliefs and practices that undergird their excellent academic writing. These scholars do important research and theorizing, and although they thoroughly understand the academic conventions, they also understand that there is more to good writing than strict adherence to those conventions. They are scholars but they are also whole persons, and what they read outside their strictly academic reading has a definite impact on their thinking and writing. They reinforce my belief in writing as an art and a craft, and—like me—they welcome those influences and the ways in which they affect the content, style, voice, aesthetic qualities, and power of their writing. So I reiterate: To write well, read everything, especially fiction!

## References

Antoniou, M., & Moriarty, J. (2008). What can academic writers learn from creative writers? Developing guidance and support for lecturers in Higher Education. *Teaching in Higher Education, 13*(2), 157–167.

Atkinson, D. (2003). Writing for publication/writing for public execution: On the (personally) vexing notion of (personal) voice. In C. P. Casanave & S. Vandrick (Eds.), *Writing for scholarly publication: Behind the scenes in language education* (pp. 159–175). Lawrence Erlbaum.

Behar, R. (1993). *Translated woman: Crossing the border with Esperanza's story.* Beacon.

Billig, M. (2013). *Learn to write badly: How to succeed in the social sciences.* Cambridge University Press.

Booth, W. C., Colomb, G. G., & Williams, J. M. (2003). *The craft of research* (2nd ed.). University of Chicago Press.

Casanave, C. P., & Vandrick, S. (2003). Introduction: Issues in writing for publication. In C. P. Casanave & S. Vandrick (Eds.), *Writing for scholarly publication: Behind the scenes in language education* (pp. 1–13). Lawrence Erlbaum.

Cox, C. (2009, Spring). Annie Proulx, The art of fiction no. 199. *The Paris Review 188.*

Curtis, A., & Romney, M. (Eds.), (2006). *Color, race, and English language teaching: Shades of meaning.* Lawrence Erlbaum.

Czarniawska, B. (2004). *Narratives in social science research.* Sage.

Ellis, C. (1997). Evocative autoethnography: Writing emotionally about our lives. In W. G. Tierney & Y. S. Lincoln (Eds.), *Representation and the text: Re-framing the narrative voice* (pp. 115–139). Southern Illinois University Press.

Kamhi-Stein, L. (Ed.). (2013). *Narrating their lives: Examining English language teachers' professional identities within the classroom.* University of Michigan Press.

Kara, H. (2013). It's hard to tell how research feels: Using fiction to enhance academic research and writing. *Qualitative Research in Organizations and Management, 8*(1), 70–84.

Kidder, T., & Todd, R. (2013). *Good prose: The art of nonfiction.* Random House.

Kingsolver, B. (1998). *The poisonwood bible.* HarperCollins.

Leki, I. (2007). *Undergraduates in a second language: Challenges and complexities of academic literacy development.* Routledge.

Lin, A., Grant, R., Kubota, R., Motha, S., Tinker-Sachs, G., Vandrick, S., & Wong, S. (2004). Women faculty of color in TESOL: Theorizing our lived experiences. *TESOL Quarterly, 38*(3), 487–504.

Prose, F. (2006). *Reading like a writer: A guide for people who love books and for those who want to write them.* HarperCollins.

Richardson, L. (1990). *Writing strategies: Reaching diverse audiences.* (Qualitative Research Methods Series 21). Sage.

Sharkey, J. (2004). Lives stories don't tell: Exploring the untold in autobiographies. *Curriculum Inquiry, 34*(4), 495–512.

Simon-Maeda, A. (2011). *Being and becoming a speaker of Japanese: An autoethnographic account.* Multilingual Matters.

Sister Scholars (2021). Strategies for Sisterhood in the language education academy. *Journal of Language, Identity, & Education.* DOI: 10.1080/15348458.2020.1833725

Stein, J. (1956, Spring). William Faulkner, The art of fiction, no. 12. *The Paris Review 12.*

Vandrick, S. (1999). ESL and the colonial legacy: A teacher faces her "missionary kid" past. In G. Haroian-Guerin (Ed.), *The personal narrative: Writing ourselves as teachers and scholars* (pp. 63–74). Calendar Islands Publishers.

Vandrick, S. (2009). *Interrogating privilege: Reflections of a second language educator.* University of Michigan Press.

Vandrick, S. (2010). Social class privilege among ESOL writing students. In M. Cox, J. Jordan, C. Ortmeier-Hooper, & G. G. Schwartz (Eds.). *Reinventing identities in second language writing* (pp. 257–272). National Council of Teachers of English.

Vandrick, S. (2013). The 'colonial legacy' and 'missionary kid' memoirs. In G. Barkhuizen (Ed.), *Narrative research in applied linguistics* (pp. 19–40). Cambridge University Press.

Vandrick, S. (2016). Feminist language teacher identity research. In G. Barkhuizen (Ed.), *Reflections on language teacher identity research* (pp. 228–233). Routledge.

Vandrick, S. (2019). *Growing up with God and empire: A postcolonial analysis of "missionary kid" memoirs.* Multilingual Matters.

Willard-Traub, M. K. (2006). Reflection in academe: Scholarly writing and the shifting subject. *College English, 68*(4), 422–432.

Yazan, B., Canagarajah, S., & Jain, R. (Eds.). (2020). *Autoethnographies in ELT: Transnational Identities, pedagogies, and practices.* Routledge.

# Contributor Bios

**Robert Kohls**

I am an associate professor of English/TESOL at San Francisco State University, where I teach courses in second language acquisition, language teaching practicum, first and second language writing theory and practice, sociolinguistics, and academic writing for multilingual writers. I have been teaching English for over twenty-five years and have taught in Canada, Colombia, and the United States. I have benefited from many brilliant mentors in my life, but the best mentors have been my students, who have taught me about more about language, culture, and learning than I taught them. My research interests are in teacher written feedback and writing teacher education. Currently, I am the coordinator of the Composition for Multilingual Writers Program at SF State, a co-editor of *The CATESOL Journal,* and book review co-editor with Christine Pearson Casanave for the *Journal of Second Language Writing.*

**Christine Pearson Casanave**

Post-PhD, I moved to Japan and taught content-based English at Keio University's SFC campus and some weekend classes in an MATESOL program at the Japan campus of Columbia University's Teachers College. My next post was in TESOL and applied linguistics in the graduate college of education at Temple University's Japan Campus (TUJ), work that continues online at the doctoral level from my home base in beautiful Monterey, California. It has been most rewarding helping the TUJ students with their studies in qualitative inquiry and their dissertation writing. I have also published numerous articles, books, and co-edited collections on topics related to academic writing, have served on several journal editorial boards, and have been book review co-editor, first with Yongyan Li and now with Robert Kohls, of the *Journal of Second Language Writing.*

**Priyavanda Abeywickrama**

I am a professor in the English Department at San Francisco State University, where I coordinate the MA TESOL program. I teach graduate courses in second language listening and speaking and curriculum and assessment development. I also often teach writing and oral communication to undergraduate multilingual students.

## Gary Barkhuizen

I am a professor at the University of Auckland, New Zealand, and an Honorary Research Fellow at the University of the Free State, South Africa. My areas of teaching and research interest are teacher education, study abroad, and narrative approaches to research in language teaching and learning.

## Diane Belcher

My academic life has been full of happy accidents. A fortuitous meeting with George Braine led to my first co-edited volume. The good fortune of working in a program with Alan Hirvela resulted in our now decades-long collaboration. My most rewarding professional accomplishments, such as recent research with my Georgia State University colleague Youjin Kim on digital multimodal composing, have been collaborations.

## Esther Chan

I have taught writing at San Francisco State University for over thirty-five years. I received my MA in TESOL and certificate to teach writing in 1985. What I enjoy most about teaching is helping students embrace their college experience and achieve self-empowerment. Teaching writing allows me to do this by helping my students find their voice, develop self-confidence, and discover their interests.

## An Cheng

I enjoy working with my students at Oklahoma State University, where I am a professor of English. Their insights on writing and genre constantly renew my understanding of these topics, leading to this chapter, various journal publications, and the volume *Genre and Graduate-level Research Writing*, also from the University of Michigan Press.

## Deborah Crusan

I've been teaching and writing about writing assessment at Wright State University in Dayton, Ohio, for some time and am often surprised by teachers who claim not to understand much about assessment. Therefore, I focus on assessment literacy in my teacher education classes. When I'm not doing that, I travel, cook, and plant scads of perennials in my garden.

## Martha Clark Cummings

I just retired from teaching writing to non-native speakers of English and training teachers in MA programs in TESOL for thirty-five years. Since I have already traveled all over the world, my plan is to find a little cabin and spend the rest of the time the world and I have left reading, writing, and being still.

## Katelyn Endow

After graduating with an MAT in TESOL from the University of Southern California, I moved to rural Japan to teach English. Then I returned to school at San Francisco State University for an MA in English Composition. I am now starting a new chapter at SFSU teaching in their Composition for Multilingual Students program.

## Guillaume Gentil

Thirty years ago, I was not expecting to be what I am today, a professor of applied linguistics and French studies at Carleton University, Ottawa, Canada. Nor did I expect to serve as a co-editor of the *Journal of Second Language Writing*. My research interests in second language writing and biliteracy in professional and postsecondary settings originate from my academic literacy experiences in France, the United States, and Canada.

## Lynn Goldstein

I am Professor Emerita, the Middlebury Institute of International Studies at Monterey (MIIS), where I taught courses in the teaching of L2 writing, writing for applied linguistics, sociolinguistics, and intercultural competence. I have been involved with L2 writing in various teaching, research, and administrative capacities and currently serve on the editorial boards of the *Journal of Second Language Writing* and the *Journal of Response to Writing*.

## Alan Hirvela

I am a professor emeritus at Ohio State University. My current scholarly interests are expertise in L2 writing instruction, the teaching and learning of argumentative writing, and literature-writing connections. I recently co-edited *Argumentative Writing in a Second Language: Perspectives on Research and Pedagogy* (University of Michigan Press) with Diane Belcher.

## Lía D. Kamhi-Stein

I am professor and coordinator of the MA in TESOL Program at California State University, Los Angeles. I have received several awards in recognition of my teaching and teacher mentoring. I am most proud of the fact that I was born and raised in Argentina, where I learned and then taught English as a foreign language.

## Penny Kinnear

I coordinate professional language development activities in the Faculty of Applied Science and Engineering, University of Toronto, where I delight in introducing engineering students to the nuances and complexities of languaging, written and oral. I co-authored *Sociocultural Theory in Second Language Education: An Introduction through Narratives*, 2nd edition (Multilingual Matters), with Merrill Swain and Linda Steinman.

## Icy Lee

I am a professor at the National Institute of Education in Nanyang Technological University, Singapore. My main research interests are second language writing and second language teacher education. My publications have appeared in numerous international journals such as the *Journal of Second Language Writing, TESOL Quarterly, System*, and *Language Teaching Research*.

## Yongyan Li

I have been working in the Faculty of Education, University of Hong Kong, for over a decade, during which my constant theme has been how I can write well and help my students to write well. It seems I write a little better now, by achieving greater coherence between my varied areas of research and teaching.

## Kimani Lincoln

I have a master's degree in English Composition and am currently teaching first-year writing courses at a university in California. I love to try and understand how the writing process works for both students and instructors to the best of my abilities.

## Hanako Okada

I am an associate professor in the Faculty of Liberal Arts at Sophia University in Tokyo, Japan, where I teach rhetoric and composition to students from diverse linguistic and cultural backgrounds. My academic interests include work infused with *life*, such as ethnography, situated qualitative research, reflexive personal narratives, and multilingual identities.

## Melinda Reichelt

I'm a Distinguished University Professor and professor of English at the University of Toledo, where I direct the ESL writing program and teach ESL writing and linguistics. My research interests include L2 writing, pronouns, and world Englishes.

## Lisya Seloni

I'm a professor of TESOL and Applied Linguistics in the Department of English at Illinois State University, where I teach courses on second language acquisition, cross-cultural issues in TESOL, and second language writing. My primary areas of research include ethnographic approaches to second language writing, genre-based instruction, narrative inquiry, and L2 writing teacher education.

## Mona Shaath

Teaching at San Francisco State University is part of my continuing education. With over a decade of teaching experience, I invite students into classrooms that are collaborative, multimodal, and challenging. I also support students as a tutor at SFSU's Tutoring and Academic Support Center. I bring a social justice perspective to composition informed by an MA in Sociology from New York University. Currently, I am pursuing an MA in Composition from SFSU. With my degree, I will encourage students to empower themselves through writing.

## Christine M. Tardy

I am a professor of English Applied Linguistics at the University of Arizona, where I teach undergraduate and graduate students in TESOL, applied linguistics, and writing. My research has focused on various areas related to academic writing, including second language writing, English for academic purposes, and genre theory and pedagogy.

## Jennifer Trainor

I am a professor in the MA Composition Program at San Francisco State University, where I teach first-year writing and graduate courses in composition theory and pedagogy. I have published in *College Composition and Communication* and *Research in the Teaching of English* and have written a book on antiracist literacy education.

### Rachael Tupper-Eoff

I recently graduated from SFSU's English Composition program and have worked at Chabot College in Hayward for over a decade, starting in the tutoring program and later teaching composition and tutor-training courses. As a teacher, I am interested in working with college tutoring and writing centers to develop innovative learning resources and services in support of student learning.

### Monique Ubungen

I am a fourth-generation Filipina American and a San Francisco native. I'm a proud Bay Area educator and college writing instructor passionate about empowering historically marginalized students in higher education. You can find me teaching first-year writing and advocating for student success at San Francisco State University, City College of San Francisco, and Skyline College.

### Stephanie Vandrick

I am a professor emerita of Rhetoric and Language at the University of San Francisco. My research focuses on social class, gender, critical and feminist pedagogies, literature, and autoethnography. My most recent book is *Growing up with God and Empire: A Postcolonial Analysis of "Missionary Kid" Memoirs* (Multilingual Matters). I blog about my passion for fiction at stephanievandrickreads.blogspot.com.

### Todd Walker

I am an instructor at multiple community colleges in the Pacific Northwest, where I teach undergraduate integrated reading and writing courses. When I'm not teaching, I prefer to be surfing the Oregon coast, making music, and enjoying nature with my wife.

### Selahattin Yilmaz

I am an English Language instructor at the School of Foreign Languages, Yildiz Technical University, Turkey. I teach pre-matriculation English as a Foreign Language as well as undergraduate-level composition and applied linguistics courses. I hold a PhD in Applied Linguistics from Georgia State University, Atlanta. In my research, I approach L2 academic writing from an English as a Lingua Franca (ELF) perspective, primarily by using corpus methods. As an L2 writer myself, I hope to continue this line of research to gain deeper insights into the ever-increasing diversity in international scientific communication today.

# Index